# Indian Cooking Unfolded

# Raghavan Iyer
# Indian Cooking Unfolded

Workman Publishing • New York

## Dedication

. . . . . . . . . . . . . . . . . . . . . . . . . . . . . . . . . . . . . .

To my son, Robert, who means the world to me.

To my partner of more than thirty years, Terry, for all the quiet support.

To my family in India, whom I always miss.

And to the tens of thousands of students over the years
from whom I continue to learn to teach.

Library of Congress Cataloging-in-Publication Data is available.

ISBN 978-0-7611-6521-7

Cover and interior design:
    Jean-Marc Troadec
Cover portrait and food photography:
    Lucy Schaeffer
Food stylist: Simon Andrews
Prop stylist: Sara Abalan
Additional photography credits on page 330.

Workman Publishing Co., Inc.
225 Varick Street
New York, NY 10014-4381
workman.com

WORKMAN is a registered trademark of Workman Publishing Co., Inc.

Printed in China
First printing July 2013

10 9 8 7 6 5 4 3 2 1

# Acknowledgments

I t's easy (well, not entirely true) for me as a teacher to stand before an audience and cook away, expounding on all the intricacies of Indian cooking, as I chop, stir, stew, and bake my creations with spicy panache. Truth be told, it's the planning and work that have transpired days before that get me to that performance kitchen to entertain and educate. So why would writing a book be any different?

Two key women formulated the course that got my attention: my brilliant, savvy, and knowledgeable agent who has been a champion and friend for all my projects, Jane Dystel. My editor, Suzanne Rafer, who, in my not-so-humble opinion, is the mother of all editors—kind, patient, insightful, and with a keen eye for detail. Any writer would kill to work with her. And I am honored to call her a friend. None of this would have been possible if it weren't for the two visionaries at Workman, the incomparable Peter Workman himself and the charming Bob Miller.

So recipe writing and testing is underway and you need a bevy of volunteers (did I say you do not get to be a millionaire writing cookbooks?) to test, taste, and critique. Katherine Kunst and Edith Pfeifer List spent some quality time with them and turned in helpful observations. A circle of friends crawl out of the woodwork just in time for dinner claiming to be experts— Dr. Jeffrey Mandel, R.J. (Molu) and Tara Singh, Raymond and Terra Vaughn, Jiten and Jennifer Gori, Ben and Zaidee Martin. So many of my colleagues and friends egg me on—Jim Dodge, Mary Evans, Meredith Deeds, Lee Dean, Paulette Mitchell, Nathan Fong, Lynne Rossetto Kasper, Beth Dooley, Sara Monick, Phyllis Louise Harris, Dorothy Long Sandercock, Leah Mann, Ellen Pruden, Ron Longe, David Joachim, Sharon Sanders, Crescent Dragonwagon, Diane Morgan, and so many more.

Now comes the part when you need someone who is meticulous, once you turn in your manuscript, to copyedit and double-check every line. You need Barbara Mateer and Carol White. Once the words are put in place, how do you make them come alive? Bring in the dazzling Jean-Marc Troadec (*bien sûr*, he is French), designer extraordinaire to shape the pages and splash colors that are vivid, warm, and downright sensuous. And did I mention the foldouts? A challenge that he mastered with great panache. He had some great material to work with in terms of photography. Photo Director Anne Kerman orchestrated it all and brought in the amazing (and very pregnant) Lucy Schaeffer to shoot the photos. And wow, did she perform! You just want to eat the pages! And yes, she delivered a beautiful baby girl (not during the shoot!), who is off the cute charts, as well. The one who made the recipes (they worked just fine, thank you very much) and fussed over the dishes for the camera was dashing and masterful food stylist Simon Andrews, ably assisted by Idan Bitton (who was a great stand-in for the author shot—much better than I). Prop stylist Sara Abalan had an eye (well, two) for grabbing the right stuff to make the food sing. Let's not forget assistant editor Erin Klabunde's ability to hold all the strings in place and the work put in by Production Manager Doug Wolff and the typesetting department,

Barbara Peragine and Jarrod Dyer. You think indexing would be a piece of cake; well think again, you are sadly mistaken—just ask Cathy Dorsey, who really knows what it takes—it can make or break a book!

All this work is fine and dandy but if it does not get the appropriate exposure, you might as well call it quits. No one will know to take that class. So in walks Executive Publicity Director Selina Meere and publicist John Jenkinson to get the job done, as did so many of my other friends at Workman. My friends and partners in my spice line (okay, time for a shameless plug—turmerictrail.com), Jennifer Leuck and Beth Gillies, who also operate a successful PR agency, pitched in. Soon word gets around and everyone wants to get in (okay, it's my fantasy).

So to all who came to class, learned, provided feedback, and left with a full belly—thank you for your support over the years. I learned as much from you as I was able to teach. Unfold this journey with me and savor the moments. You can reach me through my website, raghavaniyer.com, email me at Raghavan@raghavaniyer.com, follow me on Twitter (@660Curries), or friend me on Facebook (raghavan.iyer)—would love to chat.

# Contents

. . . . . . . . . . . . . . . . . . . . . . . . . . . . . . . . . . . . . . . . . . . . . . . . . . . . . . . . . . . .

Welcome to my cooking classroom, where you'll get a book's-eye view of everything you need to know to prepare authentic Indian cuisine with confidence and ease. How best to use this book, which contains 100 easy recipes each with 10 ingredients or less. Read up on the Indian pantry—all the ingredients are available in your local supermarket.

. . . . . . . . . . . . . . . . . . . . . . . . . . . . . . . . . . . . . . . . . . . . . . . . . . . . . . . . . . . .

Foolproof methods for preparing the cornerstones of any Indian kitchen: Steamed White Rice, Ghee (Indian-style clarified butter), Paneer (whole milk cheese), and two essential spice blends—Raghavan's Blend and Garam Masala.

. . . . . . . . . . . . . . . . . . . . . . . . . . . . . . . . . . . . . . . . . . . . . . . . . . . . . . . . . . . .

Learn to achieve layerings of flavor that only *taste* complex—but are a cinch to execute—with these pleasing bites and munchies. The recipes are organized in order from the easiest to the slightly more complex (but still containing 10 or fewer ingredients). This chapter also contains the first foldout lesson: Poppadums with Chile-Spiked Onion or Avocado Pomegranate Dip.

. . . . . . . . . . . . . . . . . . . . . . . . . . . . . . . . . . . . . . . . . . . . . . . . . . . . . . . . . . . .

A true Indian table setting does not include flatware. Use traditional, fresh-off-the-stovetop breads to transport food from plate to mouth, beginning with the second foldout lesson: All-Wheat Griddle Breads. A selection of Indian relishes make good dips and cool the heat of the upcoming meal.

Salads with a twist and soups, both chilled and warmed, combine Indian flavors with Western-style courses. The third foldout lesson, Indian Slaw, gets you started.

Breathe a little Indian flavor into main dishes that take minimal prep time. The fourth foldout lesson features what is sure to be a family and friends favorite, Ultimate Chicken Curry. Learn the proper spice blends and cooking methods for delicious beef, lamb, pork, and seafood dishes.

Indian cuisine has long been synonymous with vegetarian dishes, and this varied sampling of beans, legumes, and fresh fruits and vegetables proves why. The fifth foldout lesson highlights Smoky Yellow Split Peas, an easy *dal* dish, so important in an Indian meal.

In Indian cooking, it's the vegetables, rice, and grains that often take center stage at a meal—and deservedly so. Start with the sixth foldout lesson featuring a Sweet-Scented Pilaf—rice that packs a flavorful pow. From single-spice dishes to more heavily spiced offerings, each tempts with assertive tastes developed through simple techniques.

• • • • • • • • • • • • • • • • • • • • • • • • • • • • • • • • • • • • •

These recipes marry classic Indian flavors with both Indian and Western-style desserts, and the result is total satisfaction. Begin with the seventh foldout lesson of Funnel Cakes in Saffron Syrup, a northern Indian street food. Indulge in Creamy Rice Pudding, then whip up Chocolate Chile Brownies. The Slumdog Martini is a must.

• • • • • • • • • • • • • • • • • • • • • • • • • • • • • • • • • • • • •

Combine the dishes featured in the foldout lessons throughout the book to prepare your first full Indian meal, then try your hand at the other menus featured here. You'll never have to ask "How do I plan an Indian meal?" again. Complete with detailed instructions on what to prep when.

# Chapter I

# The Easy Breezy Indian

I WAS still exhausted from the twenty-four-hour flight as the car driven by a family friend made its way through the cornfields of southwestern Minnesota. It was the fall of 1982 and my second day in the United States. Lost in numbed thought, I was beginning to fully understand that I was alone and for the first time away from my familiar life in Mumbai. Panic washed over me as the white station wagon approached the small town of Marshall, and the four-story buildings of the university campus towered above the flat fields. What was I doing here? What was I going to do for meals? My dormitory arrangements did not include a meal plan. It quickly became obvious to me that this town would not have restaurants that served the food I was accustomed to, especially since I was, like many Indians, a sucker for spice. Why hadn't I heeded my sister's advice to learn at least the basics of cooking my childhood favorites?

An hour later, standing amid the clutter of my large suitcases in the small dorm room, I pried open a window to watch my friend drive away. I had known that leaving home would be the start of a journey, but the whiff of the chilled autumn breeze carrying the fresh-mowed-grass smell of harvested corn mixed with the acrid odor of pig farms offered no clue to the culinary odyssey ahead of me.

The first meals I conjured up in my dormitory's kitchen were pitifully pathetic. I was uneasy, but took some comfort in the contents of a white rectangular tin with green and red letters that spelled "Curry Powder" as I added it to overboiled, nutritionally devoid vegetables. Another aid was the bottle of red pepper flakes that accompanied me to restaurants. I pulled it out to perk up everything from mashed potatoes to macaroni and cheese—embarrassing my dinner companions. In the neighborhood's supermarket I found no traces of black mustard seeds, chiles, or bunches of fresh coriander leaves (called cilantro in this country, I later learned), indispensable ingredients in many of the dishes I had come to love during my childhood in Mumbai. However I discovered potatoes, onions, tomatoes, and corn were abundant and so were yellow mustard seeds (used in the ground form along with turmeric in the Western culture's production of prepared mustard), green and yellow split peas (to make split pea soup with ham hocks), ground red (cayenne) pepper (used in minimal quantities to spike deviled eggs), and parsley (the quintessential herb in providing a sprig of spring green to umpteen plates as garnish).

Without realizing it, I was learning to use readily available ingredients to create spicing techniques that brought assertive flavors into my new Midwestern American home kitchen. My education and expertise in the culinary field flourished, and I learned that in fact the everyday grocery store stock did include many of the ingredients I was familiar with from my upbringing. What struck me as being ironic

was that I, an Indian by nationality, was learning to cook the Indian way in a foreign land. Like Americans, I was experiencing firsthand the challenges Americans face in trying to procure distinctive ethnic ingredients. My task was to create the complexity of the Indian flavors I craved by using what I could find in a mainstream grocery store, eliminating the need to locate an Indian store, in person or virtually. Could it be done? The answer is an unequivocally simple "yes." And that's what this cookbook is all about.

## Enjoy This Book

Indian Cooking Unfolded presents my system for learning to cook Indian food in one hundred basic recipes, divided among eight chapters. Think of each chapter as a course. In fact, it's a course times two, since each chapter focuses on a specific course in a meal (ironic when traditional meals in India are never served in courses). Within each chapter, I've arranged the recipes from easiest to those that are a little less so, with none being really difficult at all. Each recipe teaches a technique—sometimes a cooking technique, sometimes a way to combine or prep ingredients for exceptional flavor. However, don't feel you have to follow the order I've put the recipes in. Except for the Basics chapter, which includes the recipes for ingredients—ghee (clarified butter), paneer (mild white cheese), a couple of spice blends—that show up in other recipes throughout the book, you're free to dip in wherever it pleases you. By the way, making ghee and the spice blends takes very little time and they have a long shelf life. Be sure to keep them on hand.

## What's Classic Indian and Can I Achieve Authentic Flavors with an Easy Approach?

When you look at India's culture with the realization that the civilization has existed for more than 6,000 years, it should come as no surprise that the cuisine is highly evolved. Every invasion, religious or political, has shaped in profound ways the ingredients and spices that are the backbone of regional Indian cooking. The country's geographical location, cupped by oceans to its east, south, and west and the mountains along its north

## How to Prepare the Recipes

I always give this advice to my students, either because they have asked me these questions, or because I have managed to glean their desire to know, based on how they approach my recipes in the hands-on cooking classes that I have conducted all across North America over the last 20 years.

- First, design a simple meal—if you are looking for some Indian menu ideas, flip to page 306 for some options and a plan of attack for successfully executing each menu.

- Read each recipe briskly from start to finish just so you know where I am going with it.

- Gather all your ingredients to get you started. If a recipe has a spice blend, assemble it as part of your prep. The book has only two easy blends; each takes less than 5 minutes to mix and there are options to procure them at the store if you'd rather not make them.

- Chop, measure, and arrange your ingredients in the order you need to use them. You will be amazed how this simple step (the French call it *mise en place*—put in place) makes you efficient and successful in the kitchen.

- Pour yourself a glass of wine or shake up that fantastic martini on page 301. Play your favorite music, tune out the kids and pets, and savor the process. It's cooking—it should be fun, easy, breezy, and flavorful.

side, made for open but arduous access. The single most important bounty, peppercorns, burst the spice trade dam, and Indians witnessed an unprecedented global influx of power, money, and flavors.

## Foldouts Unfolded

Now to the exciting part—the foldouts. Each chapter (except for Basics) leads off with a foldout illustrating, step-by-step, a recipe from that chapter. Not only do they clarify and simplify Indian prep work in general, but when those foldout recipes are prepared together, they add up to the perfect get-started Indian meal. Fully illustrated, easy, and straightforward, the foldouts will have you cooking Indian in no time flat. And once you've cooked one complete meal, go ahead and try the other ones I suggest that start on page 306. My kitchen is now your kitchen too. And welcome to it.

Local availability and seasonality of ingredients dictated the lay of the culinary land. Due to the cooler weather patterns in the winter months, Northerners infused their meats, vegetables, and legumes with warming spices like cloves, cinnamon, cardamom, peppercorns, and bay leaves. The opulence of the kitchens in the royal courts of the Moghul emperors led to lavish uses of nuts, golden raisins, dates, saffron, and cream, while the hearty wheat-growing farmers of the northwest peppered their mustard greens with garlic and chiles and dunked clay oven–baked flatbreads into bowls of chilelike red kidney beans.

Southerners steeped their staple seafood with indigenous cardamom, sweet cinnamon, citruslike curry leaves, nutty popped mustard seeds, and creamy coconut milk. Rice, the cash crop here, found its way into pancakes, noodles, dumplings, crepes, and steamed cakes. Lentils, beans, and peas delivered essential, body-building nutrients as well as complex flavors through unusual spice blends.

In the West, home to the largest migratory influences from the Persians, Portuguese, Buddhist, and Jewish settlers, among others, relied on cashews, peanuts, tapioca, potatoes, beef, and pork to punctuate their meals. The Gujaratis were masters of vegetarianism, drawing on their dependence on legumes and dairy to whip up simple but amazing fare. Fish, vinegar, and eggs ruled the roost, and the dizzying array of Mumbai's street foods really showed what fast food ought to be. The city drew people from all corners of India, reflecting a mosaic of cultures.

The tea plantations of the east in Darjeeling and Assam helped brew some incredible chai, while the Bengalis of Calcutta became master confectioners, sweetening their way into every belly. And their penchant for fish and seafood bore testimony to the abundance of aquatic life in the Bay of Bengal as they smothered their creations with mustard paste, poppy seed purees, and ground fennel.

## One-Stop Shopping

You will notice that I use no ingredient in this book that will require you to visit an Indian grocery store. So, spices and ingredients like fenugreek, fresh curry leaves, asafetida, and split and skinned black lentils are not present in any of the recipes. As I created and tested the recipes, I felt guilty at times but eventually found it to be an exhilarating and freeing experience. A meander down the spice aisle of numerous "regular" grocery stores across the United States, from those in small towns to large cities, showed me that five important spices used in Indian cooking were right there on the shelves and enabled me to create two blends, which helped me cook the Indian way with a spicy (as in well-seasoned) panache.

To say that every Indian dish is layered with an armload of ingredients is wrong. Oftentimes, we conjure complexities within a recipe by using the same ingredient in multiple ways as we construct the dish. It is very possible to create those sensational flavors with a small handful of key spices, as you will see in the recipes in this book. How you handle a spice makes all the difference in a recipe. I always tell my students to buy whole spices, whenever they possibly can, and store them in an airtight jar in a cool, dry area in their pantry. I never tire of mentioning the eight ways one can use a spice. Here's an example with cumin seeds.

1 When you use cumin seeds as is, you get their distinctive spice flavor.

2 When you grind the seeds and sprinkle them in a dish, the flavor is more pronounced and quite different: musky and earthy.

3 Take the whole seeds and toast them in a dry pan, with no oil, and you will experience a nutty aroma.

4 Take those toasted seeds and grind them, and they smell nothing like any of their previous incarnations.

5 Heat a little oil and roast the seeds, and you will discover yet another flavor—almost sweet smelling and smoky.

6 Grind the cumin seeds after you roast them, and they will seem to lose their smoky bouquet.

7 Soak the whole seeds in a liquid, and their presence will be surprisingly subtle.

8 And when you grind cumin seeds after you soak them, they not only take on the liquid's taste but also impart the spice's eighth flavor: The strong nutlike aroma reappears, masked by the infused flavor of the liquid.

Incidentally, once the spice is ground, even when stored in a moisture-free, well-sealed container, it will keep for only up to three months. After that, its essential oils dissipate and become rather insipid in aroma and flavor. That's when you toss the ground spice out the window and start fresh.

## The Indian Mother Hubbard's Cupboard

A typical Indian pantry brims with a plethora of spices, legumes, and grains. My bare-bones approach to cooking the Indian way saves you not only money, but space and time as well, all precious commodities. One trip to the supermarket is all you need since these ingredients are all readily available.

### FIVE INDIAN "MUST-HAVE" SPICES

• CARDAMOM PODS • CORIANDER SEEDS • CUMIN SEEDS • MUSTARD SEEDS • TURMERIC (GROUND)

**CARDAMOM PODS**
It may surprise you to know that cardamom is a close relative to ginger (and turmeric), but very much like disparate siblings, this highly aromatic spice is the expensive, high-maintenance diva of the Zingiberaceae family. Known

to have existed in India as early as 1300 BCE, cardamom was a panacea for numerous ailments, including nausea, halitosis, fever, and headaches. Cardamom is indigenous to the southwestern coast of Kerala (formerly known as the Malabar Coast) and Sri Lanka. The plump, green pods from Alleppey in Kerala, considered to be the true cardamom, are hand-picked, spread onto slow-moving, conveyor belt-type driers, packed in gunnysacks when moisture-free, and stored in sheds to ship worldwide.

Green cardamom and its seeds scent many of India's desserts; pop a few raw seeds in your mouth, they'll make your breath smell fresh and aid digestion (call it an Indian's antacid). Sizzle whole green cardamom pods in hot oil or add them to sauces and they infuse them with sweet, delicate aromas. When you pry the seeds out of the pods and gently pound them, you release a stronger aroma. Toasting and grinding the seeds from the pods extracts their optimum strength. The green pods are also sun-bleached white and sold in grocery stores as white cardamom, apparently an aesthetic measure, as the taste remains the same. When a recipe calls for just the cardamom seeds, if you don't wish to pry the seeds out of the pods yourself, you can purchase the seeds in bottles labeled "decorticated cardamom," but be prepared to secure a bank loan for that convenience.

## CORIANDER SEEDS

Introduced in northeastern India around 200 BCE by the Buddhist Indian emperor Ashoka, the seeds from the cilantro plant (called coriander leaves in India and Chinese parsley as well) are citrus-like, brownish yellow in color, and not at all similar in taste or aroma to cilantro leaves. You can't substitute coriander seeds for cilantro leaves in a dish (or vice versa), but on numerous occasions, they complement each other. Coriander seeds have a slightly sweet, fennel-like, citrus undertone and are pleasantly bitter. Cumin and coriander seeds form a cozy relationship in many spice blends, and they provide a well-balanced temperament to recipes that have large amounts of capsaicin-heavy chiles. (You can read about fresh cilantro on page 12.)

**CUMIN SEEDS**
A popular sibling of the carrot family, cumin is India's favorite spice (its Latin name is *Cuminum cyminum*). Excavated from the ruins of India's Mohenjo Daro civilization of 4000 BCE, cumin is native to the Mediterranean countries and upper Egypt (it has been found in the tombs of pharaohs dating back to 1300 BCE). Like many other spices, cumin is capable of having multiple distinct flavors based on how it is used; on page 7 you found out how to produce eight. Cumin is truly a national treasure, sizzled, toasted, roasted, soaked, and ground in recipes.

**MUSTARD SEEDS**
There is evidence that this member of the cabbage family (Brassicaceae) flourished during the civilization of Mohenjo Daro (in what is now Pakistan) around early 4000 BCE. Even in the twenty-first century, fields of mustard in northwestern India in the state of Rajasthan, and in numerous northeastern states, make mustard a cash crop in those areas. In the northern regions the greens are considered a delicacy, as well as the seeds and the oil. Three kinds of mustard plants are primarily harvested for their seeds: *Brassica nigra* produces brownish-black seeds, while *Brassica juncea* yields reddish-brown ones, and *Sinapis alba* (white or yellow mustard) is the source of light yellowish-brown seeds. The first two are widely used in Indian cooking, but because of its availability in supermarkets, I have recommended the yellow kind as an acceptable alternative. I consider these seeds to possess a split personality. When pounded, cracked, or ground and combined with a liquid, mustard seeds yield a nose-tingling sharpness. Cook the seeds in oil and let them pop (just like popcorn) and they become nutty-sweet, a crucial flavor in the cuisine of the south (India, that is).

**TURMERIC** This deep-yellow rhizome gives commercial curry powders their distinctive yellow hue. A very close sibling to fresh ginger, turmeric belongs to a species *Curcuma longa* and is probably native to India. It's mentioned in ancient Sanskrit literature around 1300 BCE and has lent its distinctive yellow to foods and medicines, as well as dye for fabrics. Turmeric, sold most often in ground form in the United States, is harsh tasting when raw and is rarely used this way. But sprinkle turmeric in oil, add some spices and vegetables, and as it cooks, its astringent taste diminishes. Strong tasting and imparting a deep color, turmeric is a spice that Indians use sparingly, albeit frequently, in many of our recipes. The fresh rhizome is also delicious when thinly sliced and pickled in bitter mustard oil, salt, and chopped fresh green chiles. In the western regions of India, its large leaves are used to wrap and steam fish.

## FIVE ESSENTIAL HERBS AND FLAVORINGS

### • CHILES, FRESH (SERRANO) AND DRIED (CAYENNE) • CILANTRO • GINGER • MINT

**CHILES** I personally would like to thank the Spanish and the Portuguese merchants and settlers who came to India and introduced us, in the early sixteenth century, to these bracing members of the capsicum family. The name for chiles is derived from the Nahuatl or Aztec name, and the word *pepper* became attached to it, thanks to Christopher Columbus. Why? He goofed up, big time! Columbus promised King Ferdinand and Queen Isabella, who funded his expedition, that he would find peppercorns. Instead he delivered the capsicum plants and called them *pimiento de las indias* (pepper of the Indies). With five species of cultivated capsicums, it is no wonder there are so many kinds of chiles in the world. In India, we grow all the five species, but in this book I have limited my selection to one or two, primarily because of their ease of availability in the grocery store.

In the world of fresh chiles, it's the capsaicin (an oil) within that pulsates with stimulating heat. Pure capsaicin is 16,000,000 Scoville units (named after a pharmacist who invented the scientific way of measuring a chile's capsaicin content). Discard the stem and slit the chile to expose the vein and the seeds, the heart of the heat. Granted, removing the vein and seeds will diminish the chile's heat, something we never do so in India as that constitutes being criminally wasteful. We do slit the chiles open but leave the vein and seeds intact to release a gentler heat. With chiles, the finer the mince, the hotter the taste, thanks to the breakdown and release of the capsaicin. Capsaicin activates endorphins in your brain that give you a sense of euphoria (high), a reason many lovers of "pain" adore chiles. The main type used in this book is serrano chiles (*Capsicum annuum*). If you wish for something hotter, use any of the more assertive varieties like habanero, Thai, or cayenne. If you live on the edge, there is always the hottest chile cultivated in India, called the ghost chile, with a Scoville unit scale that hovers around 1,600,000. More power to you!

Many types of dried chiles are plentiful in India, but here I recommend using the variety most common in grocery stores sold under the name cayenne or *chile de árbol*. These chiles are hot, as is, but treat them with heat (either by blackening them in a dry or oiled skillet) and the dried cap-

saicin from within unleashes an even more fiery taste with smoky undertones.

**CILANTRO** A curious phenomenon exists in the Western world, something I began to notice more than 20 years ago, when I started cooking and teaching Indian cuisine. Students and clients would come up to me and confess their abhorrence for sharp-tasting cilantro, known as coriander leaves in India and to some as Chinese parsley. A few people even said they were allergic to it (over the years I figured out that the allergy was actually a dislike and nothing life threatening that would require medical intervention). Some wanted to make certain I never added any to their food. Cilantro elicits a soaplike taste on certain palates. In fact, the herb contains fat molecules similar to those found in soaps and hand lotions.

How do you get someone to appreciate Indian food that, more often than not, includes these leaves? When you realize this herb's deep-rooted foothold in Indian culture and cuisine, you have to take notice of the various ways we use it to extract flavors ranging from subtle to sharp. Some recipes use cilantro as a garnish (like parsley) just before the dish reaches the table (and you can always leave it out) while other recipes incorporate cilantro at various stages of cooking. So, go ahead and have some. And what do I think of dried cilantro? Please, don't bother!

**GINGER** Ginger (botanical name *Zingiber officinale*) is a rhizome, the bulbous stem end of a plant that grows close to the ground but never burrows deep like potatoes, carrots, and onions, and calling it gingerroot is really a misnomer. Unearthed in southeast Asia (possibly China) around 6000 BCE, it did not come to India until about 1300 BCE. But once it did, its pungency (a highly aromatic one too) became a popular flavoring ingredient. Steeping slices of fresh ginger in a pot of legumes, stir-frying ginger with onions and garlic to make the base for a sauce, smashing it with herbs and spices, shredding and squeezing its juice for a mellow broth, adding julienned ginger to recipes just before serving are just a few ways to bring out its various levels of flavor.

You can find fresh ginger in the produce department of most supermarkets. Look for heavy pieces with smooth brown skin that is firm and unwrinkled. And do not be afraid of snapping off what you need at the store if the ginger is too big (no ginger police will be lurking in the aisles). Fresh ginger has a relatively long shelf life, especially when kept loosely wrapped in a plastic bag in your refrigerator's humidity-controlled vegetable bin. Do not freeze pieces of fresh ginger; it becomes unmanageable, unpalatable, and rubbery when thawed. (You can, however, freeze minced ginger.) Rinse the ginger before use. If the skin is clean and smooth, and doesn't appear dry, you don't have to bother peeling it. Simply slice off any dry ends. If the skin is tough and appears slightly woody, it's best to peel the ginger, using a swivel peeler or a paring knife.

**MINT** A weed to some, manna to others, this perennial herb is cultivated all over the world, boasting more than 24 species with hundreds of varieties (peppermint and spearmint being the most popular) within its scented umbrella. A Greek legend tells the tale of a nymph by the name of Minthe, a beautiful woman, who was a love distraction to Hades. His jealous wife transformed Minthe into a plant. It's those fresh mint leaves we consume in stews, sauces, relishes, and drinks.

## FIVE LEGUME STAPLES

- BLACK-EYED PEAS • CHICKPEAS
- KIDNEY BEANS • RED LENTILS
- YELLOW SPLIT PEAS

**CHICKPEAS** Yellow chickpeas, also commonly called garbanzo beans, were consumed in India as early as the Harappan civilization, around 4500 BCE. One of the more popular varieties among legumes, chickpeas are versatile. The fresh green ones are eaten out of the pod in India as a nutty snack. The cooked bean's nut-like texture and ability to absorb spices and herbs make it an ideal ingredient in many Indian recipes. Every supermarket carries canned cooked chickpeas, which are priceless in terms of convenience and expediency; drain and rinse them before use. You'll find information on chickpea flour on pages 22, 78 and 91.

**BLACK-EYED PEAS** Of African origin, black-eyed peas are kidney shaped and cream colored, with a small dark spot or eye on the inside curve. They gained wide acceptance all over India because of their buttery, creamy taste and nutty texture. The dried legumes are easy to cook, but in a pinch you can find canned cooked black-eyed peas at the supermarket; drain and rinse them before use. Frozen black-eyed peas are also widely available, making for a nice compromise between cooking from scratch and using canned peas.

**KIDNEY BEANS** Despite its botanical name, *Phaseolus vulgaris*, there is nothing obscene or vulgar about this robust-flavored, kidney-shaped (how obvious!) bean, which is very popular in the northern regions of India, especially in the farming communities of Punjab. There is mention of these beans as a staple among the Aryans in one of the well-known literary works, dating back to around 800 BCE. Very meaty in texture and aroma, this bean is a great alternative for someone who is looking to cut back on cholesterol-rich meats. The dried beans do take some time to soak and cook (a pressure cooker is ideal here), but if time is of the essence, the readily available canned cooked beans, drained and rinsed, are a great substitute.

**RED LENTILS** Known as red Egyptian lentils, these are in fact salmon in color. Red lentils can be prepared in just 15 minutes and become very soft and saucelike and yellow in color as they cook. This is an ideal legume for an evening meal when you are looking for something quick, meatless, cheap, and tasty.

**YELLOW SPLIT PEAS** Similar in shape to green split peas (yes, the ones that stew with salty, smoky ham hocks), yellow split peas are easy to cook from scratch. They don't require soaking and become tender and cornlike in texture, while still retaining

their shape. If unavailable (I can't imagine why), you can use green split peas as an acceptable alternative.

## The Cupboard Extended

Some of the recipes in this book also include other pantry items common in Indian kitchens and, in many cases, in your kitchen as well. Here's a look at them.

### DRIED SPICES

• BAY LEAVES • CINNAMON • CLOVES • FENNEL • NUTMEG • PEPPERCORNS • SAFFRON • SALT

**BAY LEAVES** Sharp edged, musky smelling, and dark green with a glossy sheen, the western European variety of bay leaves from the Mediterranean, with the Latin name *Laurus nobilis,* is what's found in the spice aisles of the grocery stores all across the United States. The leaves, either dried or fresh, are not poisonous as some of my students often ponder. However, what is problematic are the sharp edges that, if accidentally swallowed whole, can cause choking or possibly scratch the inside of the throat. Indians toast or roast these leaves in some of our spice blends (see Garam Masala on page 41), and pound them to accentuate their aroma. Bay leaves generate internal warmth and prove to be a crucial component in numerous versions of that blend. Stock up on fresh bay leaves when they are available, since they have an incredibly long shelf life in the refrigerator. If weeks go by and you forget they are in there, don't worry. They will become dry, further extending their use by months. Transfer the dried bay leaves to an airtight container and store them in your pantry or spice cabinet.

**CINNAMON** Around 800 CE, Jewish merchants transported silk, furs, and swords from the West to trade in the northwestern parts of India and China for cinnamon. In Indian cooking cinnamon is prized in savory dishes, not in desserts, which is exactly the opposite in the western part of the world. True cinnamon, from the bark of the *Cinnamomum verum,* also known as *Cinnamomum zeylanicum,* tree (which is indigenous to Sri Lanka and parts of southern India), is highly aromatic, with a fragrant sweetness. Most of the cinnamon sold in the Western world comes from the more inexpensive *Cinnamomum cassia,* cultivated in China for export. In India sticks of cinnamon are used most commonly to perfume oils in which meats, vegetables, and legumes simmer, or layered rice bakes. Because of the gentle warmth it produces when toasted and ground, cinnamon is a popular spice in many garam masalas, including the one on page 41.

**CLOVES** This evergreen tree bears nail-shaped flower buds (the French word for nail is *clou*), and when dried, the buds become pointed, highly aromatic, black-colored cloves. The oil adds aroma and heat to Indian dishes, especially in those from the northern regions, and also has a numbing quality to it, giving a sense of hot pungency to your tongue. In fact, clove oil is still used in numerous dentist offices for its anesthetic effect in relieving minor discomfort. As a whole spice, cloves transport sauces with their flavor when first sizzled in hot oil. When toasted and ground, and blended with other spices, the oils intensify to make an assertive presence in marinades, rubs, stir-fries, and curries.

**FENNEL** When you find evidence of spice blends from more than 6,000 years ago in the ruins of India's Mohenjo Daro civilization, mixtures that contain mustard, cumin, and the slightly bitter wild fennel, you shake your head in utter awe at the sophistication of those cooks who layered every dish they created with mouth-watering flavors. In modern day kitchens across the world, it is the sweet variety, indigenous to the Mediterranean countries, that is prized for its honeyed, angular persona. The light green seeds look similar to caraway and cumin, but their color and aroma set them apart. Although called *Foeniculum vulgare* in Latin, there is nothing foelike or vulgar about these plants that are part of the carrot family. While the leaves and the bulbous stem are abundantly consumed in Mediterranean cultures, the seeds are the favorite part in Indian spice blends.

When you are at an Indian restaurant, toasted and sugar-coated fennel seeds are either delivered to your table with the check or kept by the host stand at the entrance. A spoonful of these, after a heavy meal, is a great breath freshener and a powerful digestive.

**NUTMEG** To say that spices led countries to be attacked, robbed, possessed, and destroyed is not an understatement. Nutmeg was one of those prized possessions that drove the Dutch to trade Manhattan for the Indonesian Banda Islands back in 1700 CE. Indigenous to Indonesia, the nutmeg tree is also cultivated along India's western shores, where rich, volcanic soil and tropical conditions continue to keep these long-living trees fruiting. Pry the pear-shaped nutmeg fruit apart and you find an orange-brown web that wraps around a durable, dark brown shell. The web is the spice called mace. When the shell inside dries and is broken open, the nutmeg, a hard light brown nut with little specks of white, emerges. Just like mace, nutmeg is best when freshly ground or grated. It's always nice when a tree yields one useful spice, but when it gives you two, you want to embrace it.

### PEPPERCORNS

Sounds theatrical but it is true that this was the spice that launched the spice trade, paving the way for discovery of seas and civilizations and shaping history as we know it. It is a hefty burden for this tiny, black, oily, hot, berrylike spice. The world's top quality pepper is grown in Kerala and is known by the regions where it grows, Alleppey and the superior Tellicherry. When the green peppercorn berries on the vine are almost mature and beginning to ripen to a red color, they are picked and fermented, and spread out to dry in the sun; the heat will turn them into the familiar black peppercorns. Their volatile oils are most vivacious when freshly ground; when toasted, roasted, ground, coarsely cracked, or pounded, peppercorns exhibit different personalities. But no matter what, their ability to add heat remains relentless.

### SAFFRON

Harvested in Cyprus as early as 1600 BCE and later brought to Kashmir around 400 BCE, saffron is unequivocally the world's most expensive spice. Why? It is the handpicked, dried stigmas of the *Crocus sativus* blossom (70,000 purple crocus blooms yield a pound of beautiful, reddish-orange saffron threads), and even two to four threads, when steeped in warm liquid, can infuse a recipe that feeds four. Most of the world's saffron comes from La Mancha, Spain, but the best threads come from Kashmir. Never purchase ground saffron, as this product is inferior in quality and may be adulterated. The old adage "you get what you pay for" is true when purchasing saffron. If someone sells you "cheap" saffron, it's from dubious sources and will contain wispy thin shreds of reddish-orange-tinted tree bark.

SALT These crystals from the sea have been used as flavor enhancers, as preservatives, and for religious rituals in India for more than 6,000 years. There are three main types of "white" salt used in

Indian cooking. The first kind, rock salt, is a mined product, unearthed from the ground, processed and purified for human consumption, and sold in rock form. The extent of purification depends on the salt's end use—coarser (and cruder) rock salts are used industrially. Rock salts that are fit to eat can be pulverized into a gritty powder and then sprinkled over anything.

The second type, sea salt, is the most popular in Indian cuisine. Sea salt is available in most American supermarkets, in both crystal and powder forms. This is what I use in all my dishes, in addition to recommending the commonly available kosher salt. Conforming to Jewish dietary laws, kosher is a slightly coarse salt with uneven crystals and no additives. It can be harvested from the sea or from underground.

The third type, table salt, is the most commonly used throughout the United States and is available as a heavily processed, dense ingredient, usually with iodine—an essential trace element required by the body—added. Due to its very fine texture, I find table salt saltier in taste when compared teaspoon by teaspoon to coarse kosher or sea salt. If you are using the denser table salt when making the recipes

in the book, I suggest adding 10 to 15 percent less than the amount called for in the ingredient list. Taste. And then add more salt if needed.

## FRESH FLAVORINGS

### COCONUT

 **COCONUT** South Indian cooking without coconut is empty, discomforting, and very sad! Coconuts (there are many varieties) are used to represent marital harmony, fertility, and even the souls of departed loved ones. All parts of the coconut are used in India. The thick white meat is used for daily cooking. The coconut's abrasive husks are often saved for scrubbing pots and pans and also make their way into the shower as a loofah-style sponge. The shell, emptied of meat, oftentimes is used as a scoop for various tasks.

When selecting a coconut, choose one that has dry eyes (the three indentations on one end of the coconut indicate where it was attached to the palm tree). Shake the coconut to hear its water reverberate against the shell. If you hear silence, chances are the meat inside is rotten. To get to the coconut meat, first rinse the shell under water. Place the coconut in one hand and, holding a hammer or meat pounder in the other, gently but firmly tap the coconut around its entire midsection. As soon as the shell cracks open, the sweet white liquid inside will gush out (so make sure you have a small bowl underneath the coconut to catch it). Don't throw the liquid away. It's a great thirst quencher and is chock-full of essential electrolytes, giving sports drinks a run for their money. Then, using a sharp paring knife, score the coconut meat in large pieces. Using a firm butter knife, gently pry out pieces of the meat from the shell. Peel away the thin dark brown skin and place the meat in a food processor. Pulse the coconut chunks into small shreds. In India, we use a coconut grater (a barbaric-looking implement) to get the meat from the shell without any hassles. A medium-size coconut will yield 2 to 3 cups shredded meat. Freeze any unused portion in a freezer-safe zip-top bag for up to 2 months.

Asian grocery stores stock freshly shredded coconut meat in their freezers as do some high-end supermarkets. Dried unsweetened shredded coconut (sometimes sold as powder) is also available in major supermarkets and natural food stores. About ¾ cup of dried unsweetened coconut is comparable to 1 cup of freshly shredded coconut. I often reconstitute ¾ cup of dried unsweetened coconut in ¼ cup of hot milk to mimic the freshly shredded taste. If you are desperate, you can purchase sweetened shredded coconut: Soak it in hot water and then drain it. Repeat at least 3 or 4 times to remove as much sugar as possible.

## DRIED LEGUMES, NUTS, AND FLOURS

• CASHEW NUTS  • PEANUTS
• PISTACHIOS & ALMONDS
• CHICKPEA FLOUR

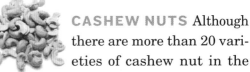

**CASHEW NUTS** Although there are more than 20 varieties of cashew nut in the world, the Portuguese settlers introduced one kind, *Anacordium occidentale* (during the latter half of 1500 CE), which thrives in India's southwestern state of Goa. The small tree bears a bell pepper–like "fruit," sometimes known as a cashew apple, and at the end of each so-called fruit is the true fruit of the tree, which is the cashew nut. The false fruit is actually a swollen stalk, and this is a delicacy in Goan cooking, stewed in curries for its astringent flavor. The nut is encased within a double shell that contains a toxic substance (corrosive acids); the shell is carefully broken open (in one piece) by roasting or boiling. The versatile nut inside, white, sweet, and addictive, is a common cooking ingredient in India and is also often eaten as a snack. I call for raw cashew nuts in my recipes, which means that they are neither roasted nor salted.

**PEANUTS** Of all the nuts, peanuts are the most popular (and affordable) in India, especially in its western and northwestern regions. These are technically legumes and are called groundnuts in India since they grow so close to the ground. Even though peanuts had been around since around 3000 BCE (they are indigenous to Peru), they did not make it to India until the late nineteenth century when two separate varieties came from Africa and China. There are four dominant kinds of peanuts in the world (Virginia, runner, Valencia, and Spanish), and in spite of India's late entry into the groundnut market, my homeland is one of the world's leading cultivators of this legume. In India we always start with raw peanuts and then toast or roast them. This draws out the oils from within, providing succulence for the tongue. Peanuts can be coarsely cracked, ground, or pureed; each technique elicits a different taste sensation. They provide nutty texture and protein in every recipe they touch.

**PISTACHIOS AND ALMONDS** Brought to India from the Mediterranean countries, pistachios and almonds remain quite pricey and relatively inaccessible to most in India. Very much a staple in the baking aisles of the supermarket, buy them as you need for the recipes. If you procure a large amount, store them in the refrigerator in a tightly sealed bag or container as they have a tendency to turn rancid rather quickly. Freezing is also an option—they will keep for up to a year.

**CHICKPEA FLOUR**
Recently, I have seen chickpea flour readily available in one-pound packages at regular grocery stores either in the flour aisle or in the health food section. Made from dried chickpeas, also known as garbanzo beans, the talcum powder–soft flour is very high in dietary fiber and proteins. Its egglike qualities make chickpea flour the perfect swathe for crisply fried vegetables. It's also ideal for making fluffy pancakes and crepes and as a nutty-tasting thickener for thin-bodied sauces.

If you have no access to the flour, here's what you can do at home. Take some dried chickpeas and pulverize them in a blender or spice grinder (like a coffee grinder). These stonelike beans won't break down easily but will resemble chunks of smaller pebbles with light yellow dust. Transfer this to a tea strainer or a sifter and allow the fine-textured flour to pass through. Then regrind the remaining kernels of beans.

Continue the sifting and grinding process until you have enough flour for the recipe. Seems a bit tedious but it works. Or you can buy one of those high-end blenders that are designed to break down grains into flours within minutes. If you don't plan to use the chickpea flour within a week or so, it can be stored in a container or sealed plastic zip-top bag in the refrigerator for up to a year. Chickpea flour does have a tendency to get rancid in your pantry rather quickly.

## Any Special Equipment?

None that an average kitchen does not already possess is the short answer. Besides a blender and or a food processor, I will mention that the addition of a spice grinder, which works like a coffee grinder, not only makes it easier to pulverize whole spices and nuts but delivers unbelievable flavors you won't get from store-bought, preground spices and blends.

The ability of electric coffee grinders to grind hard coffee beans also makes these machines ideally suited for grinding a wide range of spices, such as dried bay

leaves, cumin seeds, cloves, and broken-up cinnamon sticks. Coffee grinders can be used to grind from as little as a teaspoon of spice to as much as half a cup, and depending on how long you run them, they can produce both fine and coarse grinds. It is not necessary to clean the grinder after grinding each spice. And if a recipe calls for multiple spices to be ground, you can certainly plunk them all in and grind them together. (However, I often encourage my students to grind spices individually so they can see for themselves how different each spice smells before and after grinding. Over time, you will be able to identify a spice by smell alone.)

If you do want to clean the grinder, first unplug it. Wipe the inside with a slightly damp paper towel, taking extra care to clean underneath the metal blades. The blades are sharp, so be careful not to cut yourself. Another way to eliminate any spice residue is to grind dried bread cubes in the grinder. This not only cleans out the grinder but also provides flavored bread-crumbs that you can use to coat fish, meat, and poultry.

Blends of whole spices, whether they will be used raw, toasted, or even stir-fried in a little oil, can be ground in a spice grinder. However, fresh herbs like cilantro and mint or chiles cannot be minced or ground in a coffee grinder because of their high moisture content.

One word of caution: Do not use the same grinder for spices and coffee beans. The oils in coffee beans leave a residue that is difficult to clean out, which will affect the taste and aroma of your ground spices.

# Chapter 2

# Basics Unfolded

**LET ME JUST** put your mind at ease: You are not required to prepare all of the recipes in this chapter before you can start cooking from the book. These are grouped together to make your life easier should you wish to make a pot of rice, whip up the two spice blends, or roll out a batch of griddle breads (tortilla style). You may very well decide to go the store-bought route to stock ghee in your pantry, but rest assured there is a recipe in here if you decide to save some money and make it at home.

So here's how to get started.

# The Lesson Plan

**Lesson ❶ Steamed White Rice** The most fundamental task in Indian homes is to make rice. It's usually white but not basmati since that's a variety that is quite pricey to prepare daily. Once you follow my recommendations, you will always have perfectly cooked rice, guaranteed. And no rice cookers either—not that there is anything wrong with them!

**Lesson ❷ Ghee (Indian-style clarified butter)** Ghee is essential in so many Indian dishes. Melt butter and clarify it the Indian way. It will be nutty, rich, amber hued, and ever so slightly smoky. You can easily double the recipe and you'll have ghee on hand for months to come. The better the quality of the butter, the more succulent the ghee.

**Lesson ❸ Paneer (whole milk cheese)** When you tell your friends and family you made cheese from scratch, they will be highly impressed. They don't need to know that all you did was boil milk, curdle it with vinegar,

and weight the strained curds down to make it firm. Yes, you could buy paneer at a store that has an impressive cheese section or at an Indian store, should you happen to stumble upon one in your sojourn, but don't you want the bragging rights that come with making your own?

**Lesson ❹ Raghavan's Blend** The two spice blends that I have incorporated in some of the recipes throughout the book are easy to craft within five minutes. This blend is a mélange of whole spices pulverized in a spice grinder or clean coffee grinder (no roasting or toasting required).

**Lesson ❺ Garam Masala** This blend teaches you how to toast spices without burning them to yield a complex smelling and tasting mélange. Rest assured you will never want to buy garam masala at the store again.

# 1 Steamed White Rice

### Saada Chaawal

In my role as a cooking teacher for over twenty years, this is by far the most important question I get asked: How do you cook rice? Folks get intimidated by this grain, which has been around for more than 12,000 years. With more than 100,000 varieties of rice in the world, it does seem to cause some distress. Every variety cooks differently, every crop yields a different texture, every grain is a cherished and accessible commodity in much of the world. The following two techniques for cooking the perfect white rice—the Absorption/Steeping Method and the Pasta Method—come from years of practice, failure, more practice, and then repeated success. My failure-proof steeping method is sure to deliver a bowl of aromatic fluff, especially when you use basmati rice (see Extra Credit, page 30).

**Makes 3 cups**

**I cup Indian or Pakistani white basmati rice or long-grain white rice**

**I½ teaspoons coarse kosher or sea salt**

### ABSORPTION/STEEPING METHOD

Place the rice in a medium-size bowl. Fill the bowl with enough water to cover the rice. Gently rub the slender grains of rice between the fingers of one hand, without breaking them, to wash off any dust or light foreign objects (like loose husks), which will float to the surface. The water will become cloudy. Drain this water. You don't need a

Use your fingers to remove any dust from the rice grains.

colander for this; I just tip the bowl over the sink to pour off the water, making sure the rice stays in the bowl. Repeat this 3 or 4 times until after you rinse the grains the water remains relatively clear. Now pour in 1¾ cups of cold tap water and let the rice sit at room temperature until the kernels soften, 10 to 15 minutes.

2 Transfer the rice, water and all, to a saucepan. Stir in the salt and bring to a boil over medium-high heat. Stir the rice once or twice (just because). Let the water boil, uncovered, still over medium-high heat (and no stirring), until it has evaporated from the surface and craters are starting to appear in the rice, 5 to 8 minutes. Now (and not until now) stir once or twice to bring the partially cooked layer of rice from the bottom of the pan to the surface. Cover the pan with a tight-fitting lid and reduce the heat to the lowest possible setting. Let the rice steep for 8 to 10 minutes (8 if you are using an electric burner, 10 minutes for a gas burner). Then turn off the heat and let the pan stand (or sit, for that matter) on that burner, undisturbed, for 5 minutes.

3 Uncover the pan, fluff the rice with a fork (this lets the steam escape so it does not overcook the rice), and serve.

## Absorption/Steeping Method

**1** Once the boiling water begins evaporating, craters will appear in the surface of the rice.

**2** Stir the rice up from the bottom of the pot to ensure even cooking.

PASTA METHOD

1 Fill a large saucepan halfway with water and bring it to a rolling boil over medium-high heat.

2 While the water is heating, place the rice in a medium-size bowl. Fill the bowl halfway with water, to cover the rice, and follow the directions described in Step 1 of the absorption method for prepping the rice.

3 Add the rice to the boiling water and stir once or twice. Let the water return to a boil, then boil the rice vigorously, uncovered, stirring very rarely and only to test the kernels until they are tender, 5 to 8 minutes. Immediately drain the rice into a colander and run cold water through it to stop the rice from continuing to cook. When using this method it is crucial that you be attentive or the rice will go from just right to overcooked in mere seconds.

4 Transfer the rice to a microwave-safe dish and stir in the salt. Rewarm the rice in the microwave at full power, covered, for 2 to 4 minutes just before you serve it.

## Pasta Method

1 Boil the rice, uncovered, in plenty of water.

2 Rinsing the rice under cold water will stop the cooking process. Once it is rinsed, make sure to drain it well.

# Extra Credit

Discovered and cultivated in the foothills of the Himalayas, basmati is a much sought after aromatic variety of rice (the word *basmati* means "the perfumed one") and is the world's most expensive rice. Naturally aged for many years, like a fine wine, basmati is less starchy and more slender than other long-grain varieties, making it an ideal choice for pilafs. Not only is it a complex carbohydrate, it is also rich in amino acids and other essential nutrients, including iron, niacin, phosphorus, potassium, riboflavin, and thiamine.

Basmati from India or Pakistan is not fortified with minerals, unlike the varieties grown in the United States. The kind most widely used has the outer husk and bran removed. Brown basmati is also available, but it is rarely used in India because of its short shelf life (the bran and husk harbor oil that can turn rancid rather quickly).

Incidentally, if you do not see Indian basmati on the label, it isn't true basmati. California basmati and Texmati rice are facsimiles (poor ones in my opinion); and I find these grains to be stout, short, and starchy. But most supermarkets carry the Indian variety.

Oftentimes white basmati rice is stored in gunnysacks and sold in sacks, which means it needs to be washed. It is important to rinse the rice gently, so the grains, which are extremely thin, long, and tapering at each end, remain intact. Rinsing makes the rice less starchy and does not wash away any valuable nutrients. It is not necessary to soak basmati rice before you cook it, but I do; it guarantees a quicker cooking, dry, single-grained, fluffy result.

30

# 2 Ghee

## Indian-Style Clarified Butter

Making ghee is not rocket science. If you can melt butter, you can make ghee. Although ghee is widely available in stores, it is not easy on the pocketbook, so be prepared to plunk down your hard-earned money for the convenience of ready made. I admit I occasionally splurge and buy ghee that is imported from India, only because the cows (or water buffaloes, depending on where the milk came from) graze on a different diet and the resulting ghee has a unique flavor not found in America's dairy land. Ghee's nutty flavor, the result of gentle browning, is the key taste in many of our dishes, and often even a mere tablespoon is enough to provide succulence. Since the Vedic times of the Indo-Aryan culture (more than six thousand years ago), ghee has played a role in many facets of Hinduism, including fueling the eternal flame associated with birth, marriage, and death. Ghee evolved when there was no refrigeration (actually, many Indians still don't have refrigerators today). Milk solids and water promote rancidity in butter, and when they are removed, gone is the need for a refrigerator. Middle Eastern and Arabic *samneh* is made the same way as ghee, as is *smen* from North Africa.

**Makes about 12 ounces (1½ cups)**

**1 pound unsalted butter**

1 Line a fine-mesh strainer with a piece of cheesecloth, set it over a clean, dry 2-cup glass measuring cup or pint-size canning jar, and set it aside.

2 Melt the butter in a small, heavy-bottomed saucepan over low heat, stirring it occasionally to ensure that it melts evenly (otherwise, the bottom part of the block of butter melts and starts to bubble

## Ghee Step-by-Step

**1** Melt the butter in a heavy-bottomed pan over low heat.

**2** Stir the butter chunks regularly to ensure an even melt.

**3** Scoop out the foam from the melted butter's surface.

**4** Some of the milk solids have now settled to the bottom and are lightly browned.

**5** Clarify the amber-hued butter by spooning it through a cheesecloth-lined strainer set over a bowl.

while the top half remains firm). Once the butter has melted, you will notice that a lot of white foam gathers on the surface. Scoop the foam out with a spoon or just let it be; the melted butter will eventually stop foaming. Now you can start to carefully skim off the foam. Some of the milk solids will settle at the bottom and start to brown lightly. This light browning is what gives Indian ghee its characteristic nutty flavor. The whole process will take 15 to 20 minutes.

3 Once the liquid appears quite clear (like oil) with a light amber hue, pour the butter through the cheesecloth-lined strainer, leaving the browned milk solids behind. Discard the solids and set the melted butter aside to cool.

4 When the ghee is cool, pour it into a storage jar (if you haven't already strained it into one) and screw the lid tightly shut. Keep the ghee at room temperature, right next to your other bottled oils; it will solidify, even at room temperature. (I don't find it necessary to refrigerate ghee, but if you wish to, by all means do so. I have kept mine at room temperature for many months, without any concern for rancidity

## Extra Credit

- A few dos and don'ts. First, *don't* use margarine or any butter substitutes that want you to think they're just like the real deal. *Do* use a heavy-bottomed pan to prevent the butter from scorching. Cast iron, stainless steel, carbon steel, and ceramic-coated cast iron are all fair game. In fact, I use a cast-iron or carbon steel wok if I happen to be making a large batch; the fat seasons the pan. *Don't* turn up the heat beyond the low setting, as much as you may be tempted to do so; if you do, the milk solids in the butter will start to burn. *Do* make sure the glass jar for storing the ghee is clean and dry before pouring in the ghee. Moisture will promote the growth of mold. This is the same reason you should let the ghee cool completely before screwing on that jar's lid.

- You cannot deep-fry in butter because it has a low smoke point (that's the temperature at which oil starts to smoke). However, remove the milk solids and moisture and you have elevated butter's smoke point, making it safe for deep-frying (of course we are not talking about measuring fat calories when you do decide to splurge on foods fried this way).

or spoilage. Because ghee has no milk solids in it, and that's what can turn butter rancid, I do as millions in India do, and leave it out of the fridge.)

# ③ Paneer

## Whole Milk Cheese

The moment you tell someone you are making homemade cheese they either look at you in awe or think you are, frankly, insane. What they don't know is how easy it is, especially if there is no rennet involved or any hazardous steps of sticking your hand in boiling liquid to gather balls of creamy cheese, mozzarella style. Making whole-milk paneer, a mellow tasting, slightly creamy cheese and a common ingredient in every north Indian kitchen, is as simple as boiling milk—literally. In a country where more than a billion people exist, it seems a bit unfair that there is only one cheese (and it's the nonmelting kind). Who said life is fair? What's fair is that this cheese can also be purchased in the cheese section of some high-end supermarkets. Cut up, it's great in stir-fries, stews, or even crumbled over salads. Extra-firm tofu (drained before use) is a great stand-in for paneer. The vegan at your table will appreciate that.

**LACTO-VEGETARIAN GLUTEN FREE**

**Makes 1¼ pounds**

**1 gallon whole milk**

**About ¼ cup distilled white vinegar**

1 Line a colander with a double layer of cheesecloth or a clean dishcloth, making sure 2 to 3 inches hang over the rim of the colander. Place the colander in the sink.

2 Pour the milk into a large saucepan or Dutch oven and bring it to a boil over medium-high heat, stirring frequently to prevent the milk from scorching. When it comes to a rolling boil, stir in ¼ cup of vinegar. Remove the pan from the heat and set it aside until the milk separates into curds and a pale green, thin, watery whey, 15 to 30 seconds. Sometimes, depending on the acidic strength of the vinegar, you may need to add a bit more, 1 tablespoon at a time, until you see the separation happening.

3 Use a long-handled strainer to spoon the curds into the lined colander (or pour them in), and let drain. Once it's slightly cool to the touch, gather the edges of the cheesecloth and fold them over the curds to cover them.

4 Fill a heavy pot with water and set it directly on top of the cloth-wrapped curds in the colander. Set this aside until the curds are firm, 3 to 5 hours. (The weight will press on them and force out almost all of the moisture.)

5 Remove the weight and unwrap the firm, milky white cheese. Wrapped in plastic wrap the paneer can be refrigerated for up to 1 week. (You can also freeze the cheese, sealed in a freezer-safe plastic zip-top bag, for up to 2 months. Thaw the paneer in the refrigerator before using it.)

## Paneer Step-by-Step

1 Once the milk is boiling, it will start to foam.

2 Add vinegar to the boiling milk.

**3** The vinegar will cause the milk to separate into curds and whey.

**4** Transfer the curds to a cheesecloth-lined colander.

**5** Let the curds, now very cheeselike, cool slightly, then gather up the edges of the cheesecloth.

**6** Fold the cloth up over the curds.

**7** Weight the curds down with a heavy pot filled with water and let the cheese continue to drain and firm up.

**8** Remove the pot and unwrap the cheese. It should be nice and firm and ready to use.

# Extra Credit

- Paneer is often fried before it's used in dishes. To fry paneer, you have two options: one is deep-frying; the other is panfrying (my preferred method).

  *To deep-fry paneer,* cut the fresh cheese into 1-inch cubes (or any other size). Pour oil to a depth of 2 to 3 inches into a wok, Dutch oven, or deep medium-size saucepan. Heat the oil over medium heat until a deep-fry or candy thermometer inserted in the oil (without touching the bottom of the pan) registers 350°F. (An alternative way to see if the oil is at the right temperature for deep-frying is to stick a wooden skewer into the oil; once bubbles start to emerge from around the skewer, the oil is ready.) Line a plate or baking sheet with 3 or 4 pieces of paper towel. Once the oil is hot, gently slide in the paneer cubes. Fry them, turning occasionally, until they are golden brown and slightly crisp, 3 to 5 minutes. The oil will spatter because of some moisture in the cheese, so please be careful. Remove the fried paneer cubes from the oil with a slotted spoon and transfer them to the paper towels to drain.

  *To panfry paneer,* heat ¼ cup of vegetable oil in a large nonstick skillet over medium heat. Arrange the cubes of paneer in a single layer and cook them, turning occasionally, until all sides are honey brown and slightly crisp, 7 to 10 minutes. Transfer the fried paneer to a paper towel–lined plate to drain.

  One and a quarter pounds of fresh paneer will yield about 3 cups fried cheese (1-inch cubes). To store fried paneer, place the cubes in a bowl of water (it will keep them moist) and refrigerate them for up to a week, changing the water daily. Drain and pat dry before using. You can also freeze the cubes without immersing them in water in a freezer-safe plastic zip-top bag for up to 2 months.

- It's easy to customize paneer by folding in any array of herbs or spices you wish to add to the curds before you press them down. Some of my favorites are 3 to 4 finely chopped chiles, ½ cup each chopped cilantro and basil, ¼ cup chopped mint, 2 tablespoons garam masala, and ¼ cup fresh pomegranate seeds when in season.

#  Raghavan's Blend

Having written an authoritative book on Indian curries and having expounded on the benefits of tailoring blends for individual recipes, I hesitate to offer a panacean blend for all flavors Indian. It's like asking someone to gather the magic of Indian cuisine in a convenient bottle—after all, the British tried it more than four hundred years ago when they had their cooks in India create the phenomenon called curry powder. A sprinkle of that ubiquitous store-bought mixture to pepper your ho-hum meals seems like the easy way out of freshly grinding your own, but I offer you this version of mine for a bolder, zestier, more vibrant taste that may very well knock your socks off. All you need is a spice grinder (a coffee grinder reserved for spices is the answer) and a few ingredients purchased from your neighborhood grocery store to make this mellifluous medley that packs a punch in every recipe it touches. But, if you don't have two minutes to put this together, by all means use a store-bought Madras-style curry powder as an alternative. (Yes, I am opinionated, can you tell?)

The recipes that use this blend often instruct you to add it when you are stir-frying something. If you were to sprinkle the ground mélange directly into hot oil or a preheated naked skillet, it would yield burnt flavors and unappealing aromas. The cushion that vegetables provide is essential to safeguard the blend from burning on contact with the heat. This is not a masala (blend) that you can add as a finishing mix (see Garam Masala, page 41) since the spices need to cook for a smoother quality.

**Makes ¾ cup**

2 tablespoons coriander seeds

1 tablespoon cumin seeds

2 teaspoons black or yellow mustard seeds

1 teaspoon black peppercorns

½ teaspoon whole cloves

12 to 15 dried red cayenne chiles (like chiles de árbol), stems discarded

1 teaspoon ground turmeric

## Extra Credit

- Grinding whole spices prior to use is the best way to showcase their sensual fragrances and tastes. The aromatic oils within emerge when freshly ground, providing a greater depth of flavors. A spice grinder, essentially a coffee grinder, works well for pulverizing amounts greater than I or 2 teaspoons whole spices. If you double or triple the batch, a blender does a nice job of crushing them all at once. The narrower the base of the blender jar, the better the grind. Wide-mouthed jars are best reserved for shakes and blended cocktails.

- If you cannot procure whole dried red chiles, use 2 teaspoons ground red pepper (cayenne) instead. For a less potent blend, you can use sweet paprika for half the amount of chiles; add I teaspoon paprika plus I teaspoon ground red pepper.

Place the coriander, cumin, mustard seeds, peppercorns, cloves, and chiles in a spice grinder (you can also use a coffee grinder) and grind them to the consistency of finely ground black pepper. Stir in the turmeric, which will yellow the spice blend with its characteristic sunny bright disposition. Store the spice blend in a tightly sealed container, away from excess light, heat, and humidity, for up to 3 months. (In my opinion, refrigerating the spice blend adversely affects its flavors.)

# Garam Masala

VEGAN
GLUTEN FREE

In the Western world there is basically one "garam masala" that has become the iconic representation of Indian cuisine (*garam* means "warm" and *masala* means "blend"). Cooks sprinkle a dash of this into every dish they want to taste "Indian." It's surprising to us Indians as there are thousands of blends we use to pepper our soulful dishes. Garam masalas are usually found in the north of India, and they are as diverse as the regions they represent. In the myriad Indian versions the spices are left whole, toasted, roasted, or ground to create blends that span a rainbow of flavors.

When you buy a commercial garam masala what you are getting is a blend of raw (as in untoasted or unroasted) ground spices—a combination of such warming spices as cloves, cinnamon, cardamom, and the like. Toast the spice medley prior to grinding it to create an amazingly pleasing aroma. Garam masalas can be sprinkled either early on in a dish or even later as a finishing touch, since the spices are already "cooked." If you choose to go the store-bought route (really, it only takes a few minutes to make this from scratch), keep in mind it will have to be added in the early stages of a recipe to make sure the spices cook to yield a more refined cornucopia of tastes.

**Makes 1/3 cup**

I tablespoon coriander seeds

2 teaspoons cumin seeds

I teaspoon black peppercorns

1/2 teaspoon whole cloves

1/2 teaspoon cardamom seeds (removed from the green or white cardamom pods; see Extra Credit)

2 medium-size dried bay leaves

2 dried red cayenne chiles (like chile de árbol), stems discarded

I cinnamon stick (about 3 inches in length), broken up into smaller pieces (see Extra Credit)

Heat a small skillet over medium-high heat. While you are waiting for that

to happen, quickly combine the coriander and cumin seeds, peppercorns, cloves,

CARDAMOM

BLACK
PEPPERCORNS

CUMIN
SEEDS

CLOVES

CAYENNE

CINNAMON
STICKS

BAY
LEAVES

cardamom seeds, bay leaves, chiles, and cinnamon stick in a small heatproof bowl.

2 Once the skillet is hot (when you hold the palm of your hand close to the bottom of the skillet you will feel the heat), usually after 2 to 4 minutes, sprinkle in the spice mixture. Toast the spices, shaking the skillet every few seconds, until the coriander and cumin turn reddish brown, the cloves, peppercorns, and cardamom turn slightly ash black, the cinnamon and bay leaves appear brittle and crinkly, the chiles have blackened in spots, and the mixture is highly fragrant, 1 to 2 minutes.

3 Immediately transfer the nutty-smelling spice blend back to the small bowl to cool. (The longer the spices sit in the hot skillet, the more likely it is that they will burn, making them bitter and unpalatable.) If you don't allow the spices to cool, the ground blend will acquire unwanted moisture from the heat, making the final blend slightly "cakey." Once the spice blend is cool to the touch, place it in a spice grinder (or coffee grinder) and grind it to the consistency of finely ground black pepper.

4 Store the spice blend in a tightly sealed container, away from excess light, heat, and humidity, for up to 3 months.

## Extra Credit

- Green or white cardamom pods, a close sibling to ginger, are easy to pry open with your fingertips. Or open them as you would peel the skin of a garlic clove—place a pod on a cutting board and whack it with the flat side of a chef's knife. Discard the pod and use the tiny black seeds as directed.

  The seeds are also great to chew on as an after-dinner breath freshener and digestive. Removed from the pods, they are available at the supermarket in jars labeled decorticated cardamom. Buy them for convenience but be prepared to pay an arm and a leg for that accessibility. Because I use the pods in so many different ways, I just buy the pods and pry them open as needed.

  Once open, transfer these seeds into a mortar and pound them with a pestle to expose an aroma that will bring a smile to your face. Strong, musky, and addictive, these freshly ground seeds are more assertive than the preground cardamom. You can also grind the seeds in a spice grinder (like a coffee grinder) if you have more than a teaspoon of the seeds to grind. Any leftover ground cardamom is great dispersed among freshly ground coffee beans as you brew a heady pot in the morning.

- Most of those tightly furled sticks of brown cinnamon in the spice aisle come from China and are known as cassia. These are less expensive than cinnamon grown in Sri Lanka and southern India, but are fine to use. The sticks normally snap into pieces when you bend them but some of the sturdy ones may require a whack or two on a cutting board to break them into smaller pieces. Breaking up the cinnamon sticks ensures an even toast and makes them easier to pulverize in a grinder.

# Chapter 3

# Starters Unfolded

**WE INDIANS CANNOT** survive in a world that lacks munchies and nibbles. A stroll down the snack aisle of an Indian grocery store drives home that point as well as the array of recipes that pepper this chapter. Even though meals in India are never coursed out the way they are in American and Western home kitchens, the offerings in the following pages ease you into a style of cooking the Indian way that screams vibrant. You see, Indian food does not have to be complicated, and each recipe here (and throughout the book) achieves a complex-appearing layering of flavors without being cumbersome to execute. I have chosen these recipes to show-case classic regional flavors, some the traditional way, while others in a more contemporary way. They are laid out in an order of dishes that starts with simple ingredients and techniques, leading to creations that sing with complex-tasting blends that still require only ten ingredients or fewer to execute.

## The Lesson Plan

**Lesson ① Poppadums with Chile-Spiked Onion or Avocado Pomegranate Dip** In India, a stack of house-made and flame-toasted lentil wafers called *papads* are the most basic offering to dinner guests, next to a glass of water, especially in Sindhi-speaking homes (originally from the northwestern part of India, close to the Pakistan border). And so, they are the perfect starter for the complete Indian meal that I present throughout the book in step-by-step foldout lessons. Available as poppadums in mainstream stores, these are a simple way to experience that same hospitality, topped with pungent onion and sharp chiles. I hand-hold you through the technique of flame-toasting them to create a natural smokiness that is sure to blow your taste buds—in a good way!

Next, learn to toast and grind two spices to create a heady blend that breathes intensity into everyone's favorite, avocado (called butter fruit in India), which is punctuated with ruby red pearls of fresh pomegranate.

**Lesson ② Minty Potato Cakes** Once you master poppadums, slide into the world of cakes—ones made from potato, that is. These puffy patties contain readily available fresh herbs and just one simply ground spice. The binder is unusual—the potato cakes are held together with moistened bread slices.

**Lesson ③ Mustard and Almond Crab Cakes** Another slightly more sophisticated savory cake, this one chock-full of fresh crab meat. Binding it into a patty are ground almonds and eggs.

**Lessons 4 and 5 Plantain Chips and Crispy Okra Fries** Deep-frying has always been a source of fear and disdain among many of the students who have shared classes with me these past twenty-plus years. These recipes teach you how to do it with the correct oil, right temperature, and a spice or two, to yield ungreasy, can't-stop-at-one-bite classics like plantains that are perked with citruslike coriander seeds and fresh okra strips made red hot with cayenne.

**Lesson 6 Savory Mango Palmiers** Now you are ready to attack the world of flours and doughs through convenient packages of puff pastry sheets. First fold them, fanlike, into savory mango *palmiers* (spiceless but not tasteless).

**Lesson 7 Spinach Phyllo Samosas** Next turn phyllo sheets into samosas, those delectable pastry shells that usually cocoon spiced potatoes and peas. They are crispier and easier to assemble when made with sheets of phyllo dough. Gone is the usual starchy potato filling; instead you find delicate ribbons of spinach spiced with an easy to execute blend called garam masala.

**Lesson 8 Collard Greens Roulade** We often overlook the world of large-leafed vegetables to blanket ingredients. Here, collard greens offer a generous base in a classic steamed dish from northwestern India called *patra*. A paste of chickpea flour, cayenne, and turmeric is layered onto the collard leaves, then rolled into a convenient log, and steamed, cut into slices, panfried with cumin seeds, and soused with sweetened tomatoes.

**Lesson 9 Creamy Chicken Kebabs** Graduate from this class with honors by preparing a classic from northern India: strips of boneless chicken smothered with cream, fresh ginger, and an array of spices that bathe the kebabs with elegance so they grill to succulent and smoky perfection. These killer kebabs will rule the roost.

**Lesson 10 Pillowy Chickpea Cake** For the pièce de résistance, blow away everyone's palate with pillowy chickpea cakes, made with a surprising ingredient (Alka-Seltzer!) that adds a wonderful texture to the heat and nutty flavors in each addictive morsel. A layering of techniques creates a magical balance!

no need to turn them. Set them aside to cool. *Microwaving* poppadums on high power for 30 seconds to 1 minute is also an option.

2 The poppadums will turn crisp and brittle as they cool. You can store them in airtight plastic zip-top bags at room temperature for up to 2 weeks (but I bet they will be gone long before that).

3 To assemble the topping, combine the onion, tomato, cilantro, and chiles in a medium-size bowl. Just before serving, stir in the salt. Salting the "salsa" ahead and letting it sit for a while results in a pool of liquid at the bottom of the bowl, an unwanted result that will render the poppadums soggy.

4 To make the dip, heat a small skillet over medium-high heat. Once the skillet is hot (when you hold the palm of your hand close to the bottom of the skillet you will feel the heat), usually after 2 to 4 minutes, add the coriander and cumin seeds and toast them, shaking the skillet every few seconds, until they start to crackle and turn reddish brown and the aroma is highly nutty fragrant with citrus undertones, about 1 minute. Immediately transfer the seeds to a small heatproof bowl or plate to cool. Once cool, place the coriander and cumin seeds in a spice grinder (you can also use a coffee grinder) and grind the blend to the consistency of finely ground black pepper.

5 Place the cilantro, lime juice, salt, onion, garlic, and chiles in the bowl of a food processor and, using the pulsing action, mince the blend. Letting the processor run constantly will create an unwanted chunky puree, full of liquid.

6 Pit, peel, and cut the avocado into ¼-inch cubes (see Extra Credit, page 52). Place the avocado in a medium-size bowl and fold in the cilantro mixture, spice blend, and pomegranate seeds. Transfer the dip to a pretty serving bowl. If you are planning on serving the avocado dip later, press a piece of plastic wrap directly onto the dip's surface, making sure there are no air bubbles in between the wrap and the surface (this slows down the dip from oxidizing and turning a wee bit black). You can store the dip in the refrigerator for up to 2 days.

7 To serve, if you are making the spiked onion, place 6 poppadums on a large pretty platter. Evenly divide the onion topping among them, spreading it over the surface of each. If you are making the dip, place the poppadums in a cloth-lined basket with the dip alongside.

## Extra Credit

- Southern Indians call them poppadums. The rest of the nation refers to them as *papads*. Whatever they're called, these wafer-thin crackers made with various lentil flours are a must in every household in India. A great snack and a good substitute for bread, they are often flavored with cumin, garlic, black pepper, cayenne, or green chiles.

  Regional preferences usually dictate which lentil flour is used to prepare the poppadums. Poppadums are also made with tapioca pearls, rice flour, and even potato starch. The Sindhis from northwestern India will welcome you with a glass of water and airily crisp poppadums. They can be flame toasted, broiled, or cooked in a microwave. Or they can be fried or baked.

- Commercially prepared poppadums usually contain a spice called asafetida, which has a bit of wheat flour mixed in. So for someone who has severe wheat gluten allergies, these are not gluten free. You do have to watch out for the hidden ingredients.

- If your market doesn't sell poppadums, spread the Chile-Spiked Onion on crisp tostada shells. Serve the Avocado Pomegranate Dip with Plantain Chips (page 58) or store-bought kettle-cooked potato chips.

**VEGAN**

# Poppadums with Chile-Spiked Onion or Avocado Pomegranate Dip

## Masala Poppadums

Leave it to the Mumbaiites to come up with something this simple and additive. Poppadums are lentil wafers, usually found in the supermarket aisle with the Asian goods. Of course any crisp cracker will do but poppadum flavors are unique. You want to buy them sun-dried but uncooked. When flame toasted, they acquire a smoky quality that I find complements a spicy onion spread. In season, try incorporating unripe mango into the spread for a more sour experience (my favorite) that also cuts down on the heat from the chiles.

You can also break off pieces of poppadum and use them to scoop up a favorite dip. I served the one here made with avocado and pomegranate at my Thanksgiving table and all my friends uttered "sexy!" It was, I agreed, with that light green background of buttery avocado perked up with plump, juicy, and succulent teardrops of ruby red pomegranate seeds. If you can't choose whether to make the spread or dip, well then, make both.

. . . . . . . . . . . . . . . . . . . . . . . . . . . . . . . . . . . . . . . . . . . .

*If you are using a gas stove,* set the flame of a burner at medium-high. Holding 1 poppadum with a pair of tongs, flip it back and forth over the open flame until bumps start to appear on the surface and the poppadum turns light brown, 1 to 2 minutes. Remember to shift the tongs in order to toast the part initially covered by them. Repeat with the remaining poppadums. Set them aside to cool.

*If you are using an electric stove,* broiling is a great option. Place a rack as close as possible to the heating element, and preheat the broiler to high. Toast the poppadums until bumps appear on the surface and they turn light brown, 1 to 2 minutes. There is

Dip and topping make 2 cups each, enough for 6 poppadums each

### FOR THE POPPADUMS

**6 or 12 uncooked lentil wafers (poppadums), each at least 6 inches in diameter (before cooking; see Extra Credit)**

### FOR THE CHILE-SPIKED ONION

**½ cup finely chopped red onion**

**1 medium-size tomato, cored and finely chopped**

**¼ cup finely chopped fresh cilantro leaves and tender stems**

**1 or 2 fresh green serrano chiles, stems discarded, finely chopped (do not remove the seeds)**

**½ teaspoon coarse kosher or sea salt**

### FOR THE AVOCADO POMEGRANATE DIP

**2 teaspoons coriander seeds**

**1 teaspoon cumin seeds**

**¼ cup firmly packed fresh cilantro leaves and tender stems**

**2 tablespoons freshly squeezed lime or lemon juice**

**1 teaspoon coarse kosher or sea salt**

**1 small onion, coarsely chopped**

**3 large cloves garlic**

**2 to 3 fresh green serrano chiles, stems discarded**

**3 large ripe Hass avocados**

**½ cup fresh pomegranate seeds (see Extra Credit, page 52) or red raspberries**

**1** Hold a poppadum with a pair of tongs and pass it briskly back and forth over an open flame.

**2** The poppadums will turn brittle and crisp as they cool.

**3** Finely chop the onion, tomato, chiles, and cilantro for the Chile-Spiked Onion topping.

**4** Evenly sprinkle a portion of the topping over the cooked poppadum just before serving.

**5** Prepare all the ingredients for the Avocado Pomegranate Dip.

**6** Stir the pomegranate seeds into the minced dip and serve alongside the poppadums.

51

# Extra Credit

- Hass avocados are widely available in the supermarkets here in the United States. Dark green with a blackish exterior hue, these buttery fruits, rich in nutrients, are sold throughout the year. If possible, this is the variety to choose. If you are not planning on using them immediately, pick the ones that are lighter green and very firm to the touch. They do ripen quickly at room temperature once you get them home (they will feel soft to the touch and the skin does darken as they mature).

  To cut the fruit, place it firmly within the palm of one hand. Using a paring knife, cut all around the fruit lengthwise, slicing it in half—don't worry about the knife boring through as the hard pit in the center will prevent that from happening. Set the knife down and twist the halves in opposite directions to get a clean break, which leaves the pit wedged securely in one half. Steady the pit half with one hand and use a chef's knife to carefully whack the pit so the knife gets wedged in it. Twist your hand to loosen the pit and remove it in one clean sweep from the avocado half. Smack the knife handle against the edge of a garbage can, allowing the pit to fall freely into its newfound home. Now you can either peel the avocado or, using the paring knife, score the avocado pulp into the desired cube size. Scoop out the pulp with a spoon, leaving behind a clean, hollowed skin and perfectly cut chunks of umami-rich avocado.

- Freezing the dip is a great way to make it even 2 months ahead of when you plan to use it. The pomegranate can get a little squishy and slightly rubbery when thawed. If you wish, you can freeze the dip without the pomegranate (or raspberries) and fold those in when it is thawed.

- When pomegranates are in season, many supermarkets and larger grocery stores sell the seeds already removed from the fruit. You do pay a premium for these but if convenience is your shtick then it is worth it. I often buy pomegranates by the case, usually 6 (firm, all hues of red, applelike, and each with its glorious crown stem), and peel the fruit to get to the seeds while watching the news or listening to some music. It takes about an hour of my time but then I am rewarded (and especially so is my son) with a gigantic bowl of juicy, nutty, succulent, ruby red seeds that both of us can eat by the spoonful. (Yes, the seeds are edible.) To get the seeds and pulp out of a pomegranate, here's what I do: I cut the fruit in half lengthwise, and then cut each half again in half lengthwise. Working with one quarter at a time, I turn it inside out over a deep bowl, so the seeds and flesh are pushed out, like a puffed-up chest. Using my fingers, I cajole the juicy red seeds out into the bowl, discarding the thin off-white membranes that house them.

- Grill, broil, or pan sear a piece of wild salmon or halibut from the Pacific Northwest, and slather on some of the avocado dip for a simple dinner.

- You can use some leftover dip (I frankly cannot imagine you having any) as a spread for a sandwich and layer the bread with any toppings that fancy your taste. Smoked meats, cheeses, and grilled vegetables are particularly good.

# Minty Potato Cakes

## Aloo Kebabs

An unsuspecting eater will take a look and say "oooh, crab cakes," but looks are deceiving. These golden yellow patties dotted with fresh herbs are in fact made from potatoes and harbor assertive flavors that keep you begging for just one more bite. There is a reason they are perfect finger foods on the streets of India. These grab-and-go patties are pungent, minty, and crisp on the outside with a well-rounded finish that adroitly balances the heat from the chiles with the cool-down qualities of starchy potatoes and bread. They make an ideal accompaniment to the glasses of steaming, sweet chai sold in disposable clay cups on the streets of Mumbai and Delhi.

LACTO-VEGETARIAN (VEGAN IF YOU USE DAIRY-FREE BREAD)

**Makes 12 cakes; serves 6**

I pound russet or Yukon Gold potatoes

½ small red onion, coarsely chopped

¼ cup firmly packed fresh cilantro leaves and tender stems

2 tablespoons firmly packed fresh mint leaves

4 to 6 fresh green serrano chiles, stems discarded

5 to 7 slices (each about ½ inch thick) good-quality white bread

1½ teaspoons coarse kosher or sea salt

½ teaspoon ground turmeric

2 tablespoons canola oil, plus oil for panfrying

1  Peel the potatoes, cut them into large chunks, place them in a small saucepan, and add enough water to cover. Bring the water to a boil over medium-high heat. Reduce the heat to medium and let simmer, covered, until the potatoes are very tender, 15 to 20 minutes.

2  While the potatoes are cooking, place the onion, cilantro, mint, and chiles in the bowl of a food processor. Using the pulsing action, mince the blend to create an earthy, pungent mix that has a strong minty aroma. Letting the processor run constantly instead of using quick pulses

will break down the onion into a watery mess that will create excess liquid.

3 Once the potatoes are fall-apart tender, drain them in a colander and place them in a medium-size bowl. Mash them well. Wet the bread slices with warm tap water, then squeeze them tight to remove all excess water. Add the mass to the potatoes. Scrape the minced onion–mint medley over this mélange and sprinkle the salt and turmeric on top. Using your hand, squeeze the mixture to break apart the damp bread into smaller pieces, making sure you incorporate all of it into the potatoes to make a bumpy-feeling dough. It will be sun-yellow and speckled with green herbs.

4 Coat the dough with the 2 tablespoons of oil. Form the dough into a thick log. Cut it in half lengthwise and cut each half into 6 equal portions. Shape each portion into a ball about the size of a golf ball and press it gently between your palms to flatten it into a patty that is about 3 inches in diameter and ½ inch thick.

5 Line a plate or baking sheet with paper towels. Pour oil to a depth of ⅛ to ¼ inch into a large skillet (preferably nonstick or cast iron). Heat the oil over medium heat until it appears to shimmer. Place 6 of the

## Extra Credit

- To rewarm any leftover potato cakes, preheat the oven to 300°F and heat them uncovered on an ungreased baking sheet until they are warm all the way through, about 10 minutes. Or you may microwave them on high power for 1 to 2 minutes and stuff them into sliced pita bread nestled among shreds of romaine lettuce or spinach with a drizzle of a favorite yogurt sauce (I love the Yogurt with Grapes, page 108).

- You can also turn any leftovers into vegetarian burgers by warming them in a nonstick skillet with a slice of your favorite cheese on top. Place a lid on the skillet to melt the cheese. Then put the burgers in toasted buns and top each with a slice of red onion and tomato. Don't forget the fries. In my book, there is nothing wrong with potatoes, bread, and more potatoes for a carbohydrate overload. You will thank me for it.

patties in the skillet and panfry until the bottoms are golden brown and crisp, 3 to 5 minutes. (You are cooking only 6 because you don't want to overcrowd the skillet and get greasy results.) Turn the patties over and cook them until the second side is nicely browned, 3 to 5 minutes. Transfer the patties to the paper towels to drain. Repeat with the remaining 6 patties.

6 Serve the potato cakes warm.

# 3 Mustard and Almond Crab Cakes

## Kakra Kebabs

GLUTEN FREE

The flavors in these crab (called *kakra* in Bengali) cakes highlight one particular spice used in everyday Bengali cooking: mustard. A cash crop in the northern regions, everything about the plant is highly revered—the leaves, the seeds, and above all its oil. In Bengali-speaking homes pure mustard oil is drizzled as liberally as olive oil is in the Mediterranean countries. Some grocery stores in the U.S. (especially the upscale ones) may stock mustard oil, in which case, you should use it instead of the canola to panfry the cakes. Serve the crab cakes with any dipping sauce you like but my favorites are Tangy Mint Chutney (page 102) and Yogurt with Grapes (page 108).

**Makes 12 cakes; serves 6**

1 pound Dungeness or other high-quality crabmeat (see Extra Credit)

¼ cup finely chopped red onion

1 cup ground almond slivers or slices

2 tablespoons freshly squeezed lime or lemon juice

2 large eggs, slightly beaten

¼ cup finely chopped fresh cilantro leaves and tender stems

2 teaspoons ground mustard

1 teaspoon coarse kosher or sea salt

½ teaspoon ground red pepper (cayenne)

Canola oil, for panfrying

1 Line a tray with parchment paper.

2 Place the crabmeat, onion, almonds, lime or lemon juice, eggs, cilantro, mustard, salt, and cayenne in a medium-size bowl and stir to thoroughly combine. Divide the crab mixture into 12 equal portions. Shape each portion into a ball and press it between the palms of your hands to

form a patty about ½ inch thick. Place the patties in a single layer on the parchment paper–lined tray. Refrigerate the patties, covered, for at least 30 minutes or as long as overnight to help them set a bit.

3 When you are ready to cook the patties, line a plate or tray with paper towels. Pour oil to a depth of ⅛ to ¼ inch into a large skillet (preferably nonstick or cast iron). Heat the oil over medium heat until it appears to shimmer. Place 4 of the crab cakes in the skillet and panfry until the bottoms are golden brown and crisp, 3 to 5 minutes. Turn the patties over and cook them until the second side is nicely browned, 3 to 5 minutes. (The reason you are doing only four is because you don't want to overcrowd the pan and get soggy, greasy results.) Transfer the patties to the paper towels to drain. Repeat with the remaining patties.

4 Serve the crab cakes warm.

## Extra Credit

- You can very easily procure uncooked crabmeat (already cut up) ready for use in the recipe. Just be sure to pick it over carefully to remove any bits of shell or cartilage.

- Live blue crabs are available, usually from June through October, in any supermarket that has a decent seafood department and in Southeast Asian stores. If you wish to separate the crabmeat from live crabs here's what you do. Each 6-ounce crab yields approximately 2 ounces of usable meat, so for this recipe you'll need roughly 8 crabs to yield 1 pound of crabmeat. Bring a large pot of water to a rolling boil over medium-high heat. Drop the live crabs into the pot (this is humane—so say many fishmongers, cooks, and seafood experts). Cover the pan and let the water return to a boil. Allow it to boil for 30 seconds to 1 minute. Immediately drain the crabs (yes, they are now at peace) in a colander and run cold water over them to stop the cooking.

  Separate as much of the meat as possible from each crab: Place a crab on its back (that's top shell down) and yank off the front claws. Crack them open, remove the meat, and set it aside in a bowl.

  Pull off the flap (called the apron) on the underbelly of the crab and discard it. Now place the crab on its belly and remove the flap off the entire back; it should come off in a single piece. Discard the feathery gills inside the crab's shell. Using a sharp knife, cut the body in half from the head to the end of the crab. Lift the meat out, discarding any bits of shell and cartilage. Add this to the meat from the front claws.

  Crack the remaining back claws with a rolling pin and pull out the meat, adding it to the pile in the bowl. Cut some of the bigger chunks into bite-size morsels.

# 4 Plantain Chips

## Vazhaipazham Varuval

VEGAN
GLUTEN FREE

Y ou may be able to resist them but I can't! Just outside a bustling supermarket in suburban Mumbai, under a makeshift tent, is my favorite snack man with bags of assorted savories and sweets. My favorite are these cayenne-dusted plantain chips, crispy and highly addictive. The vendor stands poised over his gargantuan vat of bubbling coconut oil with a handheld slicer nestled in the crook of his arm, much like a violin maestro. But instead of the musical bow in the right hand, he has a peeled plantain he slices against the blade in a swift motion, deft and safe, right into the hot oil. The slices blister, crisp, and turn sunny brown as he scoops them up with a strainer and piles them onto a huge platter atop a growing pile of you-can't-just-have-one plantain chips. His assistant sprinkles them liberally with salt and cayenne and hands you a newspaper cone brimming with addiction. This is why your mouth is watering.

**Serves 4**

I tablespoon coriander seeds

½ teaspoon ground red pepper (cayenne)

½ teaspoon coarse kosher or sea salt

Canola oil, for deep-frying

2 large green plantains, peeled and cut crosswise into ¼-inch-thick coinlike slices (see **Extra Credit**)

Heat a small skillet over medium-high heat. Once the skillet is hot (when you hold the palm of your hand close to the bottom of the skillet you feel the heat), usually after 2 to 4 minutes, add in the coriander seeds and toast them, shaking the skillet every few seconds, until they turn reddish brown and smell slightly citrusy, 15 to 30 seconds. Immediately transfer the seeds to a small heatproof bowl or plate to cool. Once cool, place the coriander seeds in a spice grinder (you can also use a coffee grinder) and grind them to the consistency of finely ground black pepper. Tap

58

the ground coriander back into the same small bowl or plate and stir in the cayenne and salt.

2 Line a baking sheet or plate with paper towels. Pour oil to a depth of 2 or more inches in a wok, Dutch oven, or deep medium-size or large sauté pan. Heat the oil over medium-high heat until a deep-fry or candy thermometer inserted into the oil (without touching the bottom of the pan) registers close to 350°F.

3 Once the oil is hot add about one quarter of the plantain slices to the bubbling oil. Fry the slices, turning them periodically, until they are yellow-brown and appear crispy, 5 to 8 minutes. Scoop the plantain slices out of the oil and transfer them to the paper towels to drain. Sprinkle that batch while it is still hot with about one quarter of the spice blend.

4 Repeat with remaining plantain slices and spice blend. Serve the plantains warm or store them in an airtight container or zip-top bag at room temperature for up to 4 days. If they turn a little soggy, recrisp them on an ungreased baking sheet for about 5 minutes in an oven preheated to 300°F.

## Extra Credit

- Most supermarkets stock plantains next to the more common eating bananas. Plantains are usually longer, slightly curvaceous, firmer, and starchier. Choose the ones that feel rock hard. Peeling can be a hassle if you are not sure how to do it. Cut them in half crosswise. Steadying one of the halves with one hand, use a sharp knife to make a gash lengthwise through the skin about ¼-inch deep. Wedge your thumb and finger into the gash and neatly pull the skin back and off—it's that easy.

- For more even slices use either a mandoline or a box grater that has a slicer on one of its sides.

- My dear friend and colleague Meredith Deeds (an award-winning cookbook author and teacher) suggested something that made me like her even more: Open a bag of store-bought plain kettle-cooked potato chips, spread them out on a baking sheet, and bake them in a preheated 300°F oven for 5 minutes. Once they are warm, with that fresh-fried feel, sprinkle the coriander spice blend over the chips. Great with beer, brats, and brownies (not necessarily in that order).

# ⑤ Crispy Okra Fries

### Bhindi Kurkuré

I admit, my big weakness, next to potatoes, is fried foods. I never met a french fry I disliked (okay, the soggy ones maybe) since they cover both my addictions in one easy, crispy, fatty bite. Among vegetables, I have a fondness for okra and so does my son, who can eat two pounds of okra in one sitting, really! So when I created this recipe and tested it on him, his big eyes became wider, and with that sheepish grin, he asked me how I could possibly come up with something so good. I knew I had a winner. He did say "Papa, please add more heat next time." So there you go, if he can eat it with so much cayenne (yet ask for more heat), you certainly should be able to.

VEGAN
GLUTEN FREE

**Serves 4**

**I pound fresh okra (see Extra Credit)**

**I cup chickpea flour (see Extra Credit, page 9I)**

**¼ cup cornstarch**

**I tablespoon ground red pepper (cayenne)**

**2 teaspoons coarse kosher or sea salt, plus salt for sprinkling the okra (optional)**

**½ teaspoon ground turmeric**

**Canola oil, for deep-frying**

**Dipping sauce, such as Tamarind Date Chutney (page I03), for serving (optional)**

1 If you feel you need to rinse the okra, do so in a colander. Spread the pods out on paper towels to dry completely; they have to be bone-dry before you cut them or they will be slimy when cut. For that same reason make sure your cutting board and knife are also moisture free. Slice off the cap end of each okra pod and discard it. Cut each okra lengthwise in half and then cut each half once more, leaving you with four quarters per pod—pinkie-size okra fingers. Transfer the okra to a medium-size bowl.

2 Add the chickpea flour, cornstarch, cayenne, salt, and turmeric to the okra and give it a good mix.

## Extra Credit

Okra, a member of the hibiscus family, came to India via Africa and found a good home where the seasonings of spices and herbs could show it to best advantage.

Called lady fingers in India, okra are widely available in supermarkets in the United States, certainly in abundance in the southern states where they are revered stewed with seafood (think gumbo) or just plain batter fried with egg and bread crumbs.

When buying okra, look for the pods that are bright green and not more than 3 to 4 inches long. The more slender they are the less fibrous they can be. It is common practice among Indian women to pick each okra and snap its tail (the pointed tip opposite the cap) for freshness. If they break with a crisp sound, then they are perfect for the dinner table. If they appear flabby and just bend, chances are they are extremely fibrous. Trying to eat fibrous okra is like chewing on a jute bag (don't ask me how I know that). No wonder the senior citizens among the okra population are made into rope. Okra is rich in vitamins, iron, and dietary fiber so it's also good for you.

3 Line a baking sheet or plate with paper towels. Pour oil to a depth of 2 or more inches into a wok, Dutch oven, or deep medium-size or large sauté pan. Heat the oil over medium-high heat until a deep-fry or candy thermometer inserted into the oil (without touching the bottom of the pan) registers close to 350°F.

4 Once the oil is hot, pour about ½ cup of warm water over the floured okra and quickly stir it in. Here again I use my hand to mix. The okra will have clumps of wet, red cayenne-dyed batter clinging to its surface—that's fine. Take a handful of the okra and add it to the hot oil, using a slotted spoon to separate the slices the best you can. Don't overcrowd (or touch!) the oil or the okra will end up being greasy (adding too much at one time will lower the oil temperature by 30° to 50°F). Increase the heat to bring the oil back to the desired temperature. Once there, reduce the heat to maintain the temperature. I recommend about one quarter of the okra per batch. Deep-fry the okra fingers, turning them so they cook evenly until they appear reddish brown and crusty, 5 to 8 minutes. Transfer the cooked okra to the paper towels to drain. I usually sprinkle a little salt to taste over the okra while it is still hot. It just enlivens the flavors. Make sure that the oil temperature is back to 350°F each time you repeat with the remaining okra. I usually try and deal with the frying using my left hand so that I am not constantly washing my hand in between the handfuls of wet, sticky batter.

5 Serve the okra fingers with a dipping sauce when they are crispy hot. My favorite is the Tamarind Date Chutney.

#  Savory Mango Palmiers

I admit there is nothing in the Indian culinary scene that is even remotely close to these buttery, puffed-up morsels of pastry lodging bits of sour mango, pungent chiles, and sweet red onion. What we do have are rectangular biscuits, called *khara* biscuits, mile high, airily crisp, and chock-full of umami goodness in the name of butter. You can adapt that flaky goodness into fan-shaped *palmiers* made with convenient-to-buy frozen puff pastry sheets and stud them with the iconic ingredients in many a street vendor's bowl, like that unripe mango, onion, chiles, and cilantro, and you have a handheld addiction that tells you not to stop at just one!

LACTO-VEGETARIAN

**Makes about 36 palmiers**

½ cup finely chopped unripe mango
   (see Extra Credit)

½ cup finely chopped red onion

½ cup finely chopped fresh cilantro leaves and
   tender stems

2 fresh green serrano chiles, stems discarded,
   finely chopped (do not remove the seeds)

½ cup freshly shredded Parmigiano-Reggiano
   cheese

I package (2 sheets) frozen puff pastry, thawed
   (see Extra Credit)

½ teaspoon coarse kosher or sea salt

Parchment paper or nonfat cooking spray

Dipping sauce, such as Tangy Mint Chutney
   (page 102), for serving (optional)

1 Position a rack in the center of the oven and preheat the oven to 400°F.

2 Combine the mango, onion, cilantro, and chiles in a small bowl.

3 Sprinkle ¼ cup of the shredded cheese onto a dry cutting board or countertop so that it covers an area the length of an unfolded sheet of puff pastry.

4 Carefully unfold one of the puff pastry sheets. Place the puff pastry on top of the sprinkled cheese. Using a rolling pin, press on the puff pastry to make sure the cheese gets embedded in the underside.

5 Now add the salt to the mango medley and mix well. Waiting to add the salt until the last minute is a good thing. Salt draws moisture out of vegetables and fruits, and salting minutes or hours ahead of use will create an unwanted pool of liquid at the bottom of the bowl. Quickly spoon half of the mango medley onto the top of the puff pastry, spreading it out in an even layer. Fold the long edges of the sheet in toward the center so that the edges meet. Press the rolling pin down along the middle (the seam) to roll and press the dough out just a bit. The length of the sheet should be about 12 inches. Fold the dough in half along the middle to end up with a single rectangular piece. Chill this a bit in the freezer, 3 to 5 minutes. Meanwhile repeat with the remaining shredded cheese, puff pastry sheet, and mango medley.

## Extra Credit

- When picking a mango for this recipe, choose one that is rock hard (don't go by the color, go by the feel alone). To remove the skin, peel the unripe mango with a swivel vegetable peeler (fancy way of saying potato peeler). Now you need to separate the light-green, firm flesh from the large flat seed.

  Hold the peeled fruit firmly down with one hand so its tip is resting on the cutting board. Slice down the length of the broad side of the mango, running the knife as close as possible to the seed, to yield an oval, concave slice. Swivel the mango on its tip and repeat on the other side. Now slice off the narrower sides. (Frugal *moi* then continues to shave off as many slices as I possibly can, to leave behind a bald seed, not unlike my own pate.)

  Cut the slices into thin strips and then finely chop them when making this recipe. You don't want large chunks as they will tear the puff pastry.

- Make sure your puff pastry sheets are completely thawed before you unfold them. Even a trace of frost will end up breaking the sheets at the crease as you try to pry them open. Passing a rolling pin over the broken crease will patch it up but keep in mind you don't want to be rolling the dough that much for this recipe.

- For heaven's sake spend the extra dollars and buy the real deal when it comes to Parmigiano-Reggiano. This naturally aged crumbly cheese from the region of Parma in Italy is quite expensive, but when wrapped in parchment paper and stored in an airtight plastic zip-top bag in the refrigerator, it will keep for up to a month or even longer. Buy the smallest block possible; that way you are ensured of a fresh supply of this fruity, piquant cheese. And no matter what, don't ever buy that stuff in the green can that is labeled "parmesan."

- Fresh oregano or basil can be a shoo-in for the cilantro, ounce for ounce, in this recipe. Each herb will stand on its own and will complement the unripe mango's sourness.

6 Line 2 baking sheets with parchment paper or lightly spray the sheet with nonfat cooking spray. Slice the dough crosswise into ½-inch-wide slices. Arrange the slices cut side down on the prepared baking sheets (so they'll look V-shaped) about 1 inch apart from each other. Bake the *palmiers* until they are evenly brown, puffy, fanned out, and crisp, 20 to 25 minutes.

7 Savor the *palmiers* warm, as is, or with a dipping sauce like the Tangy Mint Chutney. They can be stored in airtight containers or zip-top bags for up to 3 days.

## Savory Mango Palmiers Step-by-Step

**1** Use a rolling pin to press down on a puffed pastry sheet that you've sprinkled with cheese.

**2** Spread half the mango filling evenly atop the pastry sheet.

**3** Fold the long edges of the sheet in toward the center so that the edges meet. Fold in half lengthwise again to form a rectangle.

**4** Slice the pastry crosswise into slices and bake them cut side down.

#  Spinach Phyllo Samosas

LACTO-VEGETARIAN (VEGAN IF YOU USE TOFU)

Samosas are flaky, crispy, and triangular-shaped pastry shells that cocoon seasoned potatoes and peas and are the most recognizable of finger foods in Indian cuisine. They are deep-fried and addictive, and I hanker for one (okay, I can devour four of them and call it a meal) quite often whenever I get homesick (funny, considering I have lived in the U.S. for more than half my life, I still think of India as home). This version of mine is just as comforting, but instead of the labor-intensive pastry shells, I use store-bought phyllo sheets, and baking replaces the deep-frying for a heart-healthy alternative. Popeye-friendly spinach, in lieu of the potatoes, adds to the "good for you" argument and you can eat more than four, guilt free.

**Makes 16**

2 tablespoons canola oil, plus oil for brushing the phyllo

I cup finely chopped red onion

8 ounces prewashed baby spinach (see Extra Credit), finely chopped

I cup shredded store-bought or homemade paneer (whole milk cheese; page 35) or drained extra-firm tofu (see Extra Credit)

2 fresh green serrano chiles, stems discarded, finely chopped (do not remove the seeds)

I teaspoon coarse kosher or sea salt

½ teaspoon garam masala, homemade (page 41) or store-bought

Parchment paper or nonfat cooking spray

I package frozen phyllo sheets, completely thawed (see Extra Credit)

1 Heat the oil in a large skillet over medium-high heat. Once the oil appears to shimmer, add the onion and stir-fry until it is slightly brown around the edges, about 2 minutes. I always tell my students to use their nose—if it smells like there is no pungency and your eyes stop tearing, the onion is slightly brown. You really can cook with a blindfold.

2 Stir in the spinach, paneer, chiles, salt, and garam masala and stir-fry until the spinach wilts, 2 to 4 minutes. Transfer the spinach filling to a colander and let

the excess liquid drain as you prepare the phyllo sheets. There is no need to save the drained liquid, but if you do, you can use it to season and flavor mashed potatoes.

3 Position a rack in the center of the oven and preheat the oven to 375°F. Line a baking sheet with parchment paper. If you don't have parchment paper, lightly spray the sheet with nonfat cooking spray.

4 Unfold the thawed phyllo sheets on a countertop. Have a clean and damp cloth on hand. Carefully peel a sheet of the phyllo from the pile and place it on a cutting board with the longer length of the rectangular sheet facing you. Brush it with some oil. Repeat 3 more times so you end up with a stack of 4 sheets of phyllo. To keep them from drying out, cover the stack of unfolded sheets with the damp cloth each time you unpeel a single sheet. Cut the 4-sheet stack into 4 equal strips.

5 Working quickly with one strip at a time, with the smaller edge facing you, spoon a tablespoon of the spinach filling onto the center of the narrow end closest to you. Here is where your flag-folding skills come in handy (good time to learn now). Form a triangle by folding the lower left-hand corner over the filling to the opposite side. Then fold the phyllo straight up. Next fold it up on the diagonal to the right side, maintaining the triangular shape. Continue folding this way until you get to the end of the strip. You should have a neat-looking triangle. If you have an uneven lip at the end, brush that lip with oil and tuck it under. Repeat with the remaining strips. You will need to repeat the 4-sheet stack,

strip cutting, and triangle folding three times more to yield 16 phyllo samosas.

6 Arrange the samosa triangles in a single layer on the prepared baking sheet so there is a little space in between them. Bake the samosas until they are golden brown, 25 to 30 minutes.

7 Serve the samosas warm, as is, or with a store-bought dipping sauce, with the the Tangy Mint Chutney (page 102) or with Tamarind Date Chutney (page 103).

## Filling and Folding a Samosa Step-by-Step

**1** Brush a sheet of phyllo with canola oil and top it with another sheet, repeating oiling the layers for a stack of 4 sheets.

**2** Cut the 4-sheet stack into 4 equal strips.

**3** Place a heaping spoonful of the spinach filling at one end of the phyllo dough strip.

**4** Fold the dough over the filling by lifting it up from the lower left-hand corner and bringing it to the opposite side.

**5** Fold the dough-covered filling straight up.

**6** Maintain a triangle, mimicking the classic flag fold.

**7** Now, fold the dough over on the diagonal back to the left-hand side.

**8** Continue in this manner until you reach the end of the strip.

**9** You will have a little strip left.

**10** Brush the remaining dough with a little oil and tuck it under, pressing on the dough to secure it.

# Collard Greens Roulade

Patra

LACTO-VEGETARIAN
GLUTEN FREE

A western Indian classic, *patra* is usually layered with elephant-eared taro leaves (not an easy leaf to access in your neighborhood supermarket), but my version uses the pervasive collard greens instead. Just as assertive, flavorful, and nutritional, collard greens *patra* is a cinch to make. You can steam the roulades up to three days ahead of when you plan to serve them, including making the embarrassingly easy sauce. Great as a starter or even a side, I love snacking on these each time that chip and dip bell goes off in my belly (now don't get me wrong, I love my chip-dip combo).

**Serves 6**

1 bunch collard greens (12 to 16 ounces, about 16 leaves)

1 cup chickpea flour (see **Extra Credit**, page 91)

1½ teaspoons ground red pepper (cayenne)

1½ teaspoons coarse kosher or sea salt

½ teaspoon ground turmeric

1 cup buttermilk

Nonfat cooking spray

¼ cup canola oil

1 teaspoon cumin seeds

1 can (14.5 ounces) diced tomatoes with their juices

2 tablespoons firmly packed dark brown sugar

1 Working with one collard leaf at a time, fold it in half lengthwise, along the stem. Slice the tough stem end off more than halfway up the leaf. When you unfold the leaf, you will have a V-shaped base with the tapered edges at the opposite end. Repeat with the remaining collard leaves. Give the leaves a good rinse under cold water to wash off any grit.

2 Place the chickpea flour into a medium-size bowl and sprinkle in 1 teaspoon of the cayenne, 1 teaspoon of the salt, and the turmeric. Slowly pour in the buttermilk,

whisking the mélange into a smooth almost pastelike orange-yellow batter.

3 Place a collard leaf on a work surface and spoon about a tablespoon of the chickpea batter on it. Using a spatula, spread the batter out to cover as much of the leaf as possible. Use a little more of the paste as needed, but do realize you have the rest of the leaves to cover. Arrange a second leaf on top of the first, its tapered end opposite the first one's, making sure the V-shapes overlap so as to form a hole-free leaf surface. Spoon another tablespoon of the chickpea batter, spreading it over the leaf. Repeat the layering with 2 more leaves. Starting from one tapered end, roll the 4 layered leaves into a tight log crosswise to meet up with the opposite end. The batter is almost gluelike and will hold the rolled log in place. Repeat the layering, smearing, and rolling with the remaining collard leaves and chickpea batter.

4 Lightly spray a steamer basket with cooking spray and insert it into a pan filled with water to a depth of 1 inch, or prepare a bamboo steamer for steaming by placing it in a wok filled halfway with water. If you are using a bamboo steamer, line the bottom with waxed paper and

## Extra Credit

- If you wish to appease the vegan at the table, you can use water instead of the buttermilk, but stir in a tablespoon of lime or lemon juice for a slight sourness to compensate for the buttermilk's absence.

- If you are planning on having leftovers, just keep the sauce and pinwheels separate. Sometimes marrying the two too early can turn the pinwheels into a soggy mess.

lightly spray the paper with cooking spray before proceeding. Place the rolled logs (you might have 4 logs) in a single layer—a little overlap is okay—in the steamer basket and place the pan or wok over medium-high heat. Once the water comes to a boil, steam the rolled logs, covered, until the leaves appear olive green and the filling peeking out from the edges has lost its wet sheen and appears opaque, 20 to 25 minutes. Transfer the steamed logs to a cutting board and let them cool, 5 to 10 minutes. Once cool, cut the rolls crosswise into ½-inch-thick slices.

5 Heat about 2 tablespoons of the oil in a large nonstick skillet over medium-high heat. Once the oil appears to shimmer,

arrange about half of the sliced pinwheel-like leaves in the skillet and cook until the bottoms are browned lightly, 3 to 5 minutes. Turn the rolls over and repeat with the second side, 3 to 5 minutes. Remove the browned slices from the pan and place them on a plate, keeping them warm under plastic wrap or aluminum foil as you finish browning the remaining pinwheels, adding the remaining 2 tablespoons of oil to the pan before doing this. Add these browned slices to the first batch.

6 There will be enough oil remaining in the skillet to make the sauce. Sprinkle the cumin seeds into the still-hot pan; they will instantly sizzle, turn reddish brown, and smell nutty, 5 to 10 seconds. Carefully pour in the tomatoes (so that they don't splatter all over you) and stir in the remaining ½ teaspoon of cayenne, ½ teaspoon of salt, and the brown sugar. Once the chunky sauce comes to a boil, carefully transfer it to a blender. Hold the blender lid in place with a towel and run the blender in pulses to puree the sauce until smooth, deep red, hot, nutty, and sweet.

7 Serve the warm sauce alongside the collard pinwheels.

#  Creamy Chicken Kebabs

## Malai Murghi Kebab

GLUTEN FREE

Kebabs in India are bite-size morsels of either spiced meats or vegetables and frankly have nothing to do with skewers. These creamy, moist, succulent chicken kebabs happen to be skewered for easy grilling or broiling but by all means pan cook them if you wish—you can still call them kebabs. Serve them as little predinner nibbles or with store-bought naans or whole-wheat flatbread and a side of vegetables for a quick-fix evening meal.

**Serves 4**

½ cup half-and-half

6 medium-size cloves garlic

4 pieces fresh ginger (each about the size and thickness of a 25-cent coin; no need to peel the skin)

1½ teaspoons coarse kosher or sea salt

1 teaspoon garam masala, homemade (page 41) or store-bought

½ teaspoon ground red pepper (cayenne)

1½ pounds skinless, boneless chicken breasts, cut at a diagonal into ½-inch-wide strips

Nonfat cooking spray

1 small red onion, cut in half lengthwise and thinly sliced

2 tablespoons finely chopped fresh cilantro leaves and tender stems

1 large lime, cut into 8 wedges

You'll also need 12 to 16 small bamboo skewers (see **Extra Credit**) or 4 or 5 long metal skewers

Pour the half-and-half into a blender and add the garlic and ginger. Puree until smooth. Scrape the half-and-half mixture into a medium-size bowl and whisk in the salt, garam masala, and cayenne to make a marinade. Add the strips of chicken to the red-hued marinade redolent of the dark spices that are part of the garam masala. Stir to mix well and refrigerate the chicken for at least 30 minutes or as

## Extra Credit

- Make sure you soak bamboo skewers in water for 30 minutes so they absorb some moisture and don't burn easily when they grill or broil.

- Even though I have used half-and-half for a lesser fat content, heavy (whipping) cream will yield a creamier kebab. For a less sweet taste add a tablespoon or two of plain yogurt to the marinade.

- Layer leftover cooked kebabs onto tortillas with some salad greens that have been dressed with vinaigrette for a quick lunch. For a great alternative to store-purchased vinaigrette, make a batch of the Golden Raisin Vinaigrette in the Braised Beet Salad recipe (page 127).

long as overnight. The longer you marinate the chicken, the deeper its flavors will be.

2 Preheat a gas or charcoal grill, or the broiler, to high.

3 While the grill or broiler heats, thread the chicken strips onto bamboo or metal skewers, weaving them on by going over and under the strip with the skewer. The bamboo skewers will hold 1 strip, the metal skewers will hold 3. Reserve any remaining marinade in the bowl. Leave about ¼ inch of space between each piece of chicken on the metal skewers to allow them to cook evenly.

4 *If you are grilling the kebabs,* lightly spray the grill rack with vegetable cooking spray. Arrange the kebabs on the grill rack, and baste the meat with the reserved marinade. Cover the grill, and grill the chicken, turning the skewers occasionally until the chicken pieces are light brown, 6 to 8 minutes. To test for doneness, slice into a piece with a paring knife; the meat should no longer be pink and the juices should run clear.

*If you are broiling the kebabs,* position a rack in the broiler so that the top of the chicken will be 2 to 3 inches from the heat. Lightly spray the rack of a broiler pan with cooking spray, place the skewers on the rack, and broil the chicken, turning the skewers occasionally and basting the meat with the reserved marinade, until the chicken pieces are light brown, the meat is no longer pink inside, and the juices run clear, 6 to 8 minutes.

5 Slide the chicken off the skewers onto a serving plate. Quickly toss the onion and cilantro together in a small bowl. Spread the onion mixture over the kebabs and serve the wedges of lime alongside.

# Pillowy Chickpea Cake

## Dhokla

Called *dhokla* in the western state of Gujarat, where this spongy soft cake is prevalent, these savory morsels pack just the right amount of heat with a hint of sugar. In Gujarat, they are considered breakfast food or a tea-time snack, but they make great starters and that's how I serve them. Chickpea cakes are a cinch to make from bare-bones ingredients. One of them will make you look twice and mutter "Alka-Seltzer!? What the . . ." This over-the-counter, effervescent antacid levitates the batter with much-needed carbon dioxide to give the steamed cake its final texture. The bonus? No indigestion from the chickpea flour since the crushed tablet is part of the recipe. So go ahead, eat some more accompanied by a tasty dipping sauce like the Tangy Mint Chutney on page 102.

**Serves 6**

Nonfat cooking spray

1 cup chickpea flour (see **Extra Credit**)

2 teaspoons granulated sugar

1 teaspoon coarse kosher or sea salt

½ teaspoon baking soda

1 cup buttermilk

1 tablespoon freshly squeezed lime or lemon juice

2 fresh green serrano chiles, stems discarded, finely chopped (do not remove the seeds)

2 tablets Alka-Seltzer (see **Extra Credit**)

1 tablespoon canola oil

1 teaspoon black or yellow mustard seeds

Pour water to a depth of 2 inches into a Dutch oven or large stockpot and bring to a rolling boil over medium-high heat. Fill a ramekin (about the size of an individual custard cup) or a small heatproof bowl with water and let it sink into the water in the stockpot. Lightly spray the insides of a soufflé dish (like a large ramekin about

## Extra Credit

- Even though these down pillow–soft cake wedges are scrumptious as is, feel free to top them off with a couple of additional toppings that are quite commonly added in western India: ¼ cup of finely chopped fresh cilantro leaves and tender stems and ¼ cup of dried unsweetened coconut reconstituted in hot tap water and drained before use.

- I have seen chickpea flour more frequently than ever at "regular" grocery stores either in the flour aisle or in the health food section in 1-pound packages. Made from dried chickpeas (garbanzo beans), the talcum powder–soft flour is very high in dietary fiber and proteins and has egglike qualities, making it perfect for fluffy pancakes and crepes, as a coating for crisp fried vegetables, and as a nutty-tasting thickener for thin-bodied sauces. If you have no access to the flour here's what you can do at home. Grind some dried chickpeas in a blender or spice grinder (like a coffee grinder). These stonelike beans won't break down easily but will resemble small pebbles with light yellow dust. Transfer this to a tea strainer or a sifter and let the flour pass through. Regrind the remaining kernels of beans. Continue with the sifting and regrinding until you have enough flour for the recipe. Seems a bit tedious but it works.

- An antacid that includes aspirin, baking soda, and citric acid, Alka-Seltzer works great in boosting the production of carbon dioxide in the batter, levitating it for an airlike texture while it steams. In India they use a product called Eno (a fruit salt) that is also used as a digestive. Effervescent Alka-Seltzer is more common here and makes this dish doable.

7½ inches round and 3 inches deep) or something similar with nonfat cooking spray. The dish should fit comfortably in the Dutch oven.

2 Combine the chickpea flour, sugar, salt, and baking soda in a medium-size bowl. Slowly pour in the buttermilk, whisking it in vigorously to make sure you don't have any lumps. Whisk in ¼ cup of water and the lime juice to thin out the batter a bit.

3 You will start to see bubbles forming in the batter, thanks to the baking soda and the lime juice interacting with each other. Fold in the chiles.

4 Now crush or grind the Alka-Seltzer in a mortar with a pestle or by placing it between layers of plastic wrap or in a plastic bag and pulverizing it with a hammer, meat pounder, or anything similar; you need about 1½ teaspoons ground Alka-Seltzer. Sprinkle this into the bubbly batter and stir to mix. You will see the batter rise immediately because of all that carbon dioxide that is created with that simple chemical reaction between the citrus (lime juice), baking soda, and the digestive (Alka-Seltzer).

5 Transfer the batter to the prepared souf-flé dish and place the dish on top of the small ramekin or bowl that is in the bubbling Dutch oven. Cover the Dutch oven and steam the batter over medium to medium-high heat until the top is opaque with little holes (similar to what you see when you cook pancakes on a griddle) and a toothpick or skewer inserted in its center comes out clean and relatively dry, 20 to 25 minutes. You will also notice that the steamed cake will appear deflated, much like a fallen soufflé, and that is okay. Carefully lift the soufflé dish out of the Dutch oven and let it cool, 10 to 15 minutes.

6 As the cake cools, heat the oil in a small skillet over medium-high heat. Once the oil appears to shimmer, add the mustard seeds, cover the pan, and cook until the seeds have stopped popping (not unlike popcorn), about 30 seconds. Turn off the heat and wait for the cake to cool.

7 When the cake is cool, turn the soufflé dish over a plate. The cake will fall easily onto the plate. Smear the oil and popped mustard seeds evenly over the cake. Cut it into wedges and serve at room temperature.

# Chapter 4

# Breads and Relishes Unfolded

**WHEN YOU REALIZE** that Indian food in India is always served all at once, appetizers through dessert, you'll probably want to understand the reasoning behind this. First off, the portions don't have to be gargantuan, especially if you have 6 to 8 things on the plate. The stir-fries, meats, curries, and dals all serve a role in the amalgamation of flavors that are colorful and aromatic and play on textural and temperature opposites. Take for instance the breads that fill our baskets to the brimful. Since flatware is never part of our table setting, the breads are ripped apart with one hand—the perfect eating utensil—wrapped around morsels of food, and popped into our eager mouths. Most of our traditional breads are flatbreads, incorporating every flour, grain, or legume you can imagine. In this chapter, I share a selection of breads that will help you explore a cornucopia of textures.

Once you've gotten past the breads, take notice of the relishes that dot the corner of the plate. These are our chutneys, pickles (*achars*), and *raitas*. They are meant to perk up something that needs a slap of bracing chiles, or, in the case of yogurt *raitas,* diffuse the heat from curries that are robust.

# The Lesson Plan

**Lesson ❶ All-Wheat Griddle Breads** Popular individual rounds of tortillalike griddle breads, called *roti,* may seem a little daunting at first, but they are easy to prepare, as you will see in the step-by-step photos. Your breads may not be perfectly round at first (no worries since they will still taste great), but with practice, you too will master that perfect roll and circle that Indian cooks replicate daily.

**Lesson ❷ Chickpea Pan Crepes with Onion** These crepes are part of the classic world of favorite Indian flatbreads. The vegan at the table will thank you as will your gluten-free pal when you serve a plateful of chickpea flour pan crepes (a cross between pancakes and crepes with respect to their texture) studded with onion and chiles.

**Lesson ❸ Naan** The next bread to try is naan, the quintessential bread from northern India. It's yeast-free, has a crackerlike crust with a slightly chewy interior, and is especially delicious with a liberal brushing of ghee.

**Lesson ❹ Potato Chile Bread** Continue to build up to the allure of stuffed flatbreads in my easy-to-roll interpretation of India's Potato Chile Bread called *aloo parantha.*

**Lesson ❺ Corn Bread with Mustard Greens** A hunk of corn bread, dripping with melted butter, is sinful at best, especially when it accompanies a bowl of hearty soup. In my rendition I teach you how to bring the ingredients of the peasant communities of northwestern India—mustard greens, chiles, and buttermilk—together in a dish we all have grown to love.

**Lessons ⑥ and ⑦  Tangy Mint Chutney and Tamarind Date Chutney**  The two chutneys you'll find here, one sweet-tart, the other minty-hot, complement each other beautifully well and are embarrassingly simple to make. Serve them both as accompaniments to either flame-toasted poppadums (as they do in those cookie-cutter north Indian restaurants that populate the Western world) or any of the starters in this book.

**Lesson ⑧  Mango Marmalade**  The recipe for mango marmalade delivers within minutes a classic mango pickle from western India called *murabba* that otherwise takes weeks of baking in the sun to produce its sugary, cayenne-hot splendor.

**Lessons ⑨ and ⑩  Yogurt with Grapes and Lady Finger Raita**  The yogurt dishes show you two polar opposites in terms of ingredients: One houses sweet grapes, the other pan-seared okra. Both cool and refresh the palate and so are tasty accompaniments to spicy dishes. However, you may very well make a bread from this chapter and both these dips and call it a night—and don't forget the wine!

**Lessons ⑪ and ⑫  Toasted Chile-Peanut Spread and Roasted Yellow Split Pea Tapenade**  The last two spreads, one made with chiles and peanuts, the other made with yellow split peas, are classic condiments that, in my mind, can be part of a "tapenade" tray alongside crostinis for a simple cocktail bash.

**1** Combine the flours and salt in a bowl.

**2** Drizzle enough water over the flour mixture to form a ball.

**3** Knead the dough to form a smooth, soft ball of dough. When the dough is blended and smooth, wrap it in plastic and let it rest.

**4** Roll the dough into a 12-inch-long log.

**5** Cut the log crosswise into 1-inch-wide pieces. Shape each piece into a ball.

**6** Press each ball flat to form a patty, then roll out a patty to form a round 5 to 6 inches in diameter.

# All-Wheat Griddle Breads

## Roti

**Makes 12 breads**

1¼ cups durum wheat flour
(also called durum semolina)

¾ cup pastry flour, plus flour for
dusting

1½ teaspoons coarse kosher or sea
salt

Ghee, homemade (page 31) or store-
bought, or melted butter,
for brushing

These griddle flatbreads are called roti or chappati in India and are an integral part of every meal all over the subcontinent (except maybe the south where rice rules the roost). Similar in function, form, and flavor (to some extent) to a tortilla, rotis are made with a high-protein whole-wheat grain similar to the durum hard wheat, used in making pastas, while tortillas rely on either cornmeal or all-purpose flour. Rotis are an Indian's silverware, used to wrap around succulent curries, stir-fries, pickles, and condiments—an easy, addictive, and well-engineered flatbread.

It's always a good idea to ask a friend or family member to help you make a batch, especially if this is your first time. Once you get the hang of rolling, cooking, and brushing with ghee, you'll be able to fly solo.

1 Thoroughly combine the durum and pastry flours and salt in a medium-size bowl.

2 Measure ¾ cup of warm water in a measuring cup. Drizzle a few tablespoons of the water over the salted flour, stirring it in as you drizzle. Repeat with a few more tablespoons of water until the flour comes together to form a soft ball. Using your hand (as long as it's clean, I think it's the best tool), gather the ball, picking up any dry flour from the bottom of the bowl, and knead it to form a smooth, soft ball of dough (do this in the bowl or on a lightly floured work surface). If the dough is a little too wet, dust it with

a little more pastry flour, kneading it in after every dusting until the dough feels smooth, dry, and supple. It should take 1 to 2 minutes. (If you used your hand to make the dough from the start, it will be caked with clumps of dough. Scrape them back into the bowl. Wash and dry your hands thoroughly, then knead the dough. You will get a much better feel for the dough's consistency with a dry hand.)

3 If you're ready to cook the bread, go to Step 4, or wrap the ball of dough in plastic wrap or cover it with a slightly dampened cloth. Let it rest at room temperature until you are ready to cook it.

4 When you are ready to cook the breads, using your hands, roll the dough into a 12-inch-long log. Cut the log crosswise into 12 coinlike pieces and shape each piece into a ball. Press each ball flat between your palms to form a round patty, about 2 inches in diameter. Cover the patties with plastic wrap. (If you wish, refrigerate the dough, each patty wrapped individually in plastic wrap, for up to 4 days. Let the dough return to room temperature before cooking.)

5 Tear off a large piece of aluminum foil, fold it in half lengthwise, and set it aside. Place the ghee near the stove and have a pastry brush handy.

**7** Place the round on a hot skillet. Once the underside is cooked, flip the round directly onto the second burner's open flame to cook the other side.

**8** Brush the roti with ghee and repeat with the remaining dough rounds.

**6** Heat a medium-size skillet (preferably nonstick or cast iron) over medium heat. *If you have a gas stove,* light another burner and keep the flame on medium heat. *If yours is an electric stove,* place a heat diffuser on a separate burner, with the heat set to medium. (If you don't have a heat diffuser, place a second skillet over medium heat.)

**7** While the skillet is heating, lightly flour a small work area near the stove and place a dough patty on it (leaving the others covered). Roll the patty out to form a round 5 to 6 inches in diameter, dusting it with flour as needed. Make sure the round is evenly thin, with no holes or rips on the surface.

**8** Lift the round and place it in the hot skillet. Cook the round until the surface forms some bumps and bubbles and the underside looks cooked and has some brown spots, 2 to 3 minutes. Immediately turn the round over directly onto the second burner's open flame or the heat diffuser or skillet. It will puff up and cook on the underside in barely 15 to 30 seconds. Lift it off with a pair of tongs, brush one or both sides with ghee, and slip it in between the foil layers to keep it warm.

**9** Repeat with the remaining dough patties, brushing them with ghee and keeping them stacked in the foil.

**10** Serve the rotis warm.

# Extra Credit

The kind of flour used to make these breads in India, called roti flour, also labeled *atta* ("flour"), is packaged in small, medium, and large bags and can be found in Indian, Pakistani, Middle Eastern, and other Asian grocery stores. It is very similar in texture to high-protein durum wheat flour (also called macaroni flour), which I find more often in small packages in the baking section of supermarkets or in the health foods aisle. The combination of durum wheat and a bit of low-protein pastry flour provides the right texture and feel of roti flour. If you do have the Indian flour, by all means use 2 cups of it (no pastry flour) in the recipe.

#  Chickpea Pan Crepes with Onion

Not as thick as pancakes and certainly not as wispy thin as crepes, these just right pan crepes (reminder to self: must trademark that term) are egglike in appearance and have that same buttery richness along with a lingering heat (in a good way) from the chiles. Great as is for breakfast, I ate all of them in one sitting with a bowl of fresh pomegranate seeds in between sips of French press coffee with cream. Serving the pan crepes with a bowl of plain yogurt will also take the edge off the heat from the chiles.

**Makes 4 pan crepes**

I cup chickpea flour (see Extra Credit)

I teaspoon coarse kosher or sea salt

½ teaspoon ground turmeric

I cup finely chopped red onion

¼ cup finely chopped fresh cilantro leaves
  and tender stems

3 to 4 fresh green serrano chiles,
  stems discarded, finely chopped
  (do not remove the seeds)

4 teaspoons canola oil

1 Combine the chickpea flour, salt, and turmeric in a medium-size bowl. Pour in about ½ cup of warm water and whisk it in quickly. The batter will be thick and you want to make sure it has no lumps. Once it is smooth, whisk in an additional ¼ cup of water. The consistency of the batter should be slightly thinner than a pancake batter.

2 Combine the onion, cilantro, and chiles in a small bowl. Stir the mixture into the batter.

3 Drizzle a teaspoon of the oil into a medium-size nonstick skillet or well-seasoned cast-iron pan and heat over medium heat. Halfway through the oil

getting warm—about 45 seconds—pour in about ½ cup of the onion-studded batter and quickly spread it evenly so it is about 6 inches in diameter (if you wait for the pan to get hot, the batter will clump up and you will be unable to spread it uniformly). Let the pan crepe cook until the top turns opaque and loses its glossy look, 2 to 3 minutes. Turn the pan crepe over and cook the second side until it has a few brown spots, 1 minute more. Transfer it to a plate. If you do not plan on serving the pan crepe right away, keep it wrapped between pieces of aluminum foil at room

## Chickpea Pan Crepes with Onion Step-by-Step

**1** Whisk the batter smooth, then add the onion-and-chile mixture.

**2** Spoon out ½ cup of the batter onto an oiled, warm cast-iron pan or nonstick griddle.

**3** Spread the batter out to about 6 inches in diameter. After 2 to 3 minutes, the top of the crepe will turn opaque.

**4** Once flipped, it just needs another minute in the pan to finish cooking.

temperature. Storing it in a preheated oven may cause it to dry out.

4 Before you make the second pan crepe, wet a piece of paper towel with cold water. Squeeze the excess water out. Wipe the hot skillet to lower its temperature then quickly drizzle a teaspoon of oil into the skillet and repeat with another ½ cup of the batter spreading, cooking, and turning the pan crepe. Repeat the process with the remaining oil and batter.

## Extra Credit

- Bob's Red Mill makes a chickpea flour that's available in supermarkets, but I also give instructions on how to make your own (see page 22).

- If you don't wish to use all the batter, you can refrigerate it, covered, for up to 3 days. The longer the batter sits the thicker it will get. Thin it down to the right consistency by whisking in ¼ cup of water. If you have made all the pan crepes, you can rewarm them, wrapped in slightly damp paper towels, in a microwave oven on high power for 30 seconds to I minute.

- Any vegetable works well with pan crepes. I usually add ribbons of fresh spinach and chopped red tomatoes for a festive look. Because of the chickpea flour's egglike quality, think of the pan crepes as a vegan's dream omelet and include mushrooms, blanched asparagus, artichoke hearts, and bell peppers. While by no means kosher, crispy bacon, ham, and pancetta are equally delicious (and certainly nonvegetarian). Add in some of your favorite shredded cheeses as the pan crepes cook and you will expand the satiating qualities.

- I often think of leftover pan crepes as a healthier alternative to tortillas (not to mention that they are gluten free). Fill them with cooked black beans, avocado, and shredded pepper Jack cheese and fold them up for a great lunch or dinner. Stack a few of them together and mince them into "scrambles." In the peak of summer, scoop out tomatoes and fill them with the scramble. Top them off with a cheese sauce and you can serve them as an elegant first course.

# ③ Naan

*aan* is northern India's classic flatbread. The dough is effortless and requires no rising time because of the absence of yeast. Naan is usually baked on the inner walls of a high-temperature, clay-lined oven called a tandoor. Here is my grilled version, so no need for a tandoor (see Extra Credit for an oven version). Crispy, chewy, tender, and toothsome, these are perfect for single servings.

LACTO-OVO
VEGETARIAN

**Makes 4 naan (each about 8-inches in diameter)**

3 cups unbleached all-purpose flour, plus additional for rolling out the dough

2 teaspoons baking powder

I teaspoon coarse kosher or sea salt plus extra for sprinkling

I large egg, slightly beaten

Canola oil, for brushing the dough

Ghee (page 3I), for the finished naan

**1** Thoroughly combine the flour, baking powder, and 1 teaspoon salt in a large bowl.

**2** Pour the beaten egg over the flour mixture and quickly stir it in. The flour will still be very dry, with a few wet spots.

**3** Pour 1 cup of warm tap water into a measuring cup. Drizzle a few tablespoons of the water over the flour mixture, stirring (you can use your hand—as long as it's clean, I think it's the best tool) it in as you drizzle. Repeat with a few more tablespoons of water until a soft, slightly sticky—but manageable—dough ball is formed. Watch the dough carefully; you don't want it so sticky you have to add more flour to make it workable.

**4** If you used your hand to make the dough, it will be caked with floury clumps. Scrape the clumps back into the bowl. Wash and dry your hands thoroughly, then knead the dough. (You'll get a much better feel for the dough's consistency with dry hands.) To knead the dough, dust your hands lightly with flour. Knead the dough to form a smooth, soft ball, 1 to 2 minutes.

5 Divide the dough into 4 equal portions. Lightly grease a plate with oil. Shape one portion into a round resembling a hamburger bun and put it on the plate. Repeat with the remaining dough.

6 Brush the tops of the dough rounds with oil, cover them with plastic wrap or a slightly dampened cloth, and let them sit at room temperature for about 30 minutes. Allowing the dough to rest softens the gluten that has formed as you knead the dough. Gluten is what gives bread its structure, and when just formed, it has a tendency to spring back into a tightness, making it difficult to roll the dough.

7 Place a pizza stone or unglazed pottery tiles on a grill rack. *If you are using a gas grill,* preheat it to the highest heat setting. *If you are using a charcoal grill,* build an intensely hot fire so the charcoal turns ash-white and red-hot. The temperature should hover between 600° and 700°F.

8 Tear off a large piece of aluminum foil, fold it in half, and set it aside.

9 Lightly flour a small work area near the grill and place a dough ball on it. Press it down to form a patty. Roll the patty out to form a round roughly 3 to 5 inches in diameter, dusting it with flour as needed. Make sure the round is evenly thin, with no tears on the surface. Sprinkle a little coarse salt over the top, and gently press it into the dough. Lift the round and flip it, salt side down, onto the hot pizza stone. Within seconds, the dough will start to bubble in spots. Cover the grill and cook until the dough turns crispy brown on the underside and the top acquires light brown patches, 2 to 3 minutes. Remove it from the stone, liberally brush the top with ghee, and slide it between the layers of foil to keep it warm.

10 Repeat with the remaining dough rounds, stacking them on top of the previously grilled naans.

## Extra Credit

It is hard to generate that same intense heat in a kitchen oven because they are not designed to go above 550°F, but you can bake the flatbread in an oven if you don't have a grill (or if it's snowing outside). If yours is a conventional oven, place the pizza stone on the lowest rack and preheat the oven to the highest temperature setting. A convection oven generates the same amount of heat but distributes it more evenly, so you can place the pizza stone on any of the racks. You will need to bake the bread a little longer than you would on an outdoor grill.

## Naan Step-by-Step

**1** Combine the flour, baking powder, and salt in a bowl, pour the lightly beaten egg over the mixture and quickly stir it in.

**2** The ball of dough should be slightly sticky but manageable. If it's too sticky, sprinkle on a bit more flour.

**3** Knead the dough to form a round, slightly sticky-soft, smooth, and easy to handle ball.

**4** Cut the ball into 4 portions. Shape each portion into a hamburger-bun-like round. Brush with oil and let rest 30 minutes.

**5** Press the dough round down and roll it out into a round 3 to 5 inches in diameter. Cook on a pizza stone on a hot grill.

**6**. Liberally brush the grilled naan with ghee and dig in.

#  Potato Chile Bread

## Aloo parantha

This is my simplified version of the more laborious, hand-stuffed flatbreads called *aloo paranthas*—chile-spiked smashed potatoes stuffed into an Indian whole wheat dough and griddle cooked. I call it *aloo paranthas* deconstructed. And the beauty of this version is that you don't need the signature *atta* flour commonly used in Indian breads, for which a trip to an Indian market would be highly probable. A combination of high-protein durum flour (from which pasta is made) and light pastry flour, both available in the flour section of your supermarket, does the trick.

LACTO-VEGETARIAN (VEGAN IF YOU USE VEGAN BUTTER OR OIL INSTEAD OF GHEE OR BUTTER)

**Makes 16 flatbreads**

I pound russet or Yukon Gold potatoes

½ cup firmly packed fresh cilantro leaves and tender stems

6 pieces fresh ginger (each about the size and thickness of a 25-cent coin; no need to peel the skin)

2 fresh green serrano chiles, stems discarded

1½ teaspoons coarse kosher or sea salt

½ teaspoon garam masala, homemade (page 41) or store-bought

I cup durum wheat flour (also called durum semolina)

½ cup pastry flour, plus flour for dusting

Ghee, homemade (page 31) or store-bought, or melted butter, for brushing

1 Peel the potatoes and place them in a small saucepan. Add water to cover and bring to a boil over medium-high heat. Reduce the heat to medium and let the potatoes simmer, covered, until they are very tender, 15 to 20 minutes.

2 While the potatoes are cooking, place the cilantro, ginger, and chiles in a food processor. Using the pulsing action, mince the blend to create an earthy, pungent mix that has a strong aroma, reminiscent of fresh mown grass (my favorite smell of

summer). If you let the processor run constantly (instead of using quick pulses), it will break down the ingredients into a watery mess with excess liquid.

3 Once the potatoes are fall-apart tender, drain them, setting aside about ½ cup of the potato cooking water. Transfer the potatoes to a medium-size bowl. Mash them well (no need for a potato ricer). Fold in the minced herb-chile blend, the salt, and the garam masala.

4 Add the durum and pastry flours and stir to mix. Now, pour a few tablespoons of the still-warm reserved potato water over the potato and flour mixture, stirring it in as you go. Keep adding water by the tablespoon until the mixture comes together to form a soft ball; you will use about ¼ cup of that potato water altogether, maybe a tablespoon more or less. Using your hand (as long as it's clean, I think it's the best tool), gather the ball, picking up any dry flour from the bottom of the bowl, and knead it to form a smooth, soft ball of dough (do this in the bowl or on a lightly floured work surface). If the dough is a little too wet, dust it with a little more pastry flour, kneading it in after every dusting until you get the right soft, dry consistency. (If you used your hand to make the dough from the start, it will be caked with clumps of dough. Scrape them back into the bowl. Wash and dry your hands thoroughly, then knead the dough. You will get a much better feel for the dough's consistency with a dry hand.) The dough consistency should be dry, smooth, almost satiny but still a bit bumpy, and speckled with herbs and spices.

5 Cover the dough with plastic wrap or a slightly dampened cloth until you are ready to make the breads (the dough will keep for a few hours).

6 When you are ready to cook the breads, use your hands to roll the dough into an 8-inch-long log (lightly flour the work surface if necessary). Cut the log crosswise into 16 pieces and shape each piece into a ball. Press each ball flat between your palms to form a round patty. Cover the patties with plastic wrap.

7 Tear off a large piece of aluminum foil, fold it in half lengthwise, and set it aside. Place the ghee near the stove and have a pastry brush handy.

**8** Heat a medium-size skillet (preferably nonstick or cast iron) over medium heat.

**9** While the skillet is heating, lightly flour a small work area near the stove and place a dough patty on it (leave the others covered). Roll the patty out to form a round 5 to 6 inches in diameter, dusting it with flour as needed. Make sure the round is evenly thin, with no tears on the surface.

**10** Lift the round and place it in the hot skillet. Cook the round until the surface has some bumps and bubbles and the underside has some brown spots and looks cooked, 2 to 3 minutes. Immediately turn the round over and cook it until the second side has brown spots, 2 to 3 minutes.

**11** Brush the round with ghee and turn it over to sear it, about 15 seconds. Brush the top with ghee and turn it over to sear the second side, about 15 seconds. Slip the griddle-cooked bread in between the foil layers to keep it warm.

**12** Repeat with the remaining dough patties, stacking the finished breads in the foil.

## Extra Credit

- Flatbreads like this one often function as edible eating utensils. You tear a piece off with your fingers, wrap it around a morsel of stir-fry or curry, and pop the whole thing in your mouth. Think outside that proverbial bun and serve the bread as an appetizer, cut into wedges, with a favorite dipping sauce. My favorite, Roasted Yellow Split Pea Tapenade (page 112), is perfect with this.

- These cooked breads freeze well for up to two months. I usually separate them with a sheet of parchment paper or waxed paper between each and slip the whole kit and caboodle into a plastic zip-top bag. When I want a few piping hot breads at a moment's notice, I wet and squeeze the excess water from a couple of paper towels. I wrap them around as many frozen breads as I wish to thaw and warm the bread in the microwave on high power for 30 seconds to 1 minute. As good as fresh!

**13** Paranthas are best served fresh and warm. They will keep, wrapped in foil and refrigerated, for up to 4 days. Reheat, still wrapped in foil, in a 250°F oven for 20 minutes. (For freezing instructions, see Extra Credit.)

# 5 Corn Bread with Mustard Greens

Y ou look at this recipe and immediately say "this is down-home cooking, southern American style," and I look at the same set of ingredients and think of the farming community of northwestern India. Based on a classic stick-to-your-ribs meal of pureed chile-spiked mustard greens and griddle-cooked cornmeal flatbread, my rendition delivers all of that in one easy bake. The night I baked this, I served Truck Stop Beans (page 213) and the combination seemed perfect in my Midwestern cozy home kitchen as the thermometer on my backyard deck dipped to -10°F. And please don't ask me why I live in the tundra.

**Serves 6**

¼ cup canola oil, plus oil for brushing the baking dish

1¼ cups unbleached all-purpose flour

¾ cup yellow cornmeal

2 tablespoons granulated sugar

2 teaspoons baking powder

I teaspoon coarse kosher or sea salt

I cup finely chopped fresh mustard greens or thawed frozen chopped leaves (see **Extra Credit**)

2 fresh green serrano chiles, stems discarded, finely chopped (do not remove the seeds)

I cup buttermilk

I large egg, slightly beaten

I Place a rack in the center of the oven and preheat the oven to 400°F. Brush the inside of a 9-inch square baking dish with oil.

2 Combine the flour, cornmeal, sugar, baking powder, and salt in a medium-size bowl. Stir in the mustard greens and chiles.

## Extra Credit

- Frozen chopped mustard greens are quite common in the freezer section of the supermarket. Once thawed and drained, chop them a bit more since the pieces can be large. And please, stay away from the canned aisle since I find mustard greens in a can quite unpalatable. One of the richest vessels of iron in the sea of greens, fresh mustard has a pleasant bitterness that titillates your nasal canal with each bite, reminiscent of horseradish and wasabi (but not that potent).

- Every part of the mustard plant (leaves, seeds, and oil) is prized in the northern regions of India and dates back to prebiblical times. Although there are more than fifteen kinds of fresh mustard greens available, each with varying degrees of bitterness, you won't find more than one kind at your neighborhood supermarket. Choose a bunch that is bright green and crisp looking (as in sharp and perky). To clean and cut up mustard greens here's what you do: Fill a medium-size bowl with cold water. Take a mustard leaf and cut it on both sides of the tough rib to remove and discard it. Slice the leaf in half lengthwise. Repeat with the remaining leaves. Stack the leaf halves, about 6 at a time, one on top of the other, and roll them into a tight log. Thinly slice the log crosswise, ending up with long, slender shreds, often referred to as a chiffonade cut. Dunk the shreds in the bowl of water to rinse off any grit. Drain the leaves in a colander. Repeat once or twice if the leaves don't appear clean.

- Leftover corn bread, when crumbled, makes for a pleasant topping for any casserole you may be baking. Turn the crumbles into stuffing at Thanksgiving by adding celery, onion, and fresh or dried sage to them. Currants, cranberries, or even golden raisins are fair game as well.

3 Place the ¼ cup oil, buttermilk, and egg in a small bowl and stir to mix. Pour this over the mustard green mixture and mix it in with a spoon to evenly incorporate everything into a thick batter.

4 Scrape the batter into the prepared baking dish and bake it, uncovered, until the top appears dry and light brown and a toothpick or skewer stuck in the center comes out clean, 25 to 30 minutes.

5 Let the corn bread cool in the pan, then cut into squares and serve warm.

# 6 Tangy Mint Chutney

Pudhina Chutney

VEGAN
GLUTEN FREE

Chutney to an Indian is a relish or a condiment. A majority of our chutneys are made with vegetables, herbs, spices, and legumes. Fruits play a small role in that world since most of our chutneys pack assertive flavors in small amounts, often leaning toward the savory side of the equation. So, don't confuse all chutneys with the world of mangoes and that jolly old Major (Grey that is). This particular relish sneaks in a nose-tingling pungency from daikon radish, reminiscent of horseradish, but not as assertive as the overbearing wasabi.

**Makes about 1 cup**

Juice from 1 large lime

1 small daikon radish (see Extra Credit)

1 medium-size tomato

½ cup firmly packed fresh mint leaves

¼ cup firmly packed fresh cilantro leaves and tender stems

1 large clove garlic

1 to 2 fresh green serrano chiles, stems discarded

1 teaspoon coarse kosher or sea salt

1 Pour the lime juice into a blender. Peel the radish with a potato peeler and lop off about ½ inch from both ends. Give the radish a good rinse and thinly slice it crosswise. Add the slices to the lime juice in the blender.

2 Core the tomato, coarsely dice it (there's no need to peel it or remove the seeds). Add the tomato to the blender along with the mint, cilantro, garlic, chile(s), and salt. Puree the herbaceous medley, scraping the inside of the blender as needed, to ensure a smooth blend.

3 Serve the chutney either at room temperature or chilled as a dipping sauce. It will keep in the refrigerator for up to a week or freeze for up to 2 months.

## Extra Credit

- Daikon radish is widely available in supermarkets and Asian grocery stores. It is a long, thick, white-fleshed radish (also called Asian radish) with a softened piquancy; it bears a textural closeness to red radish. In India, it is a common sight to see ornately cut slices of daikon radish chilling on blocks of ice on makeshift carts, beckoning passersby to nibble on them during the hot, sultry days of summer. They also end up in pickles, curries, and stir-fries. If daikon radish is unavailable, you can use red radishes as an alternative (you'll need 1 cup of sliced radishes) along with a teaspoon of prepared horseradish.

- Besides the traditional uses as a dipping sauce for appetizers and cut-up vegetables, any leftover chutney is great as a dollop atop a bowl of winter or summer soup that may require a burst of zing, similar to that from pesto and pistou in Italian and Provençal fare. Perk up a simply grilled fish with a smear of chutney or fold it into diced avocado for a bracing relish for corn chips.

# 7 Tamarind Date Chutney

Meetha Chutney

VEGAN
GLUTEN FREE

Embarrassingly simple to make, yet sophisticated in taste, this chutney, in one version or another, graces the table at all Indian restaurants in the Western Hemisphere. My version delivers four essential tastes of sour, sweet, hot, and salty with only four ingredients. A great dip for poppadums and potato chips, this is also a great glaze for barbecued pork tenderloins.

**Makes about 1½ cups**

1 teaspoon tamarind paste or concentrate (see **Extra Credit**, page 189)

1½ cups chopped seedless dates (see **Extra Credit**)

¼ teaspoon ground red pepper (cayenne)

¼ teaspoon coarse kosher or sea salt

1 Whisk the tamarind paste and 1½ cups of warm water together in a small saucepan to create a murky, dark chocolate brown colored water, sour enough to make you pucker your lips in a big way. Stir in the dates, cayenne, and salt.

2 Bring the mélange to a boil, uncovered, over medium-high heat. Once it starts to boil, lower the heat to medium and let it continue to simmer vigorously, still uncovered, stirring occasionally, until the dates soften, 6 to 8 minutes.

3 Pour the tamarind mixture into a blender, and, holding the lid in place with a towel, pulse the liquid until the dates are pureed. (Sometimes letting the blades whir nonstop will create a vacuum due to the buildup of steam that can force off the lid and trust me you don't want to clean up that mess.) Transfer the sweet and sour chutney to a glass jar (nonreactive is what you are looking for because of the acidity of the tamarind). You can store the chutney in the refrigerator for up to a week or in the freezer for up to 2 months.

4 Serve the chutney chilled as a dip for any of your favorite appetizers. It goes especially well with the Spinach Phyllo Samosas (page 67).

## Extra Credit

Dried or fresh dates are delicious in this recipe. Most of the gourmet varieties from the Middle East are available with their pits. The pits are long and narrow and are easy to remove. Pry the date apart with your fingers and pull out the pit. I prefer the variety of dates known as Medjool for their sweetness. About 15 medium-size dates will yield the amount you need for the recipe.

# Mango Marmalade

## Murabba

I know I am revealing my age when I say that during my teen years I listened to seventies disco. So while creating and testing this recipe, I just happened to catch Patti LaBelle belting out "Lady Marmalade" in her silver, moonlike, alien getup, gyrating suggestively, wondering in Creole French if I wanted to sleep with her this evening (*"Voulez-vous coucher avec moi ce soir?"*). Well, tempting as that may be, my hands were busy stirring a pan that housed crisp-tender unripe mango, puckered with natural sourness that was balanced with a smothering of sweet sugar, blood-pumping cayenne, and sensuous cardamom. I had plans for that evening that only involved my very own Lady Mango Marmalade—addictively hot, pleasingly sweet, with just the right touch of acid. I had my own hit for the night and I was slaphappy.

VEGAN (IF YOU USE UNREFINED SUGAR, SEE EXTRA CREDIT) GLUTEN FREE

**Makes about 2 cups**

**I pound unripe mango (see Extra Credit)**

**I cup granulated sugar**

**¼ cup cider vinegar**

**2 tablespoons ground red pepper (cayenne)**

**½ teaspoon ground cardamom (see Extra Credit, page 43)**

1 Peel the mango (you may need more than one) with a potato peeler. Using the large holes of a box grater or a mandoline with the shredding attachment in place, shred the mango on all sides as close as you can get to the pit without shaving the large seed. You should end up with about 4 cups of shreds.

2 Place the mango shreds in a medium-size saucepan and stir in the sugar, vinegar, cayenne, and cardamom. Let the sugar-studded shreds come to a boil over medium-high heat. Boil the mango mixture, uncovered, stirring it occasionally. Once the liquid starts to evaporate, after 8 to 10 minutes, reduce the heat to medium-low

and continue simmering, uncovered, stirring occasionally, until the sugar starts to caramelize, and look bubbly with a gorgeous reddish-brown luster and very much jamlike, 10 to 15 minutes. Remove the marmalade from the heat and let it cool.

3 Once cool, store the marmalade in a glass container (because then you can look at it and marvel at its beauty) in the refrigerator for up to a month. Whenever you wish to use the marmalade, let it come to room temperature so it spreads easily. A quick zap in the microwave or immersing the jar in hot water will expedite that.

## Extra Credit

- Refined granulated sugar is not vegan since charcoal is used in its processing. Charcoal is often derived from animal bones, making it vegan unfriendly. Unrefined sugar is a great alternative.

- When choosing an unripe mango at the grocery store, go by feel alone and not by color. The more rock hard it is the better it will be for this recipe. Keep in mind I am looking for a natural source of sourness in this dish and the unripe mango will deliver that, in addition to maintaining a noodlelike, al dente texture when stewed.

- Besides the obvious way to savor the marmalade—spread on toast—you can also serve it as a snack with pita chips, spread it on pieces of flatbread (western Indian style), or thin it down with cream for a dip. Think outside that proverbial box. Get yourself some Brie and warm it slightly in the microwave (for barely a minute). Spoon slightly warmed marmalade over the Brie and serve it with pieces of garlic crostini. Or, for an *en croûte* starter, thaw a sheet of puff pastry, wrap that around the marmalade-topped Brie, and bake it in 350°F oven until the crust is sensuously golden brown, about 30 minutes.

# Yogurt with Grapes

## Draaksh Raita

LACTO-VEGETARIAN
GLUTEN FREE

Westerners know raita as a yogurt-based accompaniment that arrives at the table in bowls alongside curries and flatbreads. Smooth, creamy, and studded with vegetables (usually cucumbers and tomatoes), these are spiked with a spice or two and serve as the heat diffuser for a kick-ass curry or stir-fry. To Indians raitas are as versatile as the regions they represent. The only common ingredient is plain yogurt; everything else is up for grabs. Any fruit, vegetable, spice, legume, and herb can bathe in the yogurt's cultured presence, providing cooling comfort to anything hot that touches your mouth. This version of mine swirls in plump grapes, sassy cilantro, and bracing cayenne, but what brings it home for me is the inclusion of toasted cumin seeds, strong but sweet, peppering relief in between mouthfuls of a fiery hot curry.

**Makes 3 cups**

2 cups plain yogurt

½ teaspoon coarse kosher or sea salt

¼ teaspoon ground red pepper (cayenne)

I teaspoon cumin seeds

½ pound green and/or red seedless grapes, sliced in half

2 tablespoons finely chopped fresh cilantro leaves and tender stems

1 Whisk together the yogurt, salt, and cayenne in a medium-size bowl.

2 Heat a small skillet over medium-high heat. Once the skillet is hot (when you hold the palm of your hand close to the bottom of the skillet you will feel the heat), usually after 2 to 4 minutes, sprinkle in the cumin seeds and toast them, shaking the skillet every few seconds, until the seeds turn reddish brown and smell incredibly nutty, 30 seconds to 1 minute. Transfer the toasted cumin to the bowl with the yogurt.

**3** Add the grapes and the cilantro, and stir to mix well. Serve the raita slightly chilled or even at room temperature. It will keep in the refrigerator, covered, for up to 5 days. Do not freeze it as the grapes will turn into a watery mess when thawed and the texture of the yogurt will deteriorate.

## Extra Credit

- Toss salad greens with any leftover raita as it makes a luscious, low-fat, oil-free dressing. Plop a spoonful atop burgers or ladle some on meatballs (for a stroganoff effect), or pass along a bowlful with wedges of pita crisps as a snack. You won't have a problem saucing it all up.

- Don't throw away any leftover grilled or boiled vegetables. Turn them into a raita—2 cups chopped vegetables will do the trick in this recipe. Snip in fresh basil or dill for a Mediterranean touch. We Indians are, after all, everywhere!

## 10 Lady Finger Raita
### Bhindi Pachadi

LACTO-VEGETARIAN
GLUTEN FREE

Okra in India are called lady fingers, their slender, delicate bodies perhaps reminiscent of ladies' appendages (but do shy away from the overly long stubby ones since they can be quite woody and fibrous). I first sampled this unusual salad when it was plopped on my banana leaf at a family wedding. I was used to the perfunctory cucumbers, tomatoes, and onions, but the inclusion of okra threw me for a loop. Yogurt accompaniments such as this one (called *raitas* in the north and *pachadis* in the south) are integral in providing cooling balance to anything at the dinner table that is chiles-hot. Great for summers, serve it as a side (Indian style), or as the center stage attention grabber for a starter alongside wedges of flatbread.

**Makes 4 cups**

2 cups plain yogurt

I teaspoon coarse kosher or sea salt

½ pound fresh okra (see **Extra Credit**, page 62)

2 tablespoons canola oil

I teaspoon black or yellow mustard seeds

¼ teaspoon ground turmeric

2 to 3 fresh green serrano chiles,
 stems discarded, finely chopped
 (do not remove the seeds)

2 tablespoons finely chopped fresh cilantro
 leaves and tender stems

1 Whisk together the yogurt and salt in a medium-size bowl.

2 If you rinse the okra, do so in a colander. Spread the pods out on paper towels to dry completely; they have to be bone-dry before you cut them or they will be slimy when cut. For that same reason make sure your cutting board and knife are also moisture free. Slice off the cap end of each okra pod and discard it. Slice each okra crosswise into coinlike ¼-inch-thick slices.

3 Heat the oil in a medium-size skillet over medium-high heat. Once the oil appears to shimmer, add the mustard seeds, cover the skillet, and wait until the seeds have stopped popping (not unlike popcorn), about 30 seconds. Stir in the okra slices and sprinkle in the turmeric along with the chiles. What you are looking for here is a high sear that will blister the okra in spots, an essential process to get rid of much of that potential slimy liquid that okra secretes. Sear the okra uncovered, stirring occasionally, until you get those blisters, 5 to 8 minutes. Reduce the heat to medium-low, cover the skillet, and cook, stirring occasionally, until the okra becomes fork-tender, about 5 minutes.

4 Transfer the cooked okra to the bowl with the whisked yogurt and stir in the cilantro. Serve the raita either at room temperature or chilled. It will keep in the refrigerator, covered for up to 5 days.

## Extra Credit

If I have some steamed white rice left over, I will often warm it up and mix it in with the okra raita for a quick lunch. Takes care of leftovers in one tasty temptation.

#  Toasted Chile-Peanut Spread

## Shengdana Mirchi Chutney

VEGAN
GLUTEN FREE

A classic spread, chutney, dip, what-have-you among the western Indian community of Maharashtrians, incorporating peanuts with smoky chiles and sweet-soft garlic, I find this an assertive, in-your-mama's-face sibling to "highbrow" Italian pesto or Provençal pistou. Even though the inclusion of so many chiles might raise an eyebrow, don't break a sweat over it—the toasting of fresh chiles actually creates a smoky flavor that masks the heat a bit, and when combined with the protein-rich peanuts, the results are downright tame. Not to mention healthy (no oils added to the recipe).

**Makes ½ cup**

**4 fresh green serrano chiles, stems discarded**

**4 medium-size cloves garlic (do not remove the papery skin)**

**I cup firmly packed fresh cilantro leaves and tender stems**

**½ cup unsalted dry-roasted peanuts**

**½ teaspoon coarse kosher or sea salt**

1 Heat a small skillet over medium-high heat. Once the skillet is hot (when you hold the palm of your hand close to the bottom of the skillet you will feel the heat), usually after 2 to 4 minutes, add the chiles and garlic. Toast them, turning each of them occasionally as the chiles blister all around, acquiring brownish black patches, and the garlic cloves steam and soften within their flimsy jackets, 8 to 10 minutes. Transfer the chiles to a food processor and the garlic to a plate to cool a bit. Once the garlic is cool enough to handle with your bare hands, slip the skins off and add the soft cloves to the chiles.

2 Pile in the cilantro, peanuts, and salt. With the machine running, process the mixture to the consistency of a thick pesto. If you wish a smoother texture, drizzle

## Extra Credit

Use the chile-peanut spread as you would pesto. Thin it down a bit with water and toss it with a half pound of your favorite pasta shape. When you drain the pasta, give it a few shakes but don't rinse it. There will be enough water clinging to the pasta to make tossing much easier, and ensure that the spread does a better job clinging to it.

about ½ cup of water through the feed tube as the spread processes.

3 Transfer the spread to a small bowl. It will keep in the refrigerator, covered, for up to 4 days or in the freezer for up to 2 months.

## 12 Roasted Yellow Split Pea Tapenade

Paruppu Tohayal

VEGAN
GLUTEN FREE

You say tapenade, I say chutney! You get the gist. A classic roasted legume chutney from the southeastern part of India, this captures the very essence of what that region is all about—nutty and hot. My grandmother used to make this on days when vegetables were sparse in her meager kitchen, mixing it with steamed white rice and a drizzle of ghee. She's been gone for more than thirty years now but I still think of her fondly, as I did the day I tested this. I did what she used to do and savored her tenacity, creativity, and love of that simple meal.

**Makes 1 cup**

. . . . . . . . . . . . . . . . . . . . . . . . . . . . . . . . . . . . .

3 tablespoons canola oil

$\frac{1}{2}$ cup dried yellow split peas

2 to 3 dried red cayenne chiles (like chile de árbol), stems discarded

$\frac{1}{4}$ cup dried unsweetened coconut shreds (see **Extra Credit**, page 121)

1 teaspoon black or yellow mustard seeds

$\frac{1}{2}$ teaspoon coarse kosher or sea salt

1 Heat 2 tablespoons of the oil in a medium-size skillet over medium-high heat. Once the oil appears to shimmer, add the split peas and chiles. Cook them, uncovered, stirring very frequently, until the peas are light brown and the chiles are slightly blackened, 3 to 4 minutes. Transfer the split peas and chiles to a blender, holding back as much of the oil as you can in the skillet. Sprinkle the coconut into the hot skillet and keep stirring it constantly over medium-high heat as it will toast sunny brown rather quickly, 30 seconds to 1 minute. Add the toasted coconut to the blender. Set the skillet aside.

2 Pour $\frac{1}{3}$ cup of water into the blender and puree the mélange until it breaks down a bit. Now pour in another $\frac{1}{3}$ cup of water and let the blades spin, turning them off and scraping the inside of the jar as needed, to make a smoother puree, albeit one still slightly grainy and nutlike. (Pouring all of the water into the blender at once results in the peas not breaking

down easily, hence the gradual addition.) Transfer the tapenade to a small bowl.

3 Heat the remaining 1 tablespoon of oil in the skillet over medium-high heat. Once the oil appears to shimmer, add the mustard seeds, cover the skillet, and wait until the seeds have stopped popping (not unlike popcorn), about 30 seconds. Immediately pour the sizzling oil, seeds and all, over the tapenade. Sprinkle the salt over all and stir.

4 Serve the tapenade at room temperature.

## Extra Credit

- The tapenade is great with rice, but you can also serve it as a spread for slices of toasted baguette. For a prettier look, swirl some finely chopped tomatoes and cilantro into the puree.

- The tapenade thickens substantially as it sits (it can be stored in the refrigerator for up to 4 days or even frozen for up to 2 months) so you will need to drizzle in some water and thin it out a bit to get to the original consistency. You may need to add a dash of salt to balance out the additional water.

# Chapter 5

# Salads and Soups Unfolded

**SALADS,** as we know them in the Western world, are never considered as such in classic Indian home kitchens across the world. There are very few vegetables in India that are consumed uncooked. You could lump the recipes in the first half of this chapter in the category of salads, even though they are served in conjunction with a curry, for instance, to infuse a textural component to the meal. I have taken some of those very same vegetables—cabbage, cucumbers, and bean sprouts to name a few—and turned them into meals all on their own. For the newbie it's a great way to test the Indian waters.

The "soupy" dishes usually fall under the curries' saucy umbrella, but restaurants in India are now setting aside a part of their menu for this all-important course and labeling them *shorbas*. Brothy, sometimes thin-bodied, but always feisty, Indian-inspired soups fill our bowls during all seasons. The six soups that I have created will appeal to omnivores, the absence of animal stock in all of them causing not even a blip in their flavor lifeline. Spices make the difference once again, peppering every spoonful that you slurp.

· · · · · · · · · · · · · · · · · · · · · · · · · · · · · · · · · · · · · · · · · · · · · · · · ·

# The Lesson Plan for Salads

**Lesson ❶ Indian Slaw** Your comfort level for making creamy coleslaws should make an easy foray into a healthier approach to dressing cabbage shreds with mustard seeds popped like popcorn and yellowed with the tint of turmeric.

**Lesson ❷ Spiced Puffed Rice with Potato and Cucumber** Next, sample a street food favorite from Calcutta with two spices (cumin and fennel) sizzled in oil that coat crispy fried potatoes. Toss these with puffed rice kernels and a sprinkle of ground mustard and marvel at the layering you've grasped with these simple spices.

**Lesson ❸ Bean Sprouts Salad with Potato Croutons** Within the confines of this flavorful

salad you create a simple spice blend (masala) with four whole spices that are toasted and ground.

**Lessons ❹ and ❺ Braised Beet Salad with Golden Raisin Vinaigrette** The last three salad recipes push you into that master level where you learn to create blends, dressings, and flavors that drape salad greens. Mustard seeds, chiles, and ginger cloak warm beets in my take on beet salad but my greens sing with a ginger and golden raisin vinaigrette. If you are that overachieving student, you can make your own cayenne-dusted candied pistachio nuts, as I explain in the Extra Credit box on page 129, and experience a textural crunch that makes the salad a showstopper.

**Lesson ⑥  Tart Chickpea Salad**  Based on a classic Delhi and Mumbai street food, this chickpea salad weaves together tamarind, brown sugar, ginger, and chiles to create a flavor masterpiece that titillates all those 10,000 taste buds (well, it feels that way!).

**Lesson ⑦  Minty Cardamom Shrimp Salad**  A similar spicing and layering concept (using different ingredients of course) with a markedly different result winds up the salad section in the Minty Cardamom Shrimp Salad.

• • • • • • • • • • • • • • • • • • • • • • • • • • • • • • • • • • • •

# The Lesson Plan for Soups

**Lesson ⑧  Chilled Watermelon Soup**  Start out with this fruity soup that is ice-cold, colorful, and chock-full of texture. One spice, dried red chiles, reconstituted in boiling water and stir-fried with another member from the capsicum family, red bell pepper, delivers a warm spark that's tamed with umami-rich, fermented, store-purchased black bean sauce. An Indo-Chinese influenced flavor combination from a community that has maintained an assertive presence in India for more than two hundred years, this is a perfect segue into cooking the Indian way.

**Lesson ⑨  Almond Pepper Soup**  The Almond Pepper Soup shows you the vibrancy of a spice that is a member of the ginger family—cardamom. When steeped with peppers and almonds, this menthol-like spice, native to India's southwest coast, elicits a "wow" from the moment your lips sip the first hot spoonful (so good you can't wait to get it out of the kitchen).

**Lesson ⑩  Chilled Cucumber Avocado Potage with Mustard**  This next potage also highlights only one spice, black or yellow mustard seeds.

The technique I'll teach you in that recipe will instantly turn you into a southern Indian cook, mastering a skill that makes nutty flavors bloom. The recipe is based on the world of Indian raitas, the yogurt accompaniments that populate many an Indian meal.

**Lesson ⑪  Popeye's Dream Soup**  This soup and the next push your culinary acumen via two spices.  Here they are mustard seeds and cumin in a spinach-rich velvety soup.

**Lesson ⑫  Ginger-Cumin Tomato Soup**  Cumin and black peppercorns are the two important spices in this soup, elevating to a whole new level the classic soup that accompanies grilled cheese sandwiches.

**Lesson ⑬  Potato Leek Soup**  Master the sophisticated spice blends of Indian cooks. My version of a commercial curry powder, made from whole spices found at your neighborhood supermarket and freshly ground in a spice grinder, delivers that "aha!" moment.

4 Heat the oil in a small skillet over medium-high heat. Once the oil appears to shimmer, add the mustard seeds, cover the skillet, and cook until the seeds have stopped popping (not unlike popcorn), about 30 seconds.

5 Remove the skillet from the heat and sprinkle in the turmeric, which will instantly bathe the oil with its yellow hue; the heat from the skillet will be just right to cook the turmeric without burning it. Pour the mustard-turmeric mixture over the cabbage. I often grab some of the cabbage from the bowl and add it to the skillet, wiping it clean with the shreds to make sure I get every last bit of spice and oil. Using tongs, spoons, or my favorite, a clean hand, thoroughly combine the slaw in the large bowl to ensure every shred of cabbage is evenly coated.

6 Serve the slaw either at room temperature (my preference) or chilled.

1 Place the cabbage half on a cutting board and remove the core using a V-shaped cut. I like to add a little red cabbage for color. Since I often make cabbage dishes, the unused portions won't go to waste in my household.

2 Cut the cabbage half in half again. Lay one of the cabbage pieces cutside down on a flat surface and cut it into thin shreds. If you wish, add some red cabbage shreds as well.

3 Place the shredded cabbage in a large bowl and add the chiles, bell pepper strips, coconut, cilantro, and salt. Sprinkle in the peanuts over all and squeeze in the lime juice.

4 Roast the mustard seeds in the hot oil. If you have a lid or protective screen, place it over the skillet so none of the popping seeds escape. Once they stop popping, add the turmeric.

# Indian Slaw

Bund Gobhi Nu Shaak

Unless your mama is from western India, chances are this is not your mother's mayo-smothered, garlic powder-ridden coleslaw. Nutty, tart, with a citrus burst, these crunchy shreds of cabbage pack just the right amount of heat from the fairly benign serrano chiles. Serve the slaw as is for a salad course or as an accompaniment to your traditional picnic fare. For an elegant presentation, I often serve the slaw after the appetizer course mounded on top of leaves from a romaine heart with, when seasonal, an edible flower as garnish.

**Makes 6 cups**

½ small head of green cabbage (about 1 pound) or 1 bag (14 ounces) coleslaw mix

Handful of shredded red cabbage (optional)

1 to 2 fresh green serrano chiles, stems discarded

¼ large red bell pepper, stemmed, seeded, and cut into thin strips

¼ cup dry-roasted peanuts

¼ cup dried unsweetened coconut shreds (see **Extra Credit**)

¼ cup finely chopped fresh cilantro leaves and tender stems

1½ teaspoons coarse kosher or sea salt

Juice from 1 medium-size lime

2 tablespoons canola oil

1 teaspoon black or yellow mustard seeds

¼ teaspoon ground turmeric

1 If you are using a half cabbage, remove the tough rib from the bottom by making diagonal cuts on either side and lifting it out in a V-shaped wedge. You will end up with a V-shaped opening at the base. Cut the cabbage half in half lengthwise. Slice both halves into shreds, as thin as you can. Place the green and red (if using) cabbage shreds in a large bowl. If you are using a preshredded coleslaw mix (which usually has a few shreds of carrots and red cabbage in it for color), empty the contents of the bag into a large bowl.

2 Slice the chiles lengthwise and then cut them into thin slices, crosswise, to form half moons of chiles that still have the rib and seeds within. Do not discard the seeds. Add the chiles to the cabbage along with the bell pepper.

3 Place the peanuts in a spice grinder (you can also use a coffee grinder), food processor or mini chopper and pulse the nuts to the consistency of coarse bread crumbs. Letting the machine run constantly will create a gummy result the consistency of peanut butter. Add the coconut, cilantro, salt, and lime juice. Sprinkle the ground peanuts over the cabbage mixture.

**5** You want to be sure to get every drop of the spice mixture, so use some of the slaw to wipe out the skillet.

**6** Toss the slaw with the spice mixture. I like to use my hands to make sure it's well mixed.

**7** Serve the slaw at room temperature—it's the best for enjoying the burst of flavors.

## Extra Credit

- A decent-size supermarket, worth its weight in gold, should stock dried unsweetened coconut either on the health foods aisle or in the baking section. If they don't, grab that bag of highly sweetened coconut shreds on the baking shelf, the one that is often a key ingredient in coconut cream pies and other coconut-based desserts like macaroons (my weakness).

  To use sweetened coconut in this recipe, place ½ cup of the sugary shreds in a medium-size bowl. Cover them with water and run your fingers through the coconut to rinse off some of the sugar. Transfer the coconut to a fine-meshed colander. Return the coconut to the bowl and repeat with the rinsing and straining. You may need to do this 3 or 4 times to make sure that all of the sugar is gone. An underlying sweetness is fine since freshly shredded coconut does have an inherent sweet taste.

- I am a sucker for cooked cabbage. Oftentimes if I have leftover slaw I will add it to a skillet along with a little water to cover the bottom of the skillet and heat the cabbage until it warms through. A little extra kick from a liberal sprinkling of ground red pepper (cayenne) takes care of my addiction for nutty, hot, crisp-tender cabbage until the next fix.

- Peanut allergy sufferers, if it is safe for you to eat other nuts, use an equal amount of a favorite as an alternative to the peanuts.

# ② Spiced Puffed Rice with Potato and Cucumber

## Moori

VEGAN
GLUTEN FREE

In this classic street food from Calcutta, India's capital city during the British regime, the cool crispness of cucumbers offsets the pungency of mustard with sweet fennel and the very forceful dried red chiles. I enjoy the presence of potatoes in this mélange and think you will too, especially when they are stir-fried long enough to acquire that croutonlike crunch.

**Serves 6**

2 tablespoons canola oil

I teaspoon fennel seeds

I teaspoon cumin seeds

3 to 4 dried red chiles (like chile de árbol), stems discarded

I medium-size russet or Yukon Gold potato, peeled, and cut into ¼-inch cubes

4 cups puffed rice (see **Extra Credit**)

I teaspoon coarse kosher or sea salt

½ teaspoon ground mustard

I large cucumber, peeled, seeded, and cut into ¼-inch cubes

2 tablespoons finely chopped fresh cilantro leaves and tender stems

**1** Position a rack in the center of the oven and preheat it to 300°F.

**2** Heat the oil in a medium-size nonstick skillet over medium-high heat. Once the oil appears to shimmer, sprinkle in the fennel, cumin, and chiles. The seeds will instantly sizzle, smell sweet, and turn reddish-brown while the chiles will exude a smoky aroma and blacken, 5 to 10 seconds. Immediately add the potato and stir-fry it, uncovered, stirring occasionally, until reddish-brown, crisp (croutonlike), and cooked through, 8 to 10 minutes.

3 While the potato browns, spread the puffed rice on an ungreased rimmed baking sheet and bake it until crisped a bit, 3 to 4 minutes. Make sure you do not keep the puffed rice in longer as it will turn brown and start to shrivel up. Remove the puffed rice from the oven and dump it into a large bowl.

4 Once the potatoes are ready, remove the pan from the burner and stir in the salt and mustard.

5 Just before you are ready to serve the salad, add the potatoes (spices and all) to the puffed rice along with the cucumber and cilantro. Stir well and serve immediately. This does not keep once everything's mixed in because the vegetables will start to soften the puffed rice.

## Extra Credit

- Puffed rice cereal, the unsweetened and unsalted variety, is rich in minerals like iron. These air-puffed grains are very popular in the snack industry all across India.

- For an untraditional presentation, serve this in bowls fashioned from endive leaves. The edible bowls are not only pretty, but they also offer an additional layer of crunch that makes the experience even more memorable.

- Although cucumbers and potatoes are classic in this street favorite, radishes, mango (I prefer the unripe sort for its sourness), fresh-hulled sweet peas, and sweet potato are all fair game.

# 3 Bean Sprouts Salad with Potato Croutons

VEGAN
GLUTEN FREE

Perfect when it's hot or cold outside, this nutritional powerhouse combines everything we in the food business look for when we hope to create unforgettable flavors. A balance of hot (from the chiles), sweet (from the cinnamon), sour (from the lime), and salty (from the salt of course) tastes; aromas from the cumin; texture from the potato croutons; and a chilled temperature (from the sprouts), this sublime salad does a mean tango in your mouth.

**Serves 4**

2 medium-size (about ½ pound) russet or
   Yukon Gold potatoes

2 to 4 dried red cayenne chiles
   (like chile de árbol), stems discarded

2 teaspoons coriander seeds

I teaspoon cumin seeds

I piece (½ inch) of cinnamon stick, broken into
   smaller pieces (see Extra Credit)

3 tablespoons canola oil

I teaspoon coarse kosher or sea salt

I bag (8 ounces) bean sprouts (do not use
   alfalfa sprouts, see Extra Credit)

¼ cup finely chopped fresh cilantro leaves and
   tender stems

Juice from I small lime

1 Peel the potatoes and cut them into ¼-inch cubes. Transfer the potatoes to a bowl large enough to hold them. Add enough cold water to cover the potatoes to prevent them from oxidizing and turning black.

2 Heat a large nonstick skillet over medium-high heat. Once the skillet is hot (when you hold the palm of your hand close to the bottom of the skillet you will feel the heat), usually after 2 to 4 minutes, add the chiles, coriander, cumin, and cinnamon stick pieces. Toast the spices, shaking the

skillet every few seconds, until the chiles blacken and smell smoky hot, the seeds turn reddish brown and smell incredibly aromatic (nutty with citrus undertones), and the cinnamon exudes a heady sweetness, 1 to 2 minutes. Immediately transfer the spice blend to a small heatproof bowl to cool, about 5 minutes.

3 Meanwhile, drain the potatoes and pat them dry with paper towels. Heat the oil over medium-high heat in the same large skillet used to toast the spices. Once the oil appears to shimmer, add the potatoes and ½ teaspoon of the salt and stir-fry until the potatoes are reddish-brown, crisp (crouton-like), and cooked through, 10 to 12 minutes. Transfer the potatoes to a medium-size bowl.

4 While the potatoes are browning, place the cooled toasted spices in a spice grinder (you can also use a coffee grinder) and grind the blend to the consistency of finely ground black pepper that gives off an aroma that is incredibly complex and layered, nothing like the whole toasted spices you smelled a few minutes back. Add the ground spice mixture to the bowl with the potatoes.

## Extra Credit

- Cinnamon sticks usually come tightly furled and are about 3 inches long. To get a small piece of one, I place it on a firm cutting board and wedge a sharp knife blade in the crack. I give the knife a good whack. It usually breaks up the cinnamon into a few shards and I grab what I need for this recipe and save the rest for use later.

- The most common form of sprouts available in supermarkets are those from a green legume called mung (or moong) beans. Off-white in color and 2 to 3 inches in length, these watery-crisp nutritional worker bees are bursting with vitamins A, B, and C. Even though they are legume-based, sprouts are much easier to digest than their unsprouted counterpart because as they sprout the complex starches convert to simple sugars, making it easy for you to process them without fear of indigestion or flatulence. Even seeds that are used as spices, namely fenugreek, produce sprouts that are also pleasantly bitter.

  For a more complex-tasting experience, purchase a mixture of bean sprouts if you see one at the market or if you happen to visit a health food store. Refrain from using the spindly alfalfa sprouts as they are much too grassy for this particular combination of ingredients.

5 Add the sprouts to the bowl with the potatoes and spice blend. Sprinkle in the remaining ½ teaspoon of salt, the cilantro, and the lime juice. Stir the salad to mix everything well. Serve at room temperature.

# Braised Beet Salad with Golden Raisin Vinaigrette

VEGAN
GLUTEN FREE

Indians are masters at extracting many flavors from a single ingredient, and here you will see ginger used in two ways—stir-fried in the beets for a sharper taste; pureed raw in the dressing for a pungency that balances sweet raisins and sour vinegar—to create a symphony of flavors. Green salads like this one are not classic regional Indian fare but the spices in the beets (mustard seeds popped the southern way) sing Indian while the beets themselves, called *chukander,* belt out the hearty north.

**Serves 4**

1½ pounds beets with their green tops

2 tablespoons canola oil

I teaspoon black or yellow mustard seeds

3 pieces fresh ginger (each about the size and thickness of a 25-cent coin; no need to peel the skin), cut into matchstick-thin shreds

I to 2 fresh green serrano chiles, stems discarded, finely chopped (do not remove the seeds)

I teaspoon coarse kosher or sea salt

Golden Raisin Vinaigrette (recipe follows)

8 ounces mixed salad greens (like mesclun)

1 Prepare the beets: Twist off the green tops of the beets. These look very similar to chard leaves and more likely than not will be gritty with sand and mud. Cut the tender ribs and leaves crosswise into thin slices and place them in a colander. Thoroughly rinse the beet tops to rid them of the gritty material. Transfer them to a salad spinner and spin them dry.

2 Peel the beets and cut them into 1-inch cubes. Rinse the cubes as well in the colander (the gush of blood-red water gives you a clue to the power of the natural dye the vegetable has within its sugary sweetness). There's no need to spin them dry.

3 Heat the oil in a medium-size saucepan over medium-high heat. Once the oil appears to shimmer, add the mustard

seeds, cover the pan, and cook until the seeds have stopped popping (not unlike popcorn), about 30 seconds. Add the ginger and chiles and stir-fry until the ginger is lightly browned and the chiles are much more pungent, 1 to 2 minutes. Add the beet greens, the cubed beets, and salt and stir well to coat them with the mustard seeds. The liquid in the beet greens will start to pool at the bottom of the pan and boil instantly, loosening the stuck-on bits of ginger and chiles, effectively deglazing the pan and releasing those flavors into the beets. Reduce the heat to medium, cover the pan, and cook, stirring occasionally, until the beets are tender when pierced with a fork, 10 to 15 minutes (the beets also will sweat, releasing some liquid, in which they will braise).

4 While the beets cook, make the vinaigrette dressing.

5 Once the beets and greens are done, make the salad: Place the mixed salad greens in a large bowl. Pour the vinaigrette dressing over the salad greens and toss to coat; I use my hands (clean) to do this. Pile the dressed salad greens onto a platter, spoon the still-warm beets and greens over them, and serve.

# Golden Raisin Vinaigrette

This vinaigrette is by far my dressing of choice to cloak a bowl of salad greens. A sweet, hot, tart, and nutty panache, the dressing incorporates plump golden raisins, which are a hallmark of northern Indian cooking.

**Makes about 1 cup**

1 teaspoon cumin seeds

¼ cup canola oil

¼ cup cider vinegar

½ cup golden raisins

¼ cup firmly packed fresh cilantro leaves and tender stems

3 pieces (each about the size and thickness of a 25-cent coin) fresh ginger (no need to peel the skin)

1 fresh green serrano chile, stem discarded

## Extra Credit

- If beets are not your thing, you can prepare exactly the same recipe with other vegetables. Root vegetables like potato, sweet potato, parsnips, turnips, carrots, or rutabagas are fair game but during summer, when green and yellow wax beans are abundant, I reach for them as well. Cooking times will of course vary with your selection. I often make this recipe with multiple varieties of beets. The challenge with that is to cook the beets separately or the red beets will pervasively coat the medley red.

- If I have the time and inclination, I crumble some paneer or feta cheese over the beet salad and top it off with candied nuts, my favorite being pistachios.

  To make a batch of candied nuts, preheat the oven to 350°F. Line a small pie plate or rimmed baking sheet with a piece of parchment paper. Toss ½ cup lightly salted pistachio nuts in a small bowl with ¼ cup firmly packed dark brown sugar and ½ teaspoon ground cayenne. (If you are using pistachios in the shell, remove the nuts and discard the shells before use—this may sound obvious but it's better to clarify—I speak from experience.) Moisten your hand with tap water and, while it is wet, mix the pistachios again to make sure some of the brown sugar adheres to the nuts.

  Spread the nuts out on the parchment paper and roast them in the oven until the sugar starts to turn dark brown and foamy, and the nuts start to have a thin, brittle-like look, 15 to 20 minutes. Remove the pistachios from the oven and let them cool.

  Once cool to the touch, break the nuts apart into separate pieces. Each nut will be glazed with some sweetness, a bit of heat, and that delectable crunch. Great even as a snack.

- If any of the beets and greens remain uneaten, you can turn them into a whipped side dish for the main course or a dip for wedges of toasted pita as an appetizer. Transfer the leftovers to a food processor and puree them with a little olive oil or even cream.

1 Heat a small skillet over medium-high heat. Once the skillet is hot (when you hold your palm close to the bottom of the skillet you will feel the heat), usually after 2 to 4 minutes, add the cumin seeds and toast them, shaking the pan every few seconds, until they start to crackle, turn reddish-brown, and smell nutty, 30 seconds to 1 minute. Immediately transfer the cumin seeds to a blender or they will start to burn in the hot skillet.

2 Pour the oil and the vinegar into the blender along with the raisins, cilantro, ginger, and whole chile and blend them into a smooth puree that is light greenish brown and sweet, sour, pleasantly hot, and highly aromatic (trust me, you will stick a finger in it, taste it, and go wow!).

# 6 Tart Chickpea Salad

## Chana Chaat

VEGAN
GLUTEN FREE

This salad is my take on the wide world of Indian street foods called *chaat*—finger-licking morsels of snack foods usually served with contrasting sauces, crunchy toppings, cooling spices, and yogurt. I simplify the dish, which usually requires elaborate prep, but don't compromise on the complex tastes. And I present it to you in a more Western way atop a bed of greens—the crunch, heat, sweet, sour, salt, succulence (umami) is there in all its glory.

**Serves 4**

**FOR THE TAMARIND DRESSING**

**1 teaspoon tamarind paste or concentrate (see Extra Credit, page 189)**

**¾ cup firmly packed dark brown sugar**

**2 fresh green serrano chiles, stems discarded, coarsely chopped (do not remove the seeds)**

**3 pieces fresh ginger (each about the size and thickness of a 25-cent coin; no need to peel), coarsely chopped**

**½ teaspoon coarse kosher or sea salt**

**FOR THE CHICKPEAS**

**1 teaspoon cumin seeds**

**1 teaspoon coarse kosher or sea salt**

**½ teaspoon ground red pepper (cayenne)**

**3 cups cooked chickpeas, or 2 cans (15 ounces each) chickpeas, rinsed and drained**

**¼ cup finely chopped fresh cilantro leaves and tender stems**

**FOR THE SALAD**

**8 ounces mixed salad greens (like mesclun)**

Start by making the tamarind dressing: Whisk the tamarind paste and 1 cup of water together in a small saucepan. Stir in the brown sugar, chiles, ginger, and ½ teaspoon salt. Bring to a boil over medium heat. Let boil, uncovered, stirring occasionally, until the dressing is slightly thickened, 10 to 12 minutes. Remove the pan from the heat and let the dressing cool for just a few minutes. Then transfer it to a blender and puree it, scraping down the inside of the blender as needed, to form a smooth, dark chocolate brown dressing. Transfer the dressing to a nonreactive bowl (like glass or stainless steel) and refrigerate it until chilled and thickened, about 30 minutes (or to speed it up, 15 minutes in the freezer).

2 As the tamarind dressing chills, prepare the chickpeas: Heat a small skillet over medium-high heat. Once the skillet is hot (when you hold the palm of your hand close to the bottom of the skillet you will feel the heat), usually after 2 to 4 minutes, add the cumin seeds, shaking the skillet every few seconds, until they turn reddish brown and smell nutty, 15 to 30 seconds. Immediately transfer the cumin seeds to a small heatproof bowl or plate to cool. Once cool, place the toasted cumin seeds in a spice grinder (you can also use a coffee grinder) and grind them to the consistency of finely ground black pepper. Tap the ground cumin back into the same small bowl or plate and stir in the 1 teaspoon of salt and the cayenne.

3 Place the chickpeas in a medium-size bowl. Sprinkle the spice blend and cilantro over them and toss to mix well.

## Extra Credit

- I find this chickpea salad a very substantial lunch dish coupled with some bread. If I serve it as a formal sit-down salad course for a nice dinner, I add some edible flowers as a garnish and serve poppadums on top as a chapeau (*oui*, that's hat in French, *bien sûr*) to crown the presentation.

- For something more hearty, crumble some feta, paneer, or goat cheese over the beans. Sliced cold meats are also fair game— keep in mind with these two options you will lose the vegan status for this dish.

4 When you are ready make the salad: Empty the salad greens into a large bowl. Pour the chilled tamarind dressing over the greens and toss to coat. I use my hands (clean) to do this. Pile the dressed salad greens onto a platter, spoon the chickpea mixture over them, and serve.

# Minty Cardamom Shrimp Salad

I adore the contrast in this salad between the warm shrimp and the cool crisp greens punctuated with creamy, minty yogurt. I often serve it with edible flowers (think purple orchids, nasturtiums, and pansies), when they are in season, and garlic-rubbed grilled crostini slices. The flavors come from a combination of techniques and ingredients common to the north and the south (India, that is). Toasting whole spices, as is done in the southern regions, is key to bringing forth an assertiveness to the dish, while invigorating, perfumed mint, a hallmark ingredient in the north, provides a calming balance, especially in the presence of plain yogurt.

GLUTEN FREE

**Serves 4**

2 teaspoons coriander seeds

½ teaspoon cardamom seeds (removed from green or white cardamom pods; see Extra Credit, page 43)

2 to 3 dried red cayenne chiles (like chile de árbol), stems discarded

1 teaspoon cumin seeds

1 pound large shrimp (21 to 25), peeled and deveined but tails left on

1½ teaspoons coarse kosher or sea salt

½ cup Greek-style plain yogurt

½ cup firmly packed fresh mint leaves, finely chopped

2 tablespoons canola oil

8 ounces mixed salad greens (like mesclun)

Heat a large skillet over medium-high heat. Once the skillet is hot (when you hold the palm of your hand close to the bottom of the skillet you will feel the heat), usually after 2 to 4 minutes, add the coriander, cardamom, and chiles. Toast the spice blend, shaking the skillet every few seconds, until the chiles blacken in patches and smell smoky hot, the coriander looks reddish-brown and smells incredibly strong with citrus tones, and the cardamom looks slightly ashy but still black, 1 to 2 minutes. Immediately transfer the spice blend to a small heatproof bowl to

## Extra Credit

- Greek-style plain yogurt is now widely available in supermarkets in the dairy section. Slightly more expensive than the common varieties, this is thick, rich, and sour cream–like in mouth-feel. If this is unavailable to you, use plain yogurt (the regular kind). Place it in a strainer lined with cheesecloth and let the excess liquid (whey) drain for 1 to 2 hours or even overnight in the refrigerator. This thickens the yogurt and provides you the same experience that Greek-style yogurt does.

- If you double the dressing ingredients, you can use it as a dip for bread, vegetables, or even fruits. For a little zing, I usually fold in coarsely cracked black peppercorns or sprinkle on some ground red pepper (cayenne).

cool, about 5 minutes (keeping the spices in the hot skillet will burn them, making them unpalatable).

2 While the skillet is still toasty hot, quickly sprinkle in the cumin seeds and toast them, shaking the skillet, until they turn reddish brown and smell nutty, 15 to 30 seconds. Immediately transfer the cumin to a separate small heatproof bowl or plate to cool.

3 Once the toasted spice blend has cooled, place it in a spice grinder (you can also use a coffee grinder) and grind the blend to the consistency of finely ground black pepper. The color will be light brown with flecks of red and the aroma will be incredibly complex and layered, nothing like the mélange of whole toasted spices you smelled a few minutes ago. Transfer the ground spice mixture to a medium-size bowl. Using the same spice grinder (no need to clean it) grind the toasted cumin seeds and tap them out into a separate medium-size bowl (nobody told you this was a one-bowl recipe).

4 Add the shrimp and 1 teaspoon of the salt to the bowl with the spice blend and stir well to make sure the shellfish gets an even coat of spice and salt. Keep the shrimp refrigerated, covered, until you are ready to cook them. You can easily do this a day before you plan to cook and serve the salad.

5 Add the remaining ½ teaspoon of salt and the yogurt and mint to the bowl with the ground cumin. Whisk them all together to create a seductively smooth, thick dressing.

6 Heat the oil in the large skillet over medium-high heat. Once the oil appears to shimmer, add the spiced shrimp, making

sure they are in a single layer. Sear the shrimp on the underside until they are saffron-hued and the tails start to curl a bit, about 3 minutes. Turn the shrimp over and sear the second side, about 3 minutes.

7 To assemble the salad, place the greens in a large bowl. Pour the dressing over the greens and toss to coat. I use my hands (clean) to do this. Pile the dressed salad greens onto a platter, arrange the warm shrimp over them, and serve.

Some of the commonly available spices, when roasted and ground, yield remarkable complexities. Included here from left to right (sort of) are cayenne peppers, cardamom pods with seeds, whole cloves, cumin seeds, black peppercorns, cinnamon sticks, ground cinnamon, dried bay leaves, and coriander seeds.

# Chilled Watermelon Soup

## Tarbooz Ka Shorba

VEGAN
GLUTEN FREE

The old adage "you eat with all your senses" holds true for this chilled and juicy wonder in the peak of summer when you don't want a reason to turn the oven on. Temperature, texture, color, aroma, and taste all come together in this bowl of sweet pieces of cold watermelon, hot chiles, bell peppers, pungent scallions, and salty-rich black bean garlic sauce. It's a great accompaniment to the Creamy Chicken Kebabs (page 75), especially if you plan to hang out grill-side and sip a martini or two.

**Makes 4 cups**

3 to 4 dried red cayenne chiles
 (like chile de árbol), stems discarded

½ cup boiling water

2½ cups cubed seedless watermelon
 (about ½-inch cubes)

3 scallions (green tops and white bulbs),
 trimmed and thinly sliced

I can (II.5 ounces) tomato juice (I½ cups)

2 tablespoons canola oil

I large red bell pepper, stem, core, ribs, and
 seeds discarded, flesh finely chopped

¼ cup finely chopped fresh cilantro leaves and
 tender stems

2 tablespoons black bean garlic sauce
 (see **Extra Credit**)

1 Place the red chiles in a small heatproof bowl, add the boiling water, and let the chiles soak at least 15 minutes (see Extra Credit). As they swell in the hot water, get everything else prepared.

2 Combine the watermelon, scallions, and tomato juice in a medium-size bowl.

3 Once the chiles are soft and swollen, fish them out of the water (save the water) and finely chop them (seeds and all).

4 Heat the oil in a medium-size skillet over medium-high heat. Once the oil appears to shimmer, add the bell pepper and the chopped reconstituted chiles

and stir-fry until the pepper pieces brown around the edges and the chiles blacken, offering a visually stunning contrast of pinks, reds, and browns, 10 to 12 minutes. And the aromas are not bad either!

5 Stir in the cilantro, the black bean sauce, and the reserved chile soaking liquid. Bring it all to a boil and cook, uncovered, stirring occasionally, until all the liquid evaporates and a deep layer of spiced oil starts to separate from the thick chocolate-colored sauce studded with ruby red peppers and flecked with green cilantro, 8 to 10 minutes.

6 Scrape this blend into the watermelon mixture and stir well. Chill the lusty soup for an hour or so before you serve it. Works great if you wish to make the soup a day before you plan to serve it.

## Extra Credit

- Dried chiles are very buoyant when they soak in water. I usually keep them submerged by forcing them down with a cup or cooking spoon. Once they start to absorb some of the water and swell up, the weight does not become necessary.

- The Asian foods section of your supermarket will have jars of black bean garlic sauce. These fermented beans, pureed with garlic and other ingredients, give a salty, umami richness to the soup.

## 9 Almond Pepper Soup
### Badam Mirchi Ka Shorba

VEGAN
GLUTEN FREE

When you rely on only one spice to be the star, it better be a showstopper. Cardamom lives up to those high expectations with its assertive presence, breathing sweet flavors into this surprisingly complex-tasting soup, considering it has only seven ingredients (including water). Indian food is not always in-your-face, complex seasonings, and this creamy, slightly smoky, nutty soup drives home that point.

Sometimes, with just the right spice, you can create a perception of having slaved over a dish for hours, when in fact all it has taken you is barely a half hour of your precious time. Slurp!

**Makes 6 cups**

1 pound red bell peppers, stems, ribs, and seeds discarded, flesh cut into 1-inch cubes

$\frac{1}{2}$ cup almond slivers or slices

6 green or white cardamom pods

3 fresh green serrano chiles, stems discarded, coarsely chopped (do not remove the seeds)

$1\frac{1}{2}$ teaspoons coarse kosher or sea salt

6 tablespoons finely chopped fresh cilantro leaves and tender stems

## Extra Credit

• The almonds play a crucial role in providing a mellow flavor (they are stewed and not roasted), fiber, and nutrients. For a more profound impact, toast them in a small skillet over medium heat, stirring them occasionally, until they are light brown and nutty-smelling, 3 to 5 minutes, before adding them to the soup.

• Any leftover soup is great as a sauce for fresh-cooked noodles. Toss the two together and serve them with shreds of your favorite cheese. I also like to reduce the soup by simmering it further until it thickens, providing a saucy topping for planks of grilled or panfried paneer (whole milk cheese; page 35) or extra-firm tofu.

   It's equally expedient and elegant with a simply grilled fillet of Pacific halibut, or wild salmon from the Pacific Northwest.

1 Pour 3 cups of water into a medium-size saucepan, add the bell peppers, almonds, cardamom, chiles, and salt, and let come to a rolling boil over medium-high heat. Cover the saucepan and reduce the heat to medium. Let simmer, stirring occasionally, until the peppers are fork-tender, the chiles look pale green, and the cardamom pods appear plump, about 15 minutes.

2 Pour half of the bell pepper mixture and its liquid into a blender. Make sure the blender is only half full (or half empty, depending on the way you look at things in life). Without adequate space, the steam from the hot contents rises and can build up pressure that can force off the lid and create a cornucopia of colors on your ceiling, walls, and anything else that gets in

the way. Please hold the blender lid in place with a towel and run the blender in pulse to puree the soup. Pour the pureed soup into a medium-size bowl. Repeat with the remaining bell pepper mixture and liquid. Add the second batch of puree to the bowl. Alternatively, if you have an immersion (or stick) blender, you can puree the soup in the pan.

3 Ladle the soup into individual bowls and serve it warm, sprinkled with the cilantro.

# 10 Chilled Cucumber Avocado Potage with Mustard

## Kakadi Ka Shorba

LACTO-VEGETARIAN
GLUTEN FREE

A bowl full of creamy chilled soup punctuated with the juicy crunch of cucumber is the ideal shield against oppressive summer heat and it is a double bonus when you don't have to slave over a hot stove. Thirty seconds of popping mustard seeds in hot oil is the extent of the cooking, but the flavors will linger for quite a bit longer.

**Makes about 6 cups**

I large cucumber

4 cups buttermilk

I large ripe Hass avocado, pulp scooped
   (see Extra Credit, page 52)

I to 2 fresh green serrano chiles,
   stems discarded

I teaspoon coarse kosher or sea salt

I tablespoon canola oil

I teaspoon black or yellow mustard seeds

¼ cup finely chopped fresh cilantro leaves
   and tender stems

1 Peel, seed, and coarsely chop the cucumber. Measure out about ¼ cup of the cucumber pieces and finely chop them. Set the finely chopped cucumber aside.

2 Pour the buttermilk into a blender and add the coarsely chopped cucumber, avocado, chiles, and salt (you may have to do this in batches). Puree the mélange to a smooth blend and pour it into a medium-size bowl.

3 Heat the oil in a small skillet over medium-high heat. Once the oil appears to shimmer, add the mustard seeds, cover the skillet, and wait until the seeds have stopped popping (not unlike popcorn), about 30 seconds. Immediately pour this sizzling oil over the soup and stir it in well so it's completely blended.

4 Chill the soup for at least 1 hour. Ladle it into individual bowls and divvy up the finely chopped cucumber among the bowls. Serve the soup sprinkled with the cilantro.

## Extra Credit

- I can hear you complaining about cilantro in this soup. You don't like it; you are allergic; you hate its smell and taste; to put it bluntly, you just can't stand it! I live with someone who has said it all. So please go ahead and use fresh basil, mint, thyme, Italian parsley (not my favorite), or tarragon, teaspoon for teaspoon as an alternative to the soapy-tasting cilantro (your words, not mine) for an equally satiating thrill.

- I love the juicy succulence of crisp cucumber against the soup's smooth backdrop. If pomegranates are in season, sprinkle some of the fresh seeds over the soup instead of, or in addition to, the cucumber for a luscious look and texture.

- Any leftover soup is great as a stand-in for your favorite salad dressing, not to mention that it's low-fat. Pour as much as you like over salad greens and toss gently. Top the salad off with fruits and nuts for a feel-good meal.

# Popeye's Dream Soup

## Palak Ka Shorba

VEGAN
GLUTEN FREE

If you crave spinach the way Popeye and I do, this creamy soup (without any cream) satisfies the hankering without adding inches to your waistline. Nutritious and chock-full of flavor with only two spices (a combination that is common to the western parts of India), every mouthful is akin to the proverbial potato chip—you can't stop at one. I often make a batch, sip a few cups as if it's tea, and then freeze the rest for up to two months. It's always on hand when the next wave of yearning flows through me. Serve it with a crusty baguette or All-Wheat Griddle Breads (page 84) for a winter dinner by a roaring fireplace.

**Makes a brimming 6 cups**

½ cup red lentils (also called Egyptian lentils; see Extra Credit, page 208)

1 medium-size russet or Yukon Gold potato, peeled and diced

1 medium-size onion, diced

2 to 3 fresh green serrano chiles, stems discarded, coarsely chopped (do not remove the seeds)

1½ teaspoons coarse kosher or sea salt

1 medium-size tomato

1 pound prewashed baby spinach leaves

1 tablespoon canola oil

1 teaspoon black or yellow mustard seeds

1 teaspoon cumin seeds

1 Place the lentils in a large saucepan or Dutch oven and add water to cover. Give the lentils a good rinse, stirring them with your fingertips; this will make the water cloudy. Drain the water (I tilt the pan over the sink to drain it). Repeat this once or twice. Then pour in 4 cups of water and add the potato, onion, chiles, salt, and the whole tomato.

2 Bring the water to a rolling boil over medium-high heat. Fish the whole tomato out of the pot; it will now look shriveled with loose skin. Transfer the tomato to a bowl.

3 Reduce the heat to medium and cover the pan. Let the lentil medley simmer, stirring occasionally, until the potato is fork-tender and the lentils are now yellow, about 15 minutes. Even though the lentils start with a beautiful salmon color, cooking them yields a yellow color (as the Indian bobble-head doll said, "Eh, it is the will of Rama"). It's the nature of these lentils and does not signify any wrongdoing on your part.

4 While the soup simmers, core the tomato and remove the loose skin, working over a bowl to catch the juices. As soon as the lentils are cooked, add the tomato, including any juices, to the pan. Pile in the spinach and cover the pan. Let the soup continue to simmer, no need to stir, until the spinach wilts, about 5 minutes.

5 Meanwhile, heat the oil in a small skillet over medium-high heat. Once the oil appears to shimmer, add the mustard seeds, cover the skillet, and cook until the seeds have stopped popping (not unlike popcorn), about 30 seconds. Turn off the heat and sprinkle in the cumin seeds, which will instantly sizzle, turn reddish brown, and smell incredibly nutty. Immediately transfer the mustard and cumin seed oil

## Extra Credit

The process of infusing oil with whole spices to flavor a pot of dal or curry is a hallmark of Indian cooking, a technique known as *tadka*. This key seasoning, usually added after the ingredients are cooked, infuses a layering of flavors that provides a sharp burst with that first mouthful. The sweetly popped mustard seeds and the aromatically nutty cumin seeds do just that in this soup.

(seeds and all) to a small heatproof bowl (the longer it sits in that hot skillet, the more burnt the spices will become).

6 Once the spinach has wilted, ladle a third of the contents of the pan into a blender. Hold the lid down and run the blender in pulses to create a bright green puree. Pour the puree into a medium-size bowl. Repeat twice until all of the soup is pureed, adding the contents each time to the soup in the bowl. Alternatively, if you have an immersion (or stick) blender, you can puree all the soup in the pan.

7 Reheat the soup over low heat, if necessary, and stir in the spiced oil, including all of the seeds. Ladle the soup into individual bowls and serve warm.

# Ginger-Cumin Tomato Soup

Tamatar Ka Shorba

LACTO-VEGETARIAN
GLUTEN FREE

You may not associate tomato soup with India, but go to any neighborhood restaurant in India that serves multiregional fare, including Continental, and you will find tomato soup on the menu. And they bring it to you replete with saltine crackers. This version of mine provides just the right heat from the black peppercorns and a pleasant nuttiness from the cumin. My son, who never likes anything tomato, had two bowls the night I tested it, and yes, there was the perfunctory ooey, gooey grilled cheese sandwich to accompany it.

**Makes 4 cups**

2 tablespoons ghee, homemade (page 31)
   or store-bought, or canola oil

I teaspoon cumin seeds

½ teaspoon black peppercorns

I small onion, diced

I slice fresh ginger (about the size of a
   25-cent coin; no need to peel the skin)

4 cups tomato juice

I tablespoon granulated sugar

I teaspoon sweet paprika

I teaspoon coarse kosher or sea salt

¼ cup heavy (whipping) cream

1 Heat the ghee in a medium-size saucepan over medium-high heat. Once the ghee appears to shimmer, sprinkle in the cumin and peppercorns and let sizzle until they smell nutty and pungent, which will be almost instantaneous at that temperature, 5 to 10 seconds.

2 Immediately add the onion and ginger and stir-fry until they are light brown around the edges, 3 to 4 minutes. Pour in the tomato juice, sprinkle in the sugar, paprika, and salt, and stir to mix. Bring the soup to a boil. Reduce the heat to medium and let the soup simmer,

uncovered, stirring occasionally, until the flavors arrive at that well-balanced juncture of tart, sweet, slightly hot, and nutty, about 15 minutes.

3 Pour half of the soup into a blender. Make sure the blender is no more than half full; without adequate space the steam from the hot soup rises and can build up pressure that can force off the lid with messy and harmful results. Hold the blender in place with a towel and run the blender in pulses until the soup is smooth. Pour the pureed soup into a medium-size bowl. Repeat with the remaining soup. Transfer the pureed soup back to the saucepan. If you have an immersion (or stick) blender, you can puree all the soup in the saucepan.

4 Stir in the cream and return the soup to a boil, uncovered, over medium heat. Serve the soup hot.

## Extra Credit

- For some optional toppings, pass around finely chopped chives, homemade croutons (they taste so much better than store-bought), and/or finely chopped fresh cilantro leaves and tender stems.

- I don't like my soups too thick but if you want a thicker body, add a medium-size peeled and diced potato or two to the onion and ginger while stir-frying. When you puree everything, the texture will be quite velvety. Because including potato brings down the heat level of the black peppercorns, I recommend also adding a fresh green serrano chile or two as you stir-fry the vegetables for a balance of tastes. Make sure you add more salt as needed.

- Any leftover soup makes a great sauce for freshly cooked pasta. If the soup is too thin it may not coat the noodles too well. One way to thicken it is to toss in freshly shredded Parmigiano-Reggiano cheese as you marry the noodles with the soup. This also adds a depth of flavor and nuttiness to the meal.

  Another option is to intensify the flavors in the soup by gently boiling it, uncovered, over medium heat, stirring occasionally, until some of the moisture evaporates, and it thickens until its volume is reduced by half, 25 to 30 minutes. I use this as a condiment, almost like ketchup, on burgers, with fries, and any appetizers that need a dipping sauce.

# Potato Leek Soup

Creamy, velvet smooth, and with just a hint of underlying heat, this comforting soup is great warm or even chilled, just like its French counterpart vichyssoise. It's hard to imagine a world without potatoes (it was the case in India prior to the sixteenth century), but now every meal (really!) in India includes the popular tuber in some shape, size, or form. Cheap, ubiquitous, available in all seasons, and abundant, no wonder potatoes are a favorite everywhere.

VEGAN (IF USING OIL INSTEAD OF GHEE OR BUTTER)
GLUTEN FREE

**Makes 6 cups**

2 pounds russet or Yukon Gold potatoes

½ pound leeks

2 tablespoons ghee, homemade (page 31) or store-bought, butter, or canola oil

¼ cup finely chopped fresh cilantro leaves and tender stems

1 to 2 fresh green serrano chiles, stems discarded, coarsely chopped (do not remove the seeds)

2 teaspoons Raghavan's Blend (page 39) or store-bought Madras curry powder

2 teaspoons coarse kosher or sea salt

1 Peel the potatoes and cut them into approximately 1-inch pieces (don't worry too much about the size since they will be eventually pureed). Transfer the potato pieces to a bowl large enough to hold them all. Add enough cold water to cover the potatoes to prevent them from oxidizing and turning black.

2 Fill a medium-size bowl three quarters full with cold water. Cut off and discard the hairy roots of the leeks. Thickly slice the green and white parts and dunk them in the water. Leeks are inherently muddy so you do need to rinse them a few times. Trust me when I say grittiness is not a desirable texture in this soup. Scoop the leeks out of the water and dump the water out. You will notice the bottom of the bowl muddied from the leeks; rinse out the bowl well. Return the leeks to the bowl and fill it up with cold water again. Repeat rinsing the leeks and dumping the water until the

water remains clear after the leeks have been rinsed. Drain the leeks.

**3** Drain the potatoes and pat them dry. Heat the ghee in a Dutch oven or a large saucepan over medium-high heat. Once the ghee appears to shimmer, add the potatoes, leeks, cilantro, chile(s), spice blend, and salt. Cook the mélange, uncovered, stirring occasionally, until some of the potato pieces brown around the edges, 8 to 10 minutes.

**4** Pour 4 cups of water into the pan and scrape the bottom to release any bits of vegetables and spices, effectively deglazing the pan and releasing those flavors back into the soup (see, you don't need any animal stock to add flavor). As soon as the liquid comes to a boil, lower the heat to medium and cover the pan. Stew the chunky contents, stirring occasionally, until the potatoes are fall-apart tender, 15 to 20 minutes.

**5** If you have an immersion (or stick) blender, puree the soup right in the pan until smooth. If not, let the soup cool a bit. Fill a blender halfway with the chunky vegetables and liquid. Holding the lid down,

## Extra Credit

- Leeks look like manly scallions or green or spring onions on steroids, but harbor a timid onion-like pungency that complements starchy potatoes. Ask the French—they created a cold version of this soup and labeled it vichyssoise. The lower part of the leeks is always muddy since they grow so close to the earth. So I cannot emphasize enough how thorough you need to be while rinsing them.

- For a textural crunch (which I always like with smoothly pureed soups) serve the soup topped with either homemade or store-bought croutons. For something unusual, panfry some slices of tofu in canola oil until they are crisp brown on the outside. Then slice them into matchstick thin pieces (julienne) and serve the soup topped with a few shreds. You get a nice balance of crispy and creamy at the same time.

run the blender in pulses to puree the soup until smooth. Pour the pureed soup into a medium-size bowl. Repeat with the remaining soup, adding the pureed soup to the bowl.

**6** Ladle into individual bowls and serve warm.

# Chapter 6

# Meat and Seafood Mains Unfolded

**HERE IN THE** Western part of the world we just about always plan our meals around the main protein source (beef, chicken, fish, and so on) and everything else falls to the side. This chapter not only fulfills the essential desire for a main dish, but many of these creations, ranging from the classic to the contemporary, involve minimal preparation times. The recipes for each protein source show you how to ease yourself into spicing the Indian way.

Contrary to popular belief, Indians do eat meats with great regularity, especially in homes that practice Islam or Christianity. The three oceans that cup the subcontinent support a fish-eating diet along the coasts. In the United States we have superior cuts of meat, so we can sprinkle in a spice or two to augment the inherently good qualities and call it an Indian night. (Keep in mind when any recipe calls for a sprinkling of one of my two spice blends, make sure you have that ready before you dig into the recipe—makes you more efficient in the kitchen.)

. . . . . . . . . . . . . . . . . . . . . . . . . . . . . . . . . . . . . . . . . . . . . . . . . . . . .

# The Lesson Plan

**Lesson ❶ Ultimate Chicken Curry** No one gets tired of chicken recipes, especially when they are curries, and this one is the right offering for your first complete Indian dinner. A liberal helping of my classic Ultimate Chicken Curry, using my signature spice blend (or you can break down and use store-bought Madras-style curry powder—don't worry, I won't judge) is delicious spooned over an accompanying pilaf (see the foldout Lesson 1 that opens the Side Dishes chapter on page 228).

**Lesson ❷ Cardamom Pepper Steak** Although beef isn't as popular as other meats in India, there are those who do enjoy it. The recipe I've included uses a prime cut of beef tenderloin, the filet mignon, and marries two very simple spices that are indigenous to the southwestern coast of India: cardamom and peppercorns. With a little salt to balance the mélange, the

result is nothing short of spectacular. Classic flavors, contemporary presentation!

**Lesson ❸ Festive Lamb Chops with Cardamom** Lamb is popular in the U.S. while in India goat meat is still the meat of choice. The spices used to punctuate goat meat are assertive and appear complex, teaching you simple layering techniques that deliver palate-pleasing results. These spices and techniques work equally well with lamb, so that is the meat I've chosen to use.

**Lesson ❹ Spiced Ground Lamb** The remaining lamb recipes feature a quintessential blend (garam masala) that will take you all of five minutes to assemble, toast, and grind. The Spiced Ground Lamb, a classic in northern Indian homes, offers comfort food on a platter, swirling in seasonal fresh (or frozen) green peas and mint.

**Lesson ⑤  Raisin-Stuffed Lamb Burgers**  Raisin-Stuffed Lamb Burgers shows off ground lamb in a more compact form and is an Indian take on an American classic sandwich. In addition to the garam masala, the recipe incorporates honeyed raisins and fiery red chiles to create the sweet-hot mélange of tastes popular in the northwestern region of India.

**Lesson ⑥  Mint-Massaged Leg of Lamb**  The Mint-Massaged Leg of Lamb showcases the elegance of Kashmir in this festive offering, weaving in complex-tasting garam masala with garlic, mint, and ginger (the three musketeers of northern Indian cooking).

**Lessons ⑦ and ⑧  Grilled Baby Back Ribs and Pork Loin with Apples and Eggplant**  Pork takes center stage after lamb and with these two recipes you'll want to take seconds without making a pig of yourself. (Even if you do, who cares?) The ribs deliver a unique flavor profile (chef talk) with ground cumin, cloves, and cayenne in the glaze, while the tenderloin with apple and eggplant showcases cool-weather ingredients with a cider vinegar–based sauce that is reflective of the Christian community from the southwestern state of Goa, a legacy of the Portuguese settlers.

**Lessons ⑨ and ⑩  Buttermilk Fried Chicken and Tandoori Chicken**  Move your favorite fried chicken recipe over and make room for one punctuated with chiles, garlic, and garam masala. I hear your thanks already! Then step up to northern India's iconic Tandoori Chicken, which, surprisingly perhaps, uses that same spice blend.

**Lesson ⑪  Panfried Fennel Tilapia**  In the world of fish and seafood, start with the simple technique of panfrying fish fillets, as I do with the Panfried Fennel Tilapia. But, instead of traditional *panko* or ho-hum bread crumbs, I use ground almonds and season the fish with east India's combination of ground mustard, fennel, and cayenne.

**Lesson ⑫  Creamy Wild Salmon with Kale**  The Portuguese Christian community of India poaches its Creamy Wild Salmon (wild salmon is not native to India, but fish is abundant) in a paste of vinegar and chiles made mellow with unsweetened coconut milk, proving that the succulence of the fish won't get masked by such assertive ingredients.

**Lesson ⑬  Coconut Mussels**  Mussels, scallops, and shrimp bring in flavors from various coastal states, reminding us why their residents are masters at dealing with the fruits from the sea. A few simple steps get mussels ready for the pot, where the traditional flavors from the southwestern state of Kerala scent the shellfish with cardamom, ginger, cinnamon, and peppercorns.

**Lesson ⑭  Cardamom Fennel Scallops**  Cardamom Fennel Scallops is an adaptation of a Bengali classic that is often made with shrimp.

**Lesson ⑮  Tamarind Shrimp**  These shrimp breathe fire against the backdrop of southeastern India's sour tamarind and nutty-popped mustard seeds.

**1** Before starting, have ready the chicken cut into nice large 2-inch cubes, the onion, garlic, and ginger coarsely chopped, and the spices measured out.

**2** Add the onions, garlic, and ginger to the oil once it's hot and shimmering.

**3** Let the onions take on some color before adding the spice blend.

**4** Add in the spice blend and stir till you smell their deepening aroma. This will only take about 10 seconds.

**5** Once the spices release their warm aroma, add the tomatoes and let them cook down and soften for 5 minutes or so.

**6** Once the tomatoes have softened, stir in the half-and-half.

# Ultimate Chicken Curry

## Tamatar Murghi

We Indians are very opinionated about everything. You mention a particular dish and chances are that someone's mother or grandmother has the best recipe and you can't argue with them on its validity, because they are defending the recipe of their nearest and dearest. Neither my mom nor my grandma could or would address this bird in their strict Brahmin vegetarian kitchen, so I took it upon myself to offer you a version that I think not only delivers a succulent dish but does so with few ingredients and some key cooking techniques. I trust it will leave you in that Oliver Twist predicament of asking for more. No worries, you will not be chastised, at least not at my table. Serve curries, such as this one, with some flatbread (either homemade All-Wheat Griddle Breads, page 84, or store-bought) and steamed rice (or a rice pilaf) to soak up all that creamy sauce vibrant with spices.

**Serves 4**

2 tablespoons canola oil

I small onion, coarsely chopped

4 medium-size cloves garlic, coarsely chopped

4 pieces fresh ginger (each about the size and thickness of a 25-cent coin; no need to peel the skin), coarsely chopped

2 teaspoons Raghavan's Blend (page 39) or store-bought Madras curry powder

½ cup canned diced tomatoes with their juices

½ cup half-and-half

1½ pounds skinless, boneless chicken breasts, cut into 2-inch cubes

I teaspoon coarse kosher or sea salt

2 tablespoons finely chopped fresh cilantro leaves and tender stems

1 Heat the oil in a large skillet over medium-high heat. Once the oil appears to shimmer, add the onion, garlic, and ginger and stir-fry until the onion is light caramel brown around the edges, 4 to 5 minutes.

2 Sprinkle the spice blend into the skillet and stir to mix. Let the spices roast in the onion medley until the aromas dramatically change, 10 seconds. Pour in the tomatoes and stir once or twice. Lower the heat and simmer the chunky sauce, uncovered, stirring occasionally, until the tomato pieces soften, the excess moisture evaporates, and some of the oils in the spices start to dot the edge of the sauce, 5 to 7 minutes.

3 Pour the half-and-half into the skillet and scrape the bottom once or twice to release any bits of onion, garlic, and ginger, effectively deglazing the skillet and releasing those flavors back into the sauce. Transfer the chunky curry to a blender. Holding the lid down, puree the curry until it is slightly curdled looking but smooth, and saffron orange-hued.

4 Return the sauce to the skillet and stir in the chicken and salt. Simmer the curry, covered, over medium-low heat, stirring occasionally, until the chicken, when cut with a fork or knife, is cooked through, no longer pinkish-red, and its juices run clear, 12 to 15 minutes.

5 Sprinkle the cilantro on top of the chicken curry and serve.

**7** Continue to stir, blending all the skillet ingredients together and scraping up any bits of onion or garlic that have stuck to the bottom of the pan.

**8** Puree the sauce in a blender, then add it back to the skillet.

**9** Add the chicken cubes and salt to the sauce and simmer, stirring from time to time, until the chicken is cooked through. This will take 12 to 15 minutes.

**10** Once cooked, the sauce will be creamy and fragrant and a deeper red, and the chicken will be moist and infused with luscious flavor.

## Extra Credit

- The other "white" meat, pork, does work well as an alternative to chicken and so will beef, lamb, and turkey. Each meat will contribute its own distinct flavors and will cook to completion at a different time.

  If you like bone-in pieces of chicken by all means use them as they will provide more succulence and a deeper flavor. Just be careful of the bones. Chicken thighs, cheaper in price but richer in taste, are an overlooked cut and will deliver a more complex gusto.

- Yes, cubed tofu or potatoes will be fine instead of the chicken for the vegetarian at your table. Tofu will be done cooking in 10 minutes; potatoes in 15 to 20 minutes, depending on the size of the cubes.

- Any leftover curry is also great when you spoon it over warm, flaky buttermilk biscuits the next morning for breakfast, giving ho-hum biscuits and gravy a run for their money.

# Cardamom Pepper Steak

GLUTEN FREE

My students and readers alike are always surprised that I include beef recipes in my cookbooks. The assumption that Indians don't eat beef is widespread, but there is a strong minority that does relish it, especially those who follow the teachings of Islam and Christianity. This particular preparation highlights some of the flavors of Syrian Christian kitchens in the coastal state of Kerala, using peppercorns and cardamom, both indigenous to this southwestern state. Saucy curries are often the norm here with beef, but when you work with the best cut of meat from the prized and pricey tenderloin, you want to make sure that you not only cook it right (if you can, serve it medium-rare but definitely cooked no more than medium) but also use spices that complement the meat's assertive presence. This should be your savory answer to the query "what's for dinner?" It's obviously beef, yes?

**Serves 4**

I tablespoon black peppercorns

I teaspoon cardamom seeds (removed from the green or white cardmom pods; see Extra Credit, page 43)

I teaspoon coarse kosher or sea salt

4 filets mignons (each 3 to 3½ inches thick and 6 to 8 ounces)

Nonfat cooking spray

1 Preheat a gas or charcoal grill to high.

2 Place the peppercorns and the cardamom seeds in a spice grinder (you can also use a coffee grinder) and grind the blend to the consistency of coarsely ground black pepper. Tap this intensely aromatic blend out on to a plate and stir in the salt.

3 Divvy up the spice blend among the four filets, pressing it on both sides of the steaks studding the meat with aroma and heat.

4 Lightly spray the grill grate with cooking spray and place the filets on the grate. *If you are using a gas grill,* reduce the heat to medium. *If charcoal is the name*

*of your game,* spread out the hot charcoal to even out the heat before placing the meat on the grate. Cover the grill, and let the meat sear and cook until done to taste, 8 to 12 minutes on each side. Use an instant-read meat thermometer to test for doneness. When done to rare the temperature of the filets will be 125°F, when done to medium-rare it will be 145°F, and when done to medium it will be 160°F.

**5** Serve the filets mignons while still hot.

## Extra Credit

- If you don't want to set up your grill, broiling is always an option. To do this, position a rack in the broiler so the tops of the filets mignons will be 2 to 3 inches from the heat. Lightly spray the rack of a broiler pan with cooking spray, place the filets on the rack, and broil them until done to taste.

- Any leftover steak is great thinly sliced and topped on salads for an extra burst of protein. Or turn it into an inviting filling for lusty sandwiches with seasonal tomatoes and lettuce— your new take on BLT, keeping the integrity of B!

# ③ Festive Lamb Chops with Cardamom

GLUTEN FREE

Many of my students get intimidated when working with lamb chops and maybe you do too. But, in fact, it is easy to work with them, especially when they are conveniently sold in mini racks that slice into individual chops. This recipe teaches you to grind a simple masala (blend) to sprinkle and press into each chop, sear the meat, and deglaze the pan with cream and spinach.

When you see the elegant rib lamb chops, with their long bone handles, cooked medium-rare, sitting on a bed of bright green spinach that's in a creamy blanket mottled with sweet cardamom, bracing mustard, and scorching red chiles, you too will

utter "festive." A simply executed dish chock-full of goodness, these chops can also be a starter for a formal sit-down meal. Usually three or four chops per person is a good portion size.

**Serves 4; makes about 16 chops**

2 racks of lamb (about 3 pounds total; see Extra Credit)

2 teaspoons black or yellow mustard seeds

1 teaspoon cardamom seeds (removed from the green or white cardamom pods; see Extra Credit, page 43)

3 to 4 dried red chiles (like chile de árbol), stems discarded

½ cup almond slices or slivers

1½ teaspoons coarse kosher or sea salt

2 to 3 tablespoons canola oil

6 medium-size cloves garlic, finely chopped

1 pound prewashed baby spinach leaves, finely shredded (see Extra Credit)

1 cup half-and-half

1 Cut the racks of lamb into individual chops by slicing in between each rib bone. You should have at least 16 chops.

2 Place the mustard seeds, cardamom seeds, and chiles in a spice grinder (you can also use a coffee grinder) and grind the blend to the consistency of finely ground black pepper. Tap the spice blend into a small bowl. Working in batches, grind the almonds in the same spice grinder to the same consistency as the spice blend and transfer them to a separate medium-size bowl. Combine ¾ teaspoon of the salt with the spice blend and the remaining ¾ teaspoon of salt with the ground almonds.

3 Place the lamb chops on a tray and sprinkle half of the spice blend on the tops of the chops (the meat part, not the bone). Press the spice blend into the meat of the chops to make sure it adheres. Turn the chops over and repeat with the remaining spice blend.

4 Heat 2 tablespoons of the oil in a large skillet over medium-high heat. Once the oil appears to shimmer, arrange half of the chops in a single layer in the hot oil. The instant sizzle and sear will cook the spices without burning them, thanks to the meaty chops. Cook the chops about 1 minute, then turn them over and repeat

· · · · · · · · · · · · · · · · · · · · · · · · · · · · · · · · · · · · · · · · · · · · · · · · · · · ·

## Extra Credit

- When I make these lamb chops, I serve some plain steamed white basmati rice alongside. Since the sauce and lamb have incredible flavors on their own, you want them to shine in the presence of a simple backdrop of uncluttered rice. A loaf of artisanal bread also does the trick.

- Racks of lamb (lamb rib chops) are common in the meat section of grocery stores and megastores. They are usually shrink-wrapped in 1½-pound packages that contain 8 chops. The excess fat has usually been trimmed off and I often don't trim

off any more since the remaining fat contributes to the meat's succulence.

- I find shredding fresh spinach leaves cathartic (okay, I don't get around much). Half the fun of cooking is doing a mundane chore while you zone out and process life, catch up on your podcasts of *This American Life*, laugh along with David Sedaris, or just listen to your favorite tunes. Stack a few spinach leaves and roll them up tight. Cut the roll crosswise into thin slices; you will end up with fine shreds of spinach, also known as chiffonade.

5 Reduce the heat to medium, add the garlic to the skillet, and stir-fry it until light brown, about 30 seconds. Sprinkle the ground almonds over the garlic and quickly stir it to make sure there are no lumps. The nuts will foam up and bubble, turning light brown quickly, about 30 seconds. Stir in handfuls of the spinach; the heat will be just right to quickly wilt the shreds. Repeat until all of the spinach has been added.

6 Pour the half-and-half into the skillet and scrape the bottom to release all of the bits of almond, spinach, and garlic, effectively deglazing the pan and releasing those flavors back into the sauce. Return all of the lamb chops to the pan, making sure that they are blanketed with the festive-looking sauce, lush green against a white backdrop. If the skillet is too small to accommodate all of the chops, place half of the chops and sauce in a separate skillet. Cover the skillet(s) and let the chops cook a bit more and absorb some of those lush favors, about 5 minutes. The chops will be medium-rare. If you want the meat to be less rare, simmer the chops, covered, an additional 3 to 5 minutes.

on the second side, about 1 minute. Transfer the chops from the skillet to a plate. If the skillet looks dry, add another tablespoon of oil. The heat of the skillet will instantly bring the added oil to the right temperature. Cook the remaining chops the same way you did the first batch. Once cooked, add them to the plate with the first batch.

7 Serve the lamb chops right away, making sure you spoon all of that satiny spinach sauce around them.

# 4 Spiced Ground Lamb

## Kheema

GLUTEN FREE

Curiously similar to the oh-so-popular children's favorite, sloppy joe, without the drenching tomato sauce, this dish packs subtle flavors with a slight kick from the chiles. Called *kheema* (which means "ground meat") in Hindi, it is comfort food to the millions who consume meat in India. The peas provide color and flavor and the fresh herbs, including mint, are the perfect mate to lamb. Serve this with some store-bought naan or pile it in hamburger buns for that American sloppy experience.

**Serves 4**

I small red onion, coarsely chopped

4 pieces fresh ginger (each about the size and thickness of a 25-cent coin; no need to peel the skin)

I to 2 fresh green serrano chiles, stems discarded

2 tablespoons canola oil

I pound ground lamb

I teaspoon garam masala, homemade (page 41) or store-bought

I teaspoon coarse kosher or sea salt

2 cups frozen green peas, thawed

¼ cup finely chopped fresh cilantro leaves and tender stems

¼ cup finely chopped fresh mint leaves

1 Place the onion, ginger, and chile(s) in the bowl of a food processor. Using the pulsing action, mince these ingredients to create a pungent-smelling blend. Letting the processor run constantly instead of using quick pulses will create an unwanted watery mélange.

2 Heat the oil in a large skillet over medium-high heat. Once the oil appears to shimmer, add the minced onion mixture to the skillet and stir-fry it until the onion is light brown around the edges and the chiles smell pungent, 2 to 3 minutes.

browned, about 5 minutes. Sprinkle in the garam masala and salt. Continue to cook the lamb, uncovered, stirring occasionally, until the spices scent the meat, 1 to 2 minutes.

4 Stir in the peas, reduce the heat to medium-low, and let the lamb simmer, uncovered, stirring occasionally, until the peas warm through, about 5 minutes.

5 Stir the cilantro and mint into the spiced lamb and serve it warm.

## Extra Credit

• Ground beef, turkey, chicken, or pork are all fair game as alternatives to the lamb in this recipe. Turkey and chicken cook faster than any of the other meats so adjust your cooking time accordingly.

• Mint and cilantro, two equally assertive herbs, when brought together form a harmonious balance and cancel each other's sharp presence. Cilantro haters won't notice the lanolin-like (yes it's the same chemical in soap) presence of their nemesis and mint loathers will be pleasantly surprised at its diminished fragrance.

Fresh tarragon and basil, in equal proportions, make a great match also.

• During the peak of summer when you have tomatoes growing out of your ears, hollow out a few of the wondrous vine fruits and stuff them with this slightly warmed lamb studded with green peas. Makes an elegant and tasty meal.

3 Add the ground lamb, breaking it up into smaller pieces with a spatula to ensure even cooking and browning, and cook, uncovered, stirring occasionally, until the lamb has lost all its liquid and has

#  Raisin-Stuffed Lamb Burgers

What is surprising about these burgers is the little hit of sweet, sour, and hot that creeps up on you when you bite into a juicy patty. I think this will give all those fast food joints that serve cheese-filled stuffed burgers a run for their money. This version, bursting with the north Indian goodness of sweet-smelling cinnamon, cardamom, and cumin (in the garam masala) and nutty almonds, packs enough punch to serve many a loved one with great satisfaction—maybe you too will have a sign that boasts over one billion satisfied folks. After all, India has that many people to give you a head start.

**Makes 4 burgers**

I pound ground lamb

¼ cup finely chopped fresh cilantro leaves and tender stems, or ¼ cup finely chopped fresh mint leaves

¼ cup ground almond slivers or raw (unroasted and unsalted) cashews (see Extra Credit)

I teaspoon garam masala, homemade (page 41) or store-bought

I teaspoon coarse kosher or sea salt

2 large cloves garlic, finely chopped

¼ cup golden raisins

2 dried red cayenne chiles (like chile de árbol), stems discarded

½ cup boiling water

I tablespoon canola oil

1 Place the lamb, cilantro or mint, almonds, garam masala, salt, and garlic in a medium-size bowl and combine well. Divide the spiced lamb into 4 equal portions.

2 Place the raisins and chiles in a small bowl and pour the boiling water over them. Let the raisins and chiles soak until the raisins swell up and the chiles soften, about 15 minutes. Drain the raisins and chiles, transfer them to the bowl of a food processor, and pulse to create a squishy mass studded with pieces of red chiles. A mini chopper works well for this because it handles smaller portions better than a full-size food processor. Finely chopping

## Extra Credit

- To get ¼ cup ground almonds, start with ¼ cup of them preground. If you wind up with a little more or less ground almonds, it will be fine.

- Ground beef and pork will also work well in this recipe, as do chicken and turkey. Because of their lower fat content you may need a bit more of the ground nuts to hold the chicken and turkey together when making the stuffed patties.

- Turn this into a complete burger experience replete with buns, greens, onion, tomato, pickles, and anything else you like. Yes, fries of course! Topping a patty with a slice of your favorite cheese as the lamb cooks will blanket the meat with an even melt. Or if you prefer the upscale sliders, now so chic on restaurant menus, shape the spiced lamb into smaller patties and sandwich them in mini buns.

- Any leftover cooked patties are great crumbled and sprinkled into tortillas (crisp or soft) along with all your favorite taco toppings. Or, do as they do in the Upper Midwest part of the United States: Fold the crumbled patties into cream of mushroom soup and bake them topped with crispy fried onions and Tater Tots. (It's called a hot dish and not a casserole—you're not from around here, are you?)

3 Working with one portion of the spiced lamb at a time, shape it into a patty. Then press the patty into a disk about 2 inches in diameter. Using your finger make a dimplelike indentation in the center of the patty and place a portion of the raisin-chile paste in it. Gather the edge of the patty and fold it over the filling, reshaping it into a patty about 1 inch thick. Repeat with the remaining portions of lamb and filling.

4 Line a large plate with paper towels. Heat the oil in a large nonstick or cast-iron skillet over medium heat. Once the oil appears to shimmer, place the 4 patties in the pan and let them sizzle and sear on the underside, about 1 minute. Then cover the skillet and continue to cook the patties until the undersides are evenly dark brown, 3 to 4 minutes. Turn the patties over and repeat with the second side, 3 to 4 minutes. You want the meat to be slightly pink in the center (done to medium). Transfer the patties to the paper towel–lined plate to drain the excess fat.

5 Serve the lamb patties warm (see Extra Credit).

the raisins and chiles together on a cutting board using a chef's knife is also an alternative. Divide the raisin and chile paste into 4 equal portions.

# Mint-Massaged Leg of Lamb

Raan

specialty of Pakistan and Lucknow (in north central India), often roasted in tandoors or makeshift grills, this bone-in leg of lamb, called *raan,* is a special-occasion dish that often requires a long marinating time because the meat used is mutton—a mature sheep—or goat. Cooks apply ground unripe papaya to the meat because the chemical papain, a natural tenderizer present in the fruit, breaks down the tough connective tissues to yield meat that falls off the bone when it is cooked. However, lamb in the United States is quite tender, making the application of papaya unnecessary. The roast is often served in India with cilantro, slivers of raw red onions, and wedges of lime and with tandoor-cooked naan alongside. You may wish to do the same here, serving homemade (page 93) or store-bought naan, from your favorite Indian restaurant. This lamb can be the center of attention at a holiday table.

**Serves 4 to 6**

I bone-in half leg of lamb (4 pounds)

½ cup firmly packed fresh mint leaves

½ cup firmly packed fresh cilantro leaves and tender stems

8 medium-size cloves garlic

6 pieces fresh ginger (each about the size and thickness of a 25-cent coin; no need to peel the skin)

I to 2 fresh green serrano chiles, stems discarded

2 teaspoons garam masala, homemade (page 41) or store-bought

1½ teaspoons coarse kosher or sea salt

Nonfat cooking spray

To prepare the lamb, make 4 to 6 slits, about ¼ inch deep, in the meat, making sure you don't hit the bone in the roast with the knife blade (it's not a good feeling, neither for the knife nor for you). Place the leg of lamb in a shallow pan and set it aside while you prepare the rub.

2 Place the mint, cilantro, garlic, ginger, chile(s), garam masala, and salt in the bowl of a food processor and pulse to create a minced rub chock-full of heady aromas, speckled with green herbs and warming spices. Grab handfuls of the herb mix and massage it over the lamb, making sure it gets into the slits. Use all of the herb medley, evenly coating all the sides of the lamb.

3 Refrigerate the lamb, covered, for at least 4 hours or, if possible, overnight to allow for the maximum infusion of flavor.

4 When you are ready to roast the lamb, position a rack in the center of the oven and preheat the oven to 450°F. Set a rack in a roasting pan and spray the rack with cooking spray.

5 Place the rub-blanketed lamb on the rack. While the oven preheats, let the lamb come to room temperature. I usually set the pan with the lamb on the kitchen counter close to the oven to quicken the process. Place the lamb in the hot oven and reduce the heat to 325°F.

The reason you reduce the heat when you put the lamb in the oven is that there is enough heat to initially sear the meat on the outside and by the time the oven gets to the lower temperature, it will be just right for slow roasting the meat to perfection. I usually pour a little water into the roasting pan before putting it in the oven so the moisture can maintain the meat's succulence and prevent the drippings from burning.

Roast the meat until done to taste, 1½ to 1¾ hours for medium-rare. To test for doneness, insert an instant-read thermometer in the center of the thickest part of the leg (make sure the thermometer does not touch the bone or you will have an incorrect reading). The internal temperature will be about 135°F for medium-rare.

6 Remove the roasting pan from the oven and let the lamb rest for 10 minutes. Its internal temperature will rise about 5 degrees. Transfer the lamb to a cutting board, cut the meat into ½-inch-thick slices, and arrange them on a serving platter.

# Grilled Baby Back Ribs

This is pure and simple "down-home" food for you lovers of grilled ribs. The technique is all-American familiar, while the seasonings belt out India. If you're at home, serve them warm, but they're also a great summer picnic offering, because these succulent, fall-apart ribs are divine even at room temperature. If you don't feel like firing up the grill outdoors, see the Extra Credit for an alternative baking method. You can use any kind of ribs, either pork or beef, for equally spectacular results.

GLUTEN FREE

**Serves 4**

FOR THE RIBS

**2 tablespoons finely chopped fresh ginger**

**I teaspoon coarse kosher or sea salt**

**½ teaspoon ground mustard**

**4 pounds baby back pork ribs**

FOR THE GLAZE

**¼ cup tomato paste**

**¼ cup maple syrup or molasses**

**I tablespoon freshly squeezed lime or lemon juice, or I teaspoon tamarind paste**

**I teaspoon ground cumin**

**I teaspoon ground red pepper (cayenne)**

**¼ teaspoon ground cloves**

**I teaspoon coarse kosher or sea salt**

**Nonfat cooking spray**

1 Prepare the ribs: Mix the ginger, 1 teaspoon of salt, and the mustard together in a small bowl. Smear this chunky rub over the meaty side of the ribs. You can cook the ribs right away or you may also choose to cover the ribs and refrigerate them overnight to allow the flavors to permeate the meat. (I usually put the ribs on a sheet pan or baking sheet, as they are easily contained in one tray and don't take up that much room in the refrigerator.)

2 Make the glaze: Combine the tomato paste, maple syrup or molasses, lime

## Extra Credit

If you don't have a grill (or it's freezing outside), use your oven to roast the ribs: Position a rack in the center of the oven and preheat the oven to 325°F. Lightly spray a broiler pan, or a rack set in a roasting pan, with cooking spray. Arrange the ribs, meat side down, on the rack and roast them until well-browned, about 45 minutes. Turn the ribs over and roast them for 30 to 45 minutes longer. The meat should be tender and almost falling off the bone. Liberally brush the ribs with all of the glaze. Continue to roast the ribs meat side up, until the glaze looks slightly opaque and the meat is very tender, 10 to 15 minutes longer. Let the ribs rest covered with aluminum foil for 5 to 10 minutes before slicing them between the bones.

Check periodically to make sure the meat drippings don't flame up and burn the ribs (if they do, I usually move the ribs to an unlit section of the grill for a few seconds until the flames die down).

6 Turn the ribs over so they are meat side up and cover the grill again. Cook until nicely browned and the meat is tender and almost falling off the bone, 20 to 25 minutes longer.

7 Liberally brush the ribs with the hot-sweet-tart glaze, using it all up. Continue to grill them, meat side up and with the grill covered, until the glaze looks slightly opaque and the meat is even more tender, 10 to 15 minutes.

8 Transfer the ribs to a cutting board, cover them with aluminum foil, and let them rest for 5 to 10 minutes.

9 Slice the ribs between the bones (it's okay to lick your fingers when no one is watching) and transfer them to a serving platter. Serve the ribs warm (this is a good time to bring out the bibs).

or lemon juice or tamarind paste, cumin, cayenne, cloves, and 1 teaspoon of salt in a small bowl and stir thoroughly.

3 When you are ready to grill the ribs, heat a gas or charcoal grill to high.

4 Lightly spray the grill grate with cooking spray. *If you are using a gas grill,* reduce the heat to medium. *If charcoal is the name of your game,* spread the hot coals to the sides for indirect heat.

5 Place the ribs on the grill grate, meat side down, and cover the grill. Cook the ribs until well-browned, 35 to 45 minutes.

# 8 Pork Loin with Apples and Eggplant

GLUTEN FREE

South of Mumbai is a state called Goa that still marches to the Portuguese settlers' tune that influenced its culinary scene, particularly among the masses who converted to Christianity. Pork, vinegar (especially the kind that is extracted from the cashew liquor called *feni*), and the local cashews appear at numerous meals alongside sweet spices like cinnamon and fiery chiles for balance. For this recipe cider vinegar steps in in lieu of the hard-to-procure cashew vinegar. Serve the pork not with the perfunctory steamed white rice but with buttered, perfectly cooked noodles (wheat, rice, or any other grain).

**Serves 4**

I teaspoon cumin seeds

3 to 4 dried red cayenne chiles (like chile de árbol), stems discarded

I cinnamon stick (about 3 inches long), broken into smaller pieces (see **Extra Credit**, page 43)

I teaspoon coarse kosher or sea salt

4 large cloves garlic, finely chopped

I pound pork tenderloin

1½ pounds eggplants (see **Extra Credit**, page 236)

2 medium-size tart apples (like Braeburn or Granny Smith)

2 tablespoons canola oil

½ cup cider vinegar

1 Place the cumin, chiles, and pieces of cinnamon stick in a spice grinder (you can also use a coffee grinder) and grind them to the consistency of finely ground black pepper. Stir in the salt.

2 Press the garlic evenly all over the pork tenderloins. Cut off and discard the stems of the eggplants, then cut the eggplants into ½-inch cubes. Core the apples and cut them into ½-inch cubes.

## Extra Credit

If you want a little color, sprinkle any fresh herbs you have lying around in the fridge over the pork before you serve it. My favorites are sage and basil, especially when I have an overflowing herb patch toward the tail end of summer.

3 Heat the oil in a large skillet over medium-high heat. Once the oil appears to shimmer, place the garlic-studded tenderloin in the pan and sear the meat on all 4 sides until it is a deep reddish-brown color, about 3 minutes per side. Transfer the browned tenderloin to a plate.

4 Reduce the heat to medium, add the eggplants and apples, and cook, stirring until they absorb some of the tenderloin flavors from the skillet, 2 to 4 minutes.

5 As soon as the eggplant and apples are tender, sprinkle the spice blend over them and cook, stirring to coat, about 1 minute. Pour the vinegar into the skillet and scrape the bottom to release any browned bits. Return the seared pork tenderloin to the skillet, spooning all that eggplant and apple chunky goodness over it. Cover the skillet and cook the pork, without stirring, until an instant-read thermometer inserted in the center registers 145° to 150°F, 10 to 12 minutes. Turn off the heat and let the pork rest, covered with aluminum foil, for 5 minutes.

6 Transfer the pork tenderloin to a cutting board and slice it into ½-inch-thick medallions, pink and juicy, bursting with succulence. Arrange the sliced tenderloin on a serving platter and spoon the eggplant and apples over it. Serve warm.

# Buttermilk Fried Chicken

hicken in India is always eaten skinless, because the skin is considered fatty and therefore unhealthy. That may be true, but when pieces of the bird are fried, there is nothing better than the crinkly-crisp skin to augment its flavors. Often chickpea flour forms the basis for batter-frying the chicken in India, but here I go the traditional American way, using all-purpose flour. However, I do spice the flour with fragrant garam masala.

A good fried chicken brings grown men and women down to their knees, their child-like cravings for crispy succulence making them barely able to contain the hot meat between their eager fingers. When my then eleven-year-old son took his first bite of this fried chicken, his big black eyes widened with unabashed glee, the spicy outside crust and moist inside providing that perfect balance of texture, temperature, and flavor. I guess I had a winner on my hands. And yes, like all great fried chicken, this too is sinful when eaten cold.

**Serves 4**

I cup buttermilk

4 large cloves garlic

2 to 3 fresh green serrano chiles, stems
  discarded

I tablespoon coarse kosher or sea salt

8 pieces bone-in, skin-on chicken (breasts,
  thighs, legs, wings; 2 to 2½ pounds total)

3 cups canola oil

¼ cup ghee, homemade (page 3I) or store-
  bought, unsalted butter, or vegetable
  shortening

2 cups all-purpose flour

2 teaspoons garam masala, homemade
  (page 4I) or store-bought

Pour the buttermilk into a blender and add the garlic and chiles. Puree until the marinade is smooth and creamy, its color is light green, and its aroma is pungent. Scrape the marinade into a large bowl and stir in 2 teaspoons of the salt, setting aside the remaining teaspoon for the flour. Add the chicken pieces to the buttermilk marinade and make sure they are all coated evenly. Refrigerate the chicken, covered, for at least an hour. Ideally, the chicken is best when marinated overnight. It's akin to brining, where the salt helps retain moisture in the meat, making it more succulent.

2 When you are ready to fry the chicken, line a tray with paper towels and place a rack (like a cake rack or grill grate) on top of the towels to drain the chicken as it comes out of the oil. The rack elevates the chicken, keeping it crisp as the excess oil drains. Heat the oil and ghee in a large sauté pan, wok, or Dutch oven over medium-high heat. A deep-fry or candy thermometer inserted in the oil (without touching the bottom of the pan) should register between 300° and 325°F.

3 As the oil heats, quickly combine the flour, garam masala, and the remaining teaspoon of salt in a medium-size bowl. Once the oil has reached the desired temperature, remove the chicken pieces from the buttermilk and place them in the spiced flour. Don't worry about patting the chicken dry with paper towels first. You need the clinging liquid for the spiced flour to stick

## Extra Credit

- Chicken in India is always consumed without the skin. If you wish the same experience take the pieces of chicken and use paper towels to pull the skin away from the meat (the chicken will slip away when held with your bare hands). Proceed with the recipe as usual. For a deeper penetration of the marinade score the meat with a knife in a few places before soaking it in the spiced buttermilk.

- If you do not have a candy or oil thermometer, to see if the oil is the right temperature for frying, stick a wooden skewer into the oil until it touches the bottom of the pan. If bubbles start to rise around the skewer, it indicates that the oil is just right for frying.

- A mess-free way of marinating the chicken is to pour the marinade in a large plastic zip-top bag and add the chicken to it. Secure the bag shut and massage the contents from the outside to make sure every piece gets well coated. You can do the same when dredging the chicken. Place the spiced flour in another plastic zip-top bag. Add two pieces of chicken at a time, keep the bag shut, and give it a good shake to coat them evenly.

to the meat. (Buttermilk has the right amount of viscosity, like what eggs provide when breading something.) Dredge each piece of chicken in the flour, making sure it gets blanketed all over.

4 Gently lower 2 of the chicken pieces into the hot oil (you don't want to overcrowd

the pan with more since that lowers the heat and makes the fried chicken greasy and soggy), frying each side until reddish brown and crisp, 5 to 7 minutes per side. Using tongs, transfer the fried chicken to the prepared rack. Repeat with the remaining pieces of chicken. Make sure the oil continues to be at the desired temperature before you fry the remaining pieces; you may need to adjust the heat to maintain the temperature.

5 Serve the fried chicken while it is still warm and crisp. If you do not plan to eat it right away, you can keep the chicken pieces warm on the rack for up to 30 minutes in an oven preheated to 175° to 200°F.

# 10 Tandoori Chicken

GLUTEN FREE

Arguably the most popular Indian dish among North Americans and Western Europeans alike, tandoori chicken has been synonymous with Indian restaurant food for centuries. Made popular by street food vendors in the narrow streets of Old Delhi, these birds spread their spicy, succulent wings and looked toward the West for acceptance, and boy, did they get it. Now every cookie-cutter restaurant that serves northern Indian food lays them out in familiar buffets or brings them out tableside sizzling in a blaze of glory on a bed of sliced onion, bell pepper, cilantro, and cayenne corralled by wedges of fresh lime. My version renders an equally scrumptious result using skinless and boneless chicken breasts that cook quickly, either on the grill or in the oven, and are a cinch to make without having to use store-bought, sodium-laden tandoori marinades that cost you an arm and a leg.

**Serves 4**

½ cup plain yogurt, preferably Greek style (full fat, or nonfat)

4 pieces fresh ginger (each about the size and thickness of a 25-cent coin; no need to peel the skin)

4 large cloves garlic

1 teaspoon garam masala, homemade (page 41) or store-bought

1 teaspoon coarse kosher or sea salt

1 teaspoon sweet paprika

½ teaspoon ground red pepper (cayenne)

1½ pounds skinless, boneless chicken breasts

Nonfat cooking spray

1 Plop the yogurt (yes, a thick yogurt makes that noise when you dump it into a pan or bowl) into a blender. Add the ginger and garlic and sprinkle in the garam masala, salt, paprika, and cayenne. Puree the marinade until it is smooth and saucy with a deep orange color. If you taste the marinade, which I hope you will, it will have a raw, robust, and sharp taste, redolent of ginger, garlic, and assertive spices.

2 Place the chicken breasts in a bowl and spread the marinade over them, coating them thoroughly. Refrigerate the chicken breasts, covered, for at least 30 minutes. If you wish, overnight would also be great.

3 To cook the chicken, heat a gas or charcoal grill to medium-high or preheat the oven to 450°F.

4 *If you are grilling the chicken,* spray the grill grate with cooking spray. Place the chicken on the grate. (Set aside any marinade for basting the chicken.) Cover the grill and cook the chicken, basting it occasionally with the remaining marinade during the first 5 minutes of cooking. Turn the breasts over after 2½ minutes so both sides get basted. Continue cooking, turning the chicken over again after about 7 minutes more. The meat is done when it is barely pink in the thickest parts and, when cut, the juices run clear, about 20 minutes total.

*If you are oven-roasting the chicken,* place a rack in a roasting pan and spray it with cooking spray. Place the chicken on the rack. (Set aside any marinade for basting the chicken.) Roast the chicken, basting it during the first 5 minutes of cooking with the remaining marinade. Turn the breasts over after 2½ minutes so both sides get basted. Continue cooking, turning the chicken over again after about 12 minutes more. The meat is done when it is barely pink in the thickest parts and, when cut, the juices run clear, 30 to 40 minutes total.

5 Serve the chicken warm or as recommended in the Extra Credit box.

# Extra Credit

• Turn these tasty tandoori treats into wraps and smother yourself with an additional layer of comfort. Plan on 2 warm tortillas per person or homemade All-Wheat Griddle Breads (page 84). Cut a small red onion in half lengthwise and then thinly slice it crosswise. Cut a medium-size green bell pepper in half lengthwise and then seed and thinly slice it. Combine the vegetables in a medium-size bowl along with ½ teaspoon ground red pepper (cayenne), ½ teaspoon coarse kosher or sea salt, and 2 tablespoons finely chopped fresh cilantro leaves and tender stems. Cut a large lime into 8 wedges. Slice the warm chicken into thin strips (about ¼ inch wide).

To wrap the whole kit and caboodle, place a tortilla on a plate and place a serving of the chicken strips in the center. Top it off with some red-hot vegetables and a squirt of lime juice. Roll the tortilla up into a neat little wrap and enjoy it with a hearty ale or a glass of viognier (a varietal wine from southern France).

• The neon reddish-pink color you see in Indian restaurants that dish out tandoori chicken comes from a few drops of red food coloring swirled into the marinade. Feel free to do the same if you wish for that look.

• For a vegetarian version, slice up ½-inch-thick planks of paneer (see page 35 for a recipe for the cheese) or extra-firm tofu and marinate it in a similar fashion. You won't have to cook them as long. Once the pieces acquire grill marks and the surface loses its glossy sheen, it is ready, usually 5 to 8 minutes. If you are roasting the paneer or tofu, do it in a preheated 450°F oven. Look for that color change to occur. It may take an additional 3 to 5 minutes in the oven.

# 11 Panfried Fennel Tilapia

## Macher Saunf

GLUTEN FREE

The Bengalis of Calcutta are connoisseurs who relish the fruits from the sea, going overboard perhaps, by serving fish at all times of the day. They will of course disagree with my two-bit opinion as they cut into subtly flavored, nut-crisp morsels of fresh-caught boneless fillets. They devour the fish panfried in pungent-tasting mustard oil, in between mouthfuls of tea brewed from the black tea leaves of the neighboring state of Assam, along with whole milk, spices, and sugar. It's teatime and dinner is nowhere in sight, so this indulgence to get them over the hunger bump is essential. Here this is main course material, especially when you augment the fish with a vegetable and/or starch.

**Serves 4**

2 large eggs, slightly beaten

4 large cloves garlic, finely chopped

I cup almond slivers or slices

2 teaspoons ground fennel

I teaspoon coarse kosher or sea salt

½ teaspoon ground mustard

½ teaspoon ground red pepper (cayenne)

Canola oil for panfrying

4 skinless boneless tilapia fillets (6 ounces each, see **Extra Credit**)

1 Position a rack in the center of the oven. Place a cake rack or something similar on a cookie sheet and set it on that oven rack. Preheat the oven to 200°F.

2 Combine the eggs and garlic in a pie plate or something shallow but ample enough to dunk the fish fillets in.

3 Working in batches, grind the almonds in a spice grinder (you can also use a coffee grinder) to the consistency of finely ground black pepper. Mix together the ground almonds, fennel, salt, mustard, and

## Extra Credit

Tilapia is not the name for one particular type of fish but a variety of freshwater species. They are prolific and are known to have low levels of mercury, making them an ideal candidate both for healthy consumption and contributing to a sustainable environment. Affordable to breed and hence accessible to the consumer, tilapia is a thin-fleshed, mild-tasting fish that cooks in mere minutes.

As an ambassador to Monterey Bay Aquarium's successful Seafood Watch program, I strongly urge you to visit its website at montereybayaquarium .org/cr/seafoodwatch .aspx where you can learn about consuming fish and seafood in terms of what's sustainable. Based on the "Best Choice" or "Good Alternative" categories for the region of the country where you live, you can choose other white-fleshed fish as an alternative to tilapia.

Keep in mind that the thickness of the fillet will determine its cooking time and allow an extra 2 to 3 minutes for thick-fleshed pieces.

5 Working with 1 tilapia fillet at a time, dip it into the garlicky egg wash, making sure it is well coated on both sides. Lift the fillet out of the egg wash and place it in the spiced ground almonds, pressing it into the nutty mélange and making sure all sides are covered.

6 Once the oil appears to shimmer, place the coated fillet in the skillet and cook it until crusty brown on the underside, 3 to 5 minutes. Turn the fillet over and cook it until crusty brown on the second side, 3 to 5 minutes. Transfer the browned fillet to the prepared rack in the oven to keep it warm as you finish dipping, coating, and panfrying the remaining fillets. Add more oil to the skillet as needed between panfrying each fillet. I can usually accommodate 2 fillets in the same skillet. Don't overcrowd the skillet or the fillets may end up with a soggy crust.

cayenne either in a separate pie plate or shallow bowl.

4 Pour enough oil into a large nonstick or cast-iron skillet to coat the bottom (you want the oil to be barely ⅛ inch deep) and heat over medium heat.

# Creamy Wild Salmon with Kale

When you use a fairly expensive, rich, and well-marbled fish like wild salmon, you want to make sure you don't clutter it with too many spices or overcook it. Coconut milk maintains that velvety mouthfeel of the fish and provides a stunning backdrop to its orange-pink vibrancy. I serve the salmon with those plump pearls of Israeli couscous that play on your senses with their caviarlike texture.

GLUTEN FREE

**Serves 4**

½ teaspoon ground turmeric

1½ pounds skinless, boneless wild salmon fillet in a single piece (such as Alaskan or Copper River)

¼ cup cider vinegar

4 dried red cayenne chiles (like chile de árbol), stems discarded, ground (do not remove the seeds; see **Extra Credit**) or 1 teaspoon ground red pepper (cayenne)

1 teaspoon coarse kosher or sea salt

¼ teaspoon ground nutmeg

1 medium-size bunch fresh kale (about 8 ounces)

2 tablespoons canola oil

6 large cloves garlic, either thinly sliced or finely chopped

1 can (13.5 to 15 ounces) unsweetened coconut milk (see **Extra Credit**)

1 Sprinkle about ¼ teaspoon of the turmeric on one side of the salmon fillet and press it into the fish. Turn the fish over and repeat with the remaining ¼ teaspoon of turmeric. Set the salmon aside as you prepare the spice paste.

2 Combine the vinegar, chiles, salt, and nutmeg in a small bowl to make a slurry. Set the slurry aside.

3 Fill up a medium-size bowl with cold water. Take a leaf of kale, cut along both sides of the tough rib, and discard it. Slice the leaf in half lengthwise. Repeat with the remaining leaves. Stack the leaf halves,

about 6 at a time, one on top of the other, and roll them into a tight log. Thinly slice the log crosswise; you will end up with long, slender shreds. When cutting the kale, you can't help notice how strong smelling and grassy it is (no wonder I love the smell of fresh-mowed grass in the summer). Dunk the shreds into the bowl of water to rinse off any grit, then scoop the shreds out and drain them in a colander. Repeat once or twice if the kale does not appear clean.

4 Heat the oil in a large skillet over medium-high heat. Once the oil appears to shimmer, add the turmeric-smeared fillet to the skillet. The instant sizzle and sear will turn the salmon light brown on the underside, about 2 minutes. Turn it over and repeat with the second side, about 2 minutes. Transfer the fish to a plate. Add the garlic to the skillet and stir-fry it until light brown and aromatic, about 1 minute.

5 Pour the vinegar-based spice slurry into the skillet and stir to mix with the garlic. Simmer, uncovered, stirring occasionally, about 2 minutes. The pungency will slap you in the face (in a good way—I promise) and the liquid will release all the browned bits of fish from the bottom of the skillet into the thin sauce.

6 Add the kale shreds and stir to coat them evenly with the liquid. Pour ½ cup of water into the skillet and stir.

## Extra Credit

- **A stout bunch, dark green and spritely, Tuscan kale stands for the epitome of winter bravado. Even though it grows all through the year, we often associate kale with cold weather, that brightness among a sea of white, very much like the evergreen Christmas tree. Curly, ornamental (those tight bases of light purple leaves with a frizzy head of green), or Russian kale— all varieties work well for this recipe. Bursting with antioxidants, vitamins A and C, and iron, kale is a nutritional powerhouse among a sea of greens. Its tough leaves make it harder to cook than some greens, but with the right amount of moisture, it turns tender within about 5 minutes.**

- **To grind the *chiles de árbol*, pulverize them in a spice grinder (like a coffee grinder) until they are the texture of finely ground black pepper. The heat from freshly ground dried chiles is much more intense than preground cayenne.**

- **Before opening a can of coconut milk, shake it well to make sure the thick milk gets dispersed evenly. If the can sits around unopened, the thicker part usually floats to the top and congeals into a creamy mass. If shaking does nothing (usually if the can has been sitting in a cool spot, this will happen), then once you open the can, scrape the contents into a small bowl, and whisk the thicker milk with the wheylike separated liquid to create an evenly thick milk.**

Lower the heat to medium, cover the skillet, and stew the kale, stirring occasionally, until the shreds are tender when tested (and tasted, I hope), 5 to 8 minutes.

7 Stir the coconut milk into the kale. Let the milk come to a boil uncovered. Add the seared salmon to the liquid, basting it to make sure it continues to poach. Cook, uncovered, scooping up the sauce and basting the fish occasionally, until it barely starts to flake, 3 to 5 minutes.

8 Transfer the fish to a serving plate. Let the sauce boil, uncovered, stirring occasionally, until it thickens, 3 to 4 minutes. Pour the sauce over the salmon and serve.

##  Coconut Mussels

### Teesri Hooman

Tight-lipped mussels are a good thing, especially if they close when tapped before you cook them. That means the mussels are alive in their cavelike home. But once you cook them, the mussel shells should open and reveal succulent meat. The thin, brothlike liquid that steeps the mussels harbors spices native to the southwestern coast of Kerala, a state that is home to many of India's indigenous spices like cinnamon, cardamom, ginger, and peppercorns. I always serve either bowls of steamed white rice or rice noodles with this dish so I can pour the flavorful broth over them and continue eating once the mussels are all gone.

**Serves 4**

5 pounds mussels, in the shells

2 tablespoons canola oil

I cup finely chopped red onion

2 green or white cardamom pods

I cinnamon stick (about 3 inches long)

2 fresh green serrano chiles, stems discarded, finely chopped (do not remove the seeds)

I cup unsweetened coconut milk (see **Extra Credit**, page 181)

I teaspoon black peppercorns, coarsely cracked

I teaspoon coarse kosher or sea salt

2 pieces fresh ginger (each about the size and thickness of a 25-cent coin; no need to peel the skin), cut into matchstick-thin strips (julienne)

1 Right before cooking, pile the mussels in a large bowl. Go through them and discard any with broken or cracked shells. Scrub each mussel (although the ones available at supermarkets are actually quite clean) and remove the beards (the 2 or 3 strands dangling from one end of the shell). Tap the mussel shell if it's slightly ajar. If it closes shut, the mussel is alive and usable. If it does not shut, discard the mussel, since this means it is dead. Place the prepared mussels in a colander and give them a good rinse under cold running water.

2 Heat the oil in a large skillet over medium-high heat. Add the onion, cardamom pods, cinnamon stick, and chiles and stir-fry until the onion is light brown around the edges, about 3 minutes.

3 Stir in the coconut milk and add the peppercorns, salt, and ginger. Once it boils, transfer the sauce to a large stockpot, stir in ½ cup of water, and let come to a boil over high heat. Add the mussels and cover the pot. Cook the mussels, shaking the pot occasionally (so they cook evenly) and ladling some of the broth over them periodically, until the mussels open, about 5 minutes. Discard any mussels that remain shut.

4 Pour the mussels and broth, including the onion, cardamon pods, cinnamon stick, and chiles, into a large bowl and serve.

## Extra Credit

Fishnet sacks of mussels are a common sight in the supermarket's fish and seafood section. Most of today's mussels come from farm-raised sources since the wild-caught ones have a tendency to harbor toxins.

#  Cardamom Fennel Scallops

## Macher Malai Curry

A trip to the fish market in Calcutta in the morning reveals bountiful fish and seafood, clean smelling, healthy looking, and inviting. A common sight of a stray cat sauntering from vendor to vendor in hopes of a morsel of sardine or any fish parts is cute to see, as his begging eyes and pitiful meows pull at many a vendor's heartstrings. The perfect balance of simple spices here yields creamy results for sweet scallops, and the combination is nothing short of perfection. Serve it with steamed white rice (preferably basmati) for a quickie (meal that is!).

**Serves 4**

I teaspoon fennel seeds

½ teaspoon black or yellow mustard seeds

¼ teaspoon cardamom seeds (removed from the green or white cardamom pods; see **Extra Credit**, page 43)

I pound large sea scallops (12 to 15; see **Extra Credit**)

4 medium-size cloves garlic, finely chopped

2 dried red cayenne chiles (like chile de árbol), stems discarded, coarsely chopped (do not remove the seeds, see **Extra Credit**)

I teaspoon coarse kosher or sea salt

2 tablespoons canola oil

½ cup unsweetened coconut milk (see **Extra Credit**, page 181)

I tablespoon finely chopped fresh cilantro leaves and tender stems

1 Place the fennel, mustard, and cardamom seeds in a spice grinder (you can also use a coffee grinder) and grind them to the consistency of finely ground black pepper. Don't forget to get a good whiff as you open the lid. Be prepared to be blown away and say wow! Transfer the spice blend to a medium-size bowl.

2 Add the scallops, garlic, chiles, and salt to the bowl with the spice blend and stir to mix, making sure you coat the scallops

well with this highly aromatic combination. Refrigerate the scallops, covered, until you are ready to cook them. Keep in mind that since there is nothing acidic in this mix, you can easily marinate the mollusks overnight.

3 When you are ready to cook the scallops, heat the oil in a large skillet over medium-high heat. Once the oil appears to shimmer, add the scallops, rub and all, to the skillet, arranging them in a single layer. Sear the scallops until they are a light reddish brown, 2 to 3 minutes per side.

4 Pour the coconut milk into the skillet and reduce the heat to medium. The coconut milk will immediately start to bubble in the hot skillet. Scrape the bottom of the skillet to release all the browned bits, effectively deglazing the skillet to create a depth of flavor in the sauce. Cover the skillet and let the scallops simmer, without stirring, until they are firm to the touch but not rubbery, 2 to 3 minutes. Transfer the scallops to a serving platter. Let the sauce continue to simmer, uncovered, stirring occasionally, until thickened, about 2 minutes. Pour the pan sauce over the scallops.

5 Serve the scallops warm sprinkled with the cilantro.

## Extra Credit

• Scallops are the abductor muscle of the mollusk (the flesh that the bivalve uses to open and shut its shell), and range in color from ivory to orange to light pink. They usually come shucked and are sold either fresh or individually quick-frozen. They vary in size, with sea scallops being larger than bay scallops and not as sweet as the latter. "Bay," "sea," "calico," "king," and "queen" are some of the varieties sold in supermarkets. Bay scallops are delicious even raw, as you can savor their natural sweetness.

The scallop shells, in bright brown and pastel colors, resemble unfurled Japanese fans and are sold in some stores as decorative pieces. I was at the house of my friend and colleague Lynne Rossetto Kasper (host of *The Splendid Table* radio show, which airs on National Public Radio) recently when she served artisanal salt in these cute shells— I thought that was very clever.

Shrimp are a great alternative to scallops, and so are chunks of lobster, wild Alaskan salmon, and cod (sustainable when fished from the waters of the Pacific U.S.).

• You can chop the dried chiles on a cutting board but do watch out for all the seeds that have a tendency to fly around with each cut. Another way is to pound the chiles in a mortar with a pestle until they break down a bit but are still in relatively large pieces.

# Tamarind Shrimp

## Imli Jhinga

GLUTEN FREE

The flavors in this shrimp, a classic from the southeastern Chettinad community, showcase various kinds and degrees of heat from two of India's prized repertoire of spices: black peppercorns (indigenous to India and the reason for the world's spice trade) and dried red chiles (introduced to India by Spanish and Portuguese traders and settlers in the early sixteenth century). Even though the amount of spice heat may seem alarming at one glance, don't be put off since the nutty split peas in the blend and the sour tamarind in the thin sauce counterbalance it to amazingly mellow results. Yes, there is that lingering heat on your palate but nothing that will make you uncomfortable. Serve the shrimp with some steamed rice and a great vegetable like Spinach with Cranberries (page 262) for a feel-good meal.

**Serves 4**

2 tablespoons yellow split peas

I teaspoon black peppercorns

2 to 3 dried red cayenne chiles
   (like chile de árbol), stems discarded
   (do not remove the seeds)

I pound large shrimp (2I to 25), peeled and
   deveined but tails left on

I teaspoon coarse kosher or sea salt

I teaspoon tamarind paste or concentrate
   (see Extra Credit)

2 tablespoons canola oil

I teaspoon black or yellow mustard seeds

2 tablespoons finely chopped fresh cilantro
   leaves and tender stems

Heat a large skillet over medium heat. Once the skillet is hot (when you hold the palm of your hand close to the bottom of the skillet you will feel the heat), usually after 2 to 4 minutes, add the split peas, peppercorns, and chiles. Toast the spice blend, shaking the skillet every few seconds, until the chiles blacken in patches and smell smoky-hot, the peppercorns look slightly ashy but still black, the peas turn brown unevenly (that's okay), and the aromas emanating from the pan are nutty-hot, 3 to 5 minutes. Transfer the spice blend to a small heatproof bowl to cool, about 5 minutes. Keeping the spices in the skillet will burn them, making them unpalatable. Once cool, place the spice blend in a spice grinder (you can also use a coffee grinder) and grind to the consistency of finely ground black pepper. The color will be light yellow and the spice blend will have an aroma that is incredibly complex and layered, nothing like the mélange of whole toasted spices you smelled a few minutes ago. Transfer the ground spice blend to a medium-size bowl.

2 Add the shrimp and salt to the spice blend and give them a good stir to make sure the shellfish gets an even coating of spice and salt. Keep the shrimp refrigerated, covered, until you are ready to cook them. You can prepare the shrimp up to this point up to a day before you plan to cook and serve them.

3 When you are ready to cook the shrimp, whisk together the tamarind paste and 2 tablespoons of warm water in a small bowl to create a murky, chocolate-colored liquid chock-full of earthy tartness.

4 Heat the oil over medium-high heat in the same large skillet used to toast the spices. Once the oil appears to shimmer, add the mustard seeds, cover the pan, and cook until the seeds have stopped popping (not unlike popcorn), about 30 seconds. Immediately add the spiced shrimp to the mustard seed oil, making sure they are in a single layer. Sear the shrimp on the underside until they are a bit saffron-hued, about 1 minute. Turn the shrimp over and repeat on the second side.

5 Stir the tamarind water one more time to make sure the paste is evenly dispersed and pour this over the shrimp. Some of the liquid will release the bits of shrimp and spice stuck to the bottom of the skillet, effectively deglazing it. Reduce the heat to medium, cover the skillet, and let the shrimp steam in the juices, stirring occasionally, until they curl and turn salmon-orange in color, 3 to 5 minutes.

6 Serve the shrimp sprinkled with the cilantro.

# Extra Credit

- Tamarind paste (or concentrate) is available in plastic jars as a brand from Thailand or India in the Asian section of the supermarket. It is extracted from the pulp of the fruit of an evergreen tree that grows wild along India's tropical coastlines (the leaves of the tree are also tart). Highly acidic and rich in vitamin C and other essential minerals, when soaked and squeezed for its juices, this pucker-your-lips sour fruit exudes complex flavors to any recipe it touches.

  There really is no credible alternative to tamarind but the closest I have come to duplicating some of its nuances is with the condiment that possesses the tough to pronounce name—Worcestershire sauce. Manufactured by Lea & Perrins (named after a pair of English scientists), this fermented condiment incorporates tamarind in its ingredient portfolio in addition to anchovies. For I teaspoon of tamarind paste dissolved in 2 tablespoons of water use 2 tablespoons of Worcestershire sauce as a substitute. Keep in mind that this commercial sauce contains malt vinegar and its inclusion will not appeal to the gluten-free guests at your table.

- If possible, please purchase either wild-caught or shrimp farmed within U.S. waters. Farm-raised or wild-caught shrimp from some of the international waters come from unsustainable fishing methods and have high levels of mercury, thus placing them on the avoid list of Monterey Bay Aquarium's highly regarded Seafood Watch program (montereybayaquarium .org/cr/seafoodwatch .aspx). As its ambassador I feel it essential to share the value that the program brings to the way we look at sustainability in today's overfished world.

Chapter 7

# Vegetarian Mains Unfolded

**TO SAY THAT** Indians are masters at vegetarianism may seem like a bold statement but I stand by it without an iota of doubt. For over 3,500 years, vegetarianism has been synonymous with Indian food. There are various reasons why an Indian follows a partial or a complete vegetarian diet—religious beliefs, dietary restrictions, and economic constraints being some of the more important ones. Hinduism, an important religion in India, dictates the abstinence from meats, fish, and poultry in one's diet. Heavy reliance is placed on beans and legumes, fresh fruits, vegetables, and dairy products like milk and yogurt. A multitude of fresh herbs and spices provide Indian cuisine with a vast array of pleasurable flavors. So what better cuisine than Indian to make the life of a vegetarian a smooth sail?

Veganism is not a practiced choice in contemporary India. For centuries dairy and dairy products have been celebrated as offerings from revered cows, and were never considered something that put the animal in harm's way. They were, in fact, manna that flowed into culinary and religious rituals in Hinduism. If Krishna, the cowherd and a reincarnation of Vishnu, had a penchant for cream, why not the common devotee?

Indian foods, especially the vegetarian offerings, are easy to "veganize," with flavorful, assertive, and vibrant results. India is after all the land of spices! What makes a cuisine like this particularly exciting for vegans is the plethora of legumes that can paint a cornucopia of textures, colors, and flavors to deliver memorable fare. Even though ghee is an intrinsic part of the cuisine, oils like mustard, unrefined sesame, and coconut can step in as replacements. To infuse creaminess in curries, think about nut purees instead of heavy cream, buttermilk, or yogurt. And extra-firm tofu can take the place of paneer, a cheese from northern India.

# The Lesson Plan

**Lesson ① Smoky Yellow Split Peas** To us Indians, the world of legumes is very important (there are over sixty varieties of lentils, peas, and beans in India), and I encourage you to start with this recipe for Smoky Yellow Split Peas. You'll see how spices that have been toasted and ground intensify in flavor, proving that succulence can be achieved without butter or oil. When cooked, the natural breakdown of the split peas and potatoes provides a creamy mouthfeel.

**Lesson ② Spicy Indian Omelets** Next time you whip eggs into a fluffy omelet, breathe a little Indian into it. One spice, cumin seeds, sizzles in hot ghee (clarified butter) to perfume it nutty-sweet. Just make sure you don't burn the seeds—it only takes a few seconds in a pan to get them perfect.

**Lesson ③ Cardamom-Scented Cheese with Peppers** Stir-frying done properly gives the onion and bell pepper a wonderful smoky sear, but what will be etched in your flavor memory is the intoxicating intensity of the freshly ground four C's (coriander, cumin, cardamom, and cayenne).

**Lesson ④ Panfried Cheese with Creamy Spinach** The simple-to-make Raghavan's Blend flavors the spinach curry and here I show you how to quickly cook the ground spices in the stir-fried onion medley without burning them to create a smooth and sophisticated variation of this favorite.

**Lesson ⑤ Sassy Chickpea Curry** Curry making does not have to be complicated as is proven by this chickpea version. Here you bruise whole spices, along with onion, ginger, and garlic (the three aunties of north Indian Punjabi curries), in a food processor to execute a simple evening meal (with rice or bread, of course).

**Lesson ⑥ Red Lentil Dal** Next, step up to the comforting world of India's dal curries. Red Lentil Dal, redolent of mustard (used in two ways), cumin, and turmeric, makes an easy main course ladled over rice with perhaps a stir-fried vegetable as a side.

**Lesson ⑦ Mustard Cannellini Beans** An unusual technique of stir-frying onion and bell pepper (as opposed to garlic), "soffrito"-style, creates the base for this curry along with fresh-ground cumin, mustard, and cayenne.

**Lesson ⑧ Black-Eyed Peas with Collard Greens** This recipe is my version of Indian fast food because it cooks up very quickly if you've got garam masala already prepared in your pantry and if you use precooked black-eyed peas (in either can or frozen form—okay with me!).

**Lesson ⑨ Truck Stop Beans** Finish off the parade of legumes with these beans, most popularly known simply as *Rajmah*. Traditional to the peasant community of northwestern India, I teach you to, instead, marry my spice blend from the south with the northern combo of ginger and garlic to create a heart-healthy classic.

**Lesson ⑩ The Mumbai Hoagie** The last section of this chapter teaches you to take the classic flavors from regional India and bring them into your contemporary Western kitchen. We all love sandwiches and this one crams in a simple, custom-made spice blend and chutney with a burst of vegetables and cheese.

**Lesson ⑪ Naan Pizzas with Roasted Vegetables** Who can resist pizzas made with naan, northern India's quintessential yeast-free bread? A weekday meal that will appeal to one and all, the inclusion of chiles, potatoes, and spinach spread a distinct pleasing Indian flavor.

**Lesson ⑫ Mac and Cheese Outsourced** A good way to introduce your kids to great Indian flavors is to perk up mundane mac and cheese with the ground spices beloved there.

**Lesson ⑬ Root Vegetable Pot Pie** This vegetable pie will earn you a doctorate, as you work with puff pastry, seasonal vegetables, and my spice blend to create a "pot pie" that will make you beam with unabashed pride.

smooth, reddish brown paste with a smoky aroma that is sure to knock your socks off.

5 Once the peas are cooked, add the tomato and spice paste to the pan. I usually pour some of the liquid from the peas into the blender and process it for a brief second to make sure I get every last bit of the tomato paste, and then pour it back into the pan. Stir in the cilantro and salt.

6 Increase the heat to medium-high and let the dal boil vigorously, uncovered, stirring occasionally, until the flavors mingle and the sauce thickens slightly, 12 to 15 minutes. If you would like the sauce to be thicker, mash some of the peas and potatoes with the back of your spoon. Serve the dal warm.

1 Once you've cubed the potatoes, rinse the peas in water, draining them after each rinse, until the water remains pretty clear.

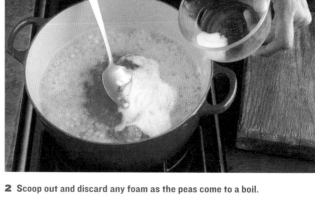

2 Scoop out and discard any foam as the peas come to a boil.

3 Add the potatoes and the turmeric to the peas.

4 Cook the potatoes and peas, stirring occasionally, until the potatoes and peas are tender.

# Smoky Yellow Split Peas

## Tamatar Chana Dal

Dals are a cornerstone of India's meals since they are an inexpensive way of infusing proteins, fiber, and bodybuilding nutrients into one's diet, vegetarian or otherwise. Common to find, yellow split peas are easy to cook and do not require any presoaking. The spicing techniques in this recipe hail from the southeastern region of India where roasting spices to yield nutty-hot flavors is key to creating a layered experience. I have simplified the number of spices used but have kept the authenticity in terms of assertiveness and balance. Oh, and best of all, no added fat! For the foldout meal I have chosen a rice pilaf to accompany the dal, but for an everyday meal, be sure to have some steamed white rice (page 27) to absorb all that saucy goodness.

**Makes 6 cups; serves 6**

I pound potatoes, russet or Yukon Gold

I cup yellow split peas

¼ teaspoon ground turmeric

2 to 4 dried red cayenne chiles (like chile de árbol), stems discarded

I tablespoon coriander seeds

I teaspoon cumin seeds

I medium-size tomato, cored and diced

2 tablespoons finely chopped fresh cilantro leaves and tender stems

1½ teaspoons coarse kosher or sea salt

1 Peel the potatoes and cut them into ½-inch cubes. Transfer the cubed potatoes to a bowl large enough to hold them. Add enough cold water to cover the potatoes to prevent them from oxidizing and turning black.

2 Place the split peas in a medium-size saucepan. Add water to cover and rinse the peas, rubbing them between your fingertips (I just use the fingers of one hand to do this). The water will become cloudy and may have some debris like the odd skin from the peas (even though they are skinless) or dust from the packaging. Drain this water. Repeat 3 to 4 times

until the water, upon rinsing the peas, remains clearer. Add 4 cups water to the pan with the peas and let it come to a boil over medium-high heat. You will see some foam rise to the surface; scoop it out and discard it.

3 Drain the potatoes and add them with the turmeric to the peas, stirring once or twice. Reduce the heat to medium-low and cover the pan. Cook the mélange, stirring occasionally, until the peas are tender but still firm looking and the potatoes are cooked, 20 to 25 minutes.

4 Meanwhile, heat a small skillet over medium-high heat. Once the skillet feels hot (when you hold the palm of your hand close to the bottom of the skillet you will feel the heat), usually after 2 to 4 minutes, add the chiles, coriander, and cumin. Toast the spices, shaking the skillet every few seconds, until the chiles blacken and smell smoky hot and the seeds turn reddish brown and smell incredibly aromatic (nutty with citrus undertones), 1 to 2 minutes. Immediately transfer the spice blend to a blender and plunk in the tomato. Puree, scraping the insides of the blender as needed, to make a

**5** Toast the chiles and coriander and cumin seeds.

**6** Add the pureed tomatoes and the toasted spice blend to the cooked peas and potatoes.

**7** Continue to cook the dal vigorously to allow the flavors to mingle and to thicken the sauce.

**8** For a thicker sauce, mash some of the potatoes and peas with the back of your spoon.

# Extra Credit

- Dals are great spooned over a bed of steamed rice, but try them by dunking in wedges of flatbread. Dals also make a great appetizer served warm with a crusty baguette or another yeast bread, warmed, sliced, and served alongside.

- The yellow split peas that are available here in every supermarket are different from the ones in India—I find those grown here to be nuttier and very cornlike in texture. The ones in India are from a variety of garbanzo beans that have a dark brown to almost blackish skin. When the skin is removed and the grain split in half, you get the variety of yellow split peas called *chana dal*. Green split peas (what are generally used for split pea soup) are a perfect stand-in for the yellow variety.

- Puree any leftover dal in a blender or a food processor to yield an almost pâtélike spread. Try and drain off a bit of the excess liquid before you do that. The result reminds me of a Greek *skordalia* (potato puree with garlic) but with more texture.

# ② Spicy Indian Omelets

Pora

These fluffy omelets are common in many home kitchens across India, especially in the Parsi community (of Persian-Iranian decent) from Mumbai where they're called *pora*. When scrambled, the eggs become the signature breakfast fare called *akuri*. I love the simplicity of this universal pocket of rich tastes studded with vegetables, and the hint of heat is just right in awakening early morning taste buds. No wonder these are also popular stuffed into grab-and-go white-bread sandwiches on the streets. No golden arches above those vendors' carts where people are served inexpensively, with expediency, and with assertive flavors.

**Makes 4 omelets**

12 large eggs

¼ cup heavy (whipping) cream

1 teaspoon coarse kosher or sea salt

¼ cup ghee, homemade (page 31) or store-bought, or butter

2 teaspoons cumin seeds

½ cup finely chopped red onion

4 fresh green serrano chiles, stems discarded, finely chopped (do not remove the seeds)

1 medium-size tomato, cored and finely chopped (no need to remove the seeds)

¼ cup finely chopped fresh cilantro leaves and tender stems

1 Crack the eggs into a blender. Pour in the cream and add the salt. Blend the eggs until they are slightly frothy, 1 to 2 minutes.

2 To make one omelet, heat 1 tablespoon of the ghee in a medium-size nonstick skillet over medium heat. Once the ghee appears to shimmer, sprinkle in ½ teaspoon of the cumin seeds, which will almost instantly sizzle, smell nutty, and turn reddish-brown, 5 to 10 seconds. Add 2 tablespoons of the chopped onion and a quarter

of the chopped chiles and stir-fry until the onion is light brown around the edges, 1 to 2 minutes. Stir in a quarter of the chopped tomato.

3 Pour a quarter of the egg mixture into the skillet with the tomato medley and swirl it around a bit to make sure it coats the pan evenly. Now tilt the skillet and lift the edges a bit as the omelet starts to set so the liquid on top starts to pool under the lifted edges, making the top start to look opaque. Continue doing this until all of the omelet is cooked to your liking. This should take 3 to 5 minutes. Sprinkle a tablespoon of the cilantro over the top. Fold the omelet in half and serve right away.

4 Repeat with the remaining ingredients to make 3 more omelets.

## Extra Credit

- Any filling that suits your fancy for your usual omelet fix is perfectly fine in this recipe. The mishmash I have given you is typically Indian. If you have vegetables left over from a previous meal, this omelet is a creative way to use them up.

- The frothy beating of the eggs is key to a fluffy, pillow-soft omelet. The hint of heavy cream in it certainly helps with the succulence factor.

**3** # Cardamom-Scented Cheese with Peppers

## Mirchi Paneer

A simple stir-fry can yield incredible flavors with the right pan and an appropriate heat level. The process of searing vegetables over high heat delivers a smoky punch and a handful of accessible spices pushes the combination over the top. Reminiscent of a sizzling platter of fajitas, the fresh ground spices in this dish deliver that wow factor with each bite.

**Serves 4**

½ pound store-bought or homemade paneer (whole milk cheese; page 35) or drained extra-firm tofu

1 medium-size green bell pepper

1 small to medium-size red onion

2 teaspoons coriander seeds

1 teaspoon cumin seeds

½ teaspoon cardamom seeds (removed from the green or white cardamom pods; see Extra Credit, page 43)

1½ teaspoons coarse kosher or sea salt

½ teaspoon ground red pepper (cayenne)

3 tablespoons canola oil

1 Slice the paneer or tofu crosswise into ¼-inch-thick slabs. Stack 2 or 3 slabs together and cut them into thin strips about ½ inch wide. You should end up with strips that measure about 2 inches long, ½ inch wide, and ¼ inch thick. Transfer them to a plate.

2 Discard the stem from the bell pepper. Slice the pepper in half lengthwise and remove the seeds and ribs (those are the white, slightly spongy pieces that look like flimsy half-open partitions). Cut each half lengthwise into thin strips about ½ inch wide. Add the bell pepper slices to the plate with the paneer.

3 Slice the onion in half lengthwise. Cut each half into thin slices, also lengthwise. Add the onion to the pile of bell pepper and cheese.

4 Place the coriander, cumin, and cardamom seeds in a spice grinder (you can also use a coffee grinder) and grind the blend to the consistency of finely ground black pepper. Stir in the salt and cayenne. Set the spice blend aside.

5 Heat the oil in a large skillet over high heat. Once the oil appears to shimmer, add the medley of paneer, bell pepper, and onion. Stir-fry to sear them all; you will hear them sizzle with a slightly smoky aroma. Cook until the onion slices turn light purple-brown, the bell peppers look blistered, and the paneer turns an uneven reddish-brown, 6 to 8 minutes.

6 Turn off the heat, sprinkle in the spice blend, and stir once or twice. The heat in the pan is just right for cooking the ground spices without burning them. Trust me, the aromas will drive you pleasantly insane. Serve the paneer mixture warm.

## Extra Credit

A dish like this begs to be turned into a fajita party. Start with a stack of warmed-up whole wheat tortillas or store-bought flatbreads called *rotis*. Or, if you are so inclined, make a batch of All-Wheat Griddle Breads (page 84). Cut a lime into wedges and finely chop a handful of fresh cilantro leaves and tender stems. Either open a jar of store-bought salsa or pull out your favorite homemade version of one from the refrigerator. Dish up a bowl of my Avocado Pomegranate Dip (page 49) or slice up some just-ripe avocado. Sour cream or my favorite, crème fraîche, should be the dollop of satiny goodness on top.

There you have it. A warm tortilla or roti as the base followed by the paneer and bell pepper strips, a scoop of avocado, salsa, a sprinkle of cilantro, a dollop of sour cream, and a squeeze of fresh lime. Gather everything into a convenient pouchlike fold. You won't stop at one, I promise.

# Panfried Cheese with Creamy Spinach

Saag Paneer

LACTO-VEGETARIAN
GLUTEN-FREE

A steadfast favorite on every north Indian menu in restaurants across North America, *saag paneer* is a cinch to replicate, with far better flavors, in your home kitchen. I prefer my spinach to be left whole (and not pureed as they do in those eating establishments) since I like some texture in the sauce. This rendition of mine is smooth, creamy, replete with juicy paneer and iron-rich goodness from the spinach. What's not to love?

**Makes 6 cups; serves 4 as a main dish or 6 as a side dish**

¼ cup canola oil

1 pound store-bought or homemade paneer (whole milk cheese; page 35) or drained extra-firm tofu, cut into 1-inch cubes (see Extra Credit)

1 medium-size onion, coarsely chopped

3 fresh green serrano chiles, stems discarded, coarsely chopped (do not remove the seeds)

1 tablespoon Raghavan's Blend (page 39) or store-bought Madras curry powder

1 teaspoon coarse kosher or sea salt

1 cup tomato sauce

1 pound prewashed baby spinach leaves

1 cup half-and-half

Heat the oil in a large nonstick skillet or a well-seasoned cast-iron pan over medium heat. Add the paneer cubes in a single layer and cook them until reddish brown (when they turn this color they signify they are ready to be turned over by "spitting" a bit of moisture) on all sides, 5 to 8 minutes. Using a slotted spoon, transfer the cooked paneer from the skillet to a plate, leaving the oil in the skillet.

2 While the paneer browns, place the onion and chiles in a food processor and, using the pulsing action, mince them. Letting the processor run constantly will create unwanted excess moisture and make the blend pulpy.

3 Once you have removed the browned paneer from the skillet, scrape the minced onion and chiles into the hot oil. Stir-fry over medium heat until the onion is light brown around the edges and the chiles smell sharp (if you cough once or twice it is a good sign), 5 to 7 minutes.

4 Sprinkle in the spice blend and the salt, stirring them and letting them roast, 15 to 30 seconds. Ground spices do not take much time to roast so you do want to make sure that your next ingredient is ready to go. Pour in the tomato sauce, which will boil instantly. Reduce the heat to medium-low and simmer, uncovered, stirring occasionally, until some of the liquid in the sauce evaporates and you start to see slightly sheenlike drops of oil around the sauce, 8 to 10 minutes.

5 Increase the heat to medium-high and take a handful of the spinach leaves, piling them into the skillet. Cook, stirring,

## Extra Credit

- Students often ask me how to slice up paneer or tofu into a specific cube size, in this case 1-inch cubes. Cut it first into 1-inch-thick slabs. Cut each slab into 1-inch-wide strips and then cut each strip crosswise into 1-inch pieces to yield 1-inch cubes.

- For the vegan at your table, tofu of course is the way to go, but to create the creamy texture and mouthfeel of half-and-half, puree ½ cup of raw cashews with ½ cup of water in a blender until smooth. Drizzle in just enough additional water to bring the paste to measure 1 cup. Push the blender button once or twice to mix in the added water and create a creamy liquid that will take the place of the half-and-half in the recipe.

- If you use tofu, drain it, place it between paper towels, and press down hard with your hand to get rid of the excess moisture. It will make for a relatively splatter-free panfrying.

until the spinach wilts. Repeat with the remaining spinach until all of it has wilted, which should take 5 to 7 minutes.

6 Pour in the half-and-half and add the paneer. Stir everything well and continue to simmer, uncovered, stirring occasionally, until the creamy sauce thickens slightly, 3 to 5 minutes. Serve warm.

#  Sassy Chickpea Curry

## Chana Masala

VEGAN
GLUTEN FREE

A staple in north Indian restaurant menus across the world, this chickpea classic, called *chana masala,* raises the humble chickpeas, also referred to as garbanzo beans, to a level that commands a respectable devotion on account of the vibrancy in every morsel. Hearty, comforting, and redolent of just two fresh-bruised whole spices, the combination works with some store-bought flatbread or homemade All-Wheat Griddle Breads (page 84) or plain steamed white rice (page 27).

**Makes 4 cups; serves 4**

I small onion, coarsely chopped

4 pieces fresh ginger (each about the size and thickness of a 25-cent coin; no need to peel the skin)

2 large cloves garlic

2 fresh green serrano chiles, stems discarded, coarsely chopped (do not remove the seeds)

I tablespoon coriander seeds

2 teaspoons cumin seeds

2 tablespoons canola oil

I cup canned diced tomatoes with their juices

I¹/₂ teaspoons coarse kosher or sea salt

2 cans (about I5 ounces each) chickpeas, rinsed and drained

1 Place the onion, ginger, garlic, chiles, coriander, and cumin in a food processor. Using the pulsing action, mince these ingredients to create a pungent and aromatic blend. The spices will look bruised but still be fairly whole. Letting the processor run constantly instead of using quick pulses will create an undesired watery and coarse puree.

2 Heat the oil in a medium-size saucepan over medium heat. Once the oil appears to shimmer, scrape the processor bowl's contents into the pan and stir-fry until bits

of onion, spice, and some of the overall good schmutz browns and sticks to the bottom of the pan, about 15 minutes.

3 Stir in the tomatoes with their juices and the salt, scraping the bottom of the pan to release the bits of onion and spices, effectively deglazing the pan and releasing those flavors back into the sauce.

4 Pour in 1 cup of water and add the chickpeas, giving the curry a few stirs. Once the sauce comes to a rolling boil reduce the heat to medium-low. Cover the pan and let the chickpeas simmer, stirring occasionally, until the curry sauce slightly thickens, about 15 minutes. Serve the curry warm.

## Extra Credit

- Here's why I prefer using pans that have a heavy bottom without a nonstick surface. With a nonstick pan things don't stick to the bottom. The technique of adding liquid to a pan after things brown and stick to a pan, referred to as deglazing, adds a depth of flavor (called *fond* in French), that je ne sais quoi we all hanker for in each mouthful.

- This is by no means a scientifically proven statement, but there is something to say about the benefits of being short (I am average, thank you very much). When you stir-fry a medley that harbors chiles, the pungent aromas that waft from the pan tend to reach for higher points. If you happen to be tall, chances are your coughing and sneezing bout might be more intense than the cute little dog that hovers close to the ground looking for anything that resembles food (I have seen our little Ms. Emma sneeze but never cough). So, do all the tall humans a favor and turn on that exhaust fan while cooking with chiles.

- *Chana masala* in India is often served with thinly sliced raw red onion, slivers of punchy chiles, and wedges of juicy lime. Feel free to do the same. The contrast of the warm cooked food and crunchy raw vegetables is a hallmark of north Indian cuisine.

- Turn any remaining curry into a delicious appetizer dip. Fold in some of your favorite shredded cheese(s) and a tablespoon or 2 of thinly sliced scallion. Heat the mixture in a microwave on high power until the cheese melts and the dip warms through, 2 to 3 minutes. Serve the dip with a basket of your favorite chips (in my case it is always kettle-cooked potato chips).

# Red Lentil Dal

## Adraki Masoor Dal

VEGAN
GLUTEN FREE

These lentils are a favorite among the northern communities in India. The lentils' creamy texture offers a great backdrop for some heavy-duty chiles and mustard (the mustard is used in two ways, one yielding sweet nutty flavors, the other exacerbating its pungency). Red lentils are great ladled over steamed white rice (page 27). If serving brown rice, I recommend you add more spice to the dal or the texture of the brown rice will blunt the stout taste of the seasoned lentils. You can also turn the dal into a soup course. Brush thin slices of baguette with butter and toast them. Serve the toast on top of each cup of soup and watch the accolades come flowing toward you.

**Makes 4 brimming cups; serves 4**

**I cup red lentils (also called Egyptian lentils, see Extra Credit)**

**2 teaspoons black or yellow mustard seeds (see Extra Credit)**

**2 tablespoons canola oil**

**2 tablespoons finely chopped fresh ginger**

**2 fresh green serrano chiles, stems discarded, thinly sliced crosswise (do not remove the seeds)**

**2 teaspoons ground cumin**

**I teaspoon coarse kosher or sea salt**

**½ teaspoon ground turmeric**

**I can (14.5 ounces) diced tomatoes with their juices**

**2 tablespoons finely chopped fresh cilantro leaves and tender stems**

Place the lentils in a medium-size saucepan. Add water to cover and rinse the lentils, rubbing them between your fingertips (I just use the fingers of one hand to do this). The water will become cloudy and may have some debris like the odd skin from the lentils (even though they are skinless) or dust from the packaging. Drain this water. Repeat 3 to 4 times until the water, upon rinsing the lentils, remains clearer.

## Extra Credit

- Red lentils are one of the quickest cooking lentils I have ever worked with. They need no prior soaking and turn into mush (in a good way) within 15 minutes. When elliptical brown lentils are skinned and split, the result is these salmon-colored lentils. If you don't find red lentils in your store, use the brown ones (sometimes labeled as French lentils) instead. They will require a longer cooking time and you may need to add a bit more water.

- My students often ask me why I don't cook the seasonings first in a saucepan and then add the lentils and water to that pan and proceed to cook them. Oftentimes the amount of water it takes to cook the lentils dilutes the spicing and the resulting flavors. So it is better to wait until much of that water is absorbed, yielding a heartier base for the potent spices.

- If you don't have or can't find mustard seeds, use 1½ teaspoons of preground mustard instead.

that's just the nature of this particular variety of legume.

3 Meanwhile, place 1 teaspoon of the mustard seeds in a spice grinder (you can also use a coffee grinder) and grind them to the consistency of finely ground black pepper. Heat the oil in a small skillet over medium-high heat. Once the oil shimmers, add the remaining teaspoon of mustard seeds, cover the skillet, and wait until the seeds have stopped popping (not unlike popcorn), about 30 seconds. Add the ginger and chiles and cook, stirring, until they are browned and smell pungent, about 1 minute. Stir in the ground mustard seeds, cumin, salt, and turmeric, which will instantly sizzle and cook. Very quickly add the tomatoes with their juices, which will stop the ground spices from burning. Let the tomato mixture simmer, uncovered, stirring occasionally, until the tomatoes soften and the flavors mingle, 5 minutes.

2 Add 3 cups of water to the pan with the lentils and let it come to a boil over medium-high heat. You will see some foam rise to the surface; scoop it out and discard it. Reduce the heat to medium and let the lentils simmer, uncovered, stirring occasionally, until they are very tender and almost mushy, about 15 minutes. You will see the lentils change from a salmon color to a pale yellow once they begin to cook;

4 Once the lentils are cooked, don't drain them. Just add the robust and chunky tomato sauce to the pan with the lentils and give them a good stir. Let the spiced dal simmer over medium heat, uncovered, stirring occasionally, until the flavors meld, about 5 minutes. Serve sprinkled with the cilantro.

# Mustard Cannellini Beans

Simla Mirch Saféd Rajmah

Oftentimes we reach for that ubiquitous combination of onion and garlic as the building block for a sauce. Here bell peppers step up to the plate and offer an unusual base with sweet results. Uncluttered with spices yet complex tasting, this cannellini bean curry can be the only ticket for the evening meal alongside a plate of steamed white rice or a small stack of flatbreads, either homemade (page 84) or store-brought (whole wheat tortillas work just as well). I devoured the curry with a few slices of hearty, crusty sourdough baguette and an unhealthy amount of house-churned butter speckled with sea salt. What can I say? Wish you were here.

**Makes 4 cups; serves 4**

2 tablespoons canola oil

I large onion, finely chopped

I large green bell pepper, stem, ribs, and seeds discarded, flesh finely chopped

2 teaspoons cumin seeds

2 teaspoons black or yellow mustard seeds

I teaspoon ground red pepper (cayenne)

I½ teaspoons coarse kosher or sea salt

I cup tomato sauce

2 cans (19 ounces each) cannellini beans, rinsed and drained

1 Heat the oil in a large skillet over medium-high heat. Once the oil appears to shimmer, add the onion and bell pepper and stir-fry until the onion is light brown around the edges and the pieces of pepper appear slightly soft and shriveled, 5 to 7 minutes.

2 As the vegetables cook, quickly place the cumin and mustard seeds in a spice grinder (you can also use a coffee grinder) and grind the blend to the consistency of finely ground black pepper. Stir in the cayenne and salt to concoct your very own masala (spice blend).

209

will be just right to cook the spices without burning them, 5 to 10 seconds. Add the tomato sauce, 1 cup of warm water, and the cannellini beans and stir a few times to incorporate. Let the curry come to a boil. Then reduce the heat to medium and simmer the curry, uncovered, stirring occasionally, until the sauce thickens slightly and the flavors get a chance to mingle, 10 to 15 minutes.

3 Once the onion and bell pepper are ready, stir in the spice blend; the heat

4 Serve the beans warm.

## 8 Black-Eyed Peas with Collard Greens

### Lobhia Aur Saag

VEGAN IF YOU USE CANOLA OIL
GLUTEN FREE

It may seem that this is a heart-healthy version of the southern American classic so typical of soul food. It could be, but it is also a classic peasant dish among the farmers of northwestern India, often accompanying stacks of griddle-cooked corn bread and fresh fried hot chiles for an extra zing. Whenever I am there visiting family and friends, I make sure I include these in one of my five-meals-a-day plan. Yes, to answer your unspoken question, I do return with a few extra pounds tucked under my layered shirt.

**Makes 4 brimming cups; serves 4**

1 bunch (12 to 16 ounces) collard greens

2 tablespoons ghee, homemade (page 31) or
  store-bought, butter, or canola oil

2 tablespoons finely chopped fresh ginger

4 large cloves garlic, finely chopped

2 teaspoons garam masala, homemade
  (page 41) or store-bought

1 teaspoon coarse kosher or sea salt

½ teaspoon ground red pepper (cayenne)

3 cups cooked black-eyed peas
  (see Extra Credit)

1 can (14.5 ounces) diced tomatoes with
  their juices

1 Fill a medium-size bowl with cold water. Take a collard leaf and cut along both sides of the tough rib to remove and discard it. Slice the leaf in half lengthwise. Repeat with the remaining leaves. Stack the leaf halves, about 6 at a time, one on top of the other, and roll them into a tight log. Thinly slice the log crosswise; you will end up with long, slender shreds. Dunk the collard shreds in the bowl of water to rinse off any grit, then scoop the leaves out and drain them in a colander. Repeat once or twice if the collard greens don't appear clean.

2 Heat the ghee in a medium-size saucepan over medium-high heat. Once the ghee appears to shimmer, add the ginger and garlic and stir-fry until fragrant and light brown, 1 to 2 minutes. Sprinkle in the garam masala, salt, and cayenne, and stir once or twice; the heat from the pan will be just right to cook the spices immediately.

3 Take handfuls of the collard greens and stir them into the pan. Once they wilt, add a second handful, repeating until all of the greens are wilted. Stir in the black-eyed peas and tomatoes. Reduce the heat to medium and let the stew simmer, covered, stirring occasionally, until the flavors meld and soak into the black-eyed peas, 20 to 25 minutes. Serve the black-eyed peas and collard greens warm.

# Extra Credit

- Cabbagelike in flavor, collards' tough leaves and versatility appeal to my style of cooking. Part of the Brassica family, these leaves are available year round, although they are primarily associated with the cuisine of the southern United States. In India collards are common in the northern regions and thrive well in colder climates. Thinly sliced cabbage, kale, mustard greens, winter spinach, and turnip greens are some great alternatives for collards in this dish.

- Black-eyed peas, also known as cowpeas, are easy to find in the grocery store in the aisle with the canned beans. Drain them in a colander and rinse well before use. I am not a big fan of all the brine but the convenience of a product like this makes the weekday evening meal a whole lot quicker. Two cans (15 ounces each) will yield 3 cups of peas.

  Frozen black-eyed peas are also available (cook them according to the package directions before using them in the recipe). Or you can use dried black-eyed peas. To cook these, rinse and pick them over well first. Since these peas are quick cooking, they do not require any presoaking. Place I cup of rinsed peas in a small saucepan and add enough water to cover them. Bring the water to a boil and simmer the peas over medium-low heat, covered, stirring occasionally, until they are tender, 40 to 45 minutes. Drain the peas and use as directed in the recipe. A cup of dried peas will yield 3 cups cooked.

- Even though leftovers are delicious rewarmed on their own, I also turn them into a hearty filling for quesadillas. Spread the peas and greens on a tortilla, trying not to include any excess liquid, and liberally sprinkle them with cheese. Top with a second tortilla and griddle cook the quesadilla until it is brown and crispy on both sides. Cut the quesadilla into slices and dunk them in some hot salsa—triple extra hot if you eat like me! The peas and collards are also great as a topping for a green salad, giving it that nutritious boost we all need at times.

# Truck Stop Beans

## Tamatar Rajmah

Truck stops in India are generally run-down edifices that beckon lorry drivers with hungry bellies to descend from their festooned trucks with the promise of camaraderie from fellow deliverymen. At these weather-beaten truck stops you won't find an attached gas station or any gum-chewing, beehive-haired waitresses asking, in that raspy, tobacco-abused voice, whether you want black coffee. What you will find instead is mayhem next to serene fields of mustard. Amid a clutter of makeshift tables and plastic chairs, the drivers find savory comfort in a cacophony of aromas, mouthwatering platters of garlicky beans, mounds of white rice, a pile of tandoor-cooked naan, brimming clay-pot bowls of pureed mustard greens dotted with white butter, and tall tumblers of frothy buttermilk laced with salt, black pepper, and toasted cumin. These particular beans, kidney shaped and dark red, mottled with ginger, garlic, and bell pepper, are boisterous and appeal to the swarthy, mustachioed, turbaned truck drivers as they wrap morsels of flatbreads around them and chase them down with a bite of vinegar-pickled red onion and fresh chile.

**Makes 4 cups; serves 4**

I medium-size green bell pepper, stem, core, ribs, and seeds discarded, flesh coarsely chopped

3 large cloves garlic

3 pieces fresh ginger (each about the size and thickness of a 25-cent coin; no need to peel the skin)

2 fresh green serrano chiles, stems discarded

2 tablespoons canola oil

I tablespoon Raghavan's Blend (page 39) or store-bought Madras curry powder

2 cans (about 16 ounces each) dark red kidney beans, drained and rinsed

I cup canned stewed tomatoes with their juices

I teaspoon coarse kosher or sea salt

## Extra Credit

- As they do in the roadside diners in northwest India, toss this curry with steamed white rice, a drizzle of ghee, and finely chopped fresh cilantro leaves and tender stems. Adding a bowlful of plain yogurt and a stack of *papads* (poppadums, page 48) and fiery pickles makes it extraspecial and brings you home to India.

- Any cooked beans will work as alternatives to the red kidney beans in this curry but will impart their own distinct taste and texture to the mix.

- Have some bean curry left over? Think the hearty classic American chili. I warm the beans up with a generous handful of shredded cheeses and serve them with tortilla chips as a snack. Ladle some over Corn Bread with Mustard Greens (page 100) for a savory breakfast wake-up call to your sleeping taste buds.

1 Place the bell pepper, garlic, ginger, and chiles in a food processor. Using the pulsing action, mince the vegetables. Letting the processor run constantly instead of using quick pulses will create a watery, pulpy mess not suitable for browning in oil.

2 Heat the oil in a medium-size saucepan over medium-high heat. Once the oil appears to shimmer, add the minced pepper medley to the hot oil and stir-fry until brown around the edges, about 5 minutes. Make sure you use the exhaust hood to address the pungent aromas that are sure to emanate from the pan.

3 Stir in the spice blend. The heat from the pan will be just right to cook the spices without burning them in 10 to 15 seconds. Add the kidney beans, tomatoes with their juices, and salt. Pour in 1 cup of water and stir the bean curry, scraping the bottom of the pan to incorporate the browned bits of spices and pepper into the curry. Let the curry come to a boil. Reduce the heat to medium-low and simmer, covered, stirring occasionally, until the flavors come together and the sauce thickens, about 15 minutes.

4 Serve the bean curry warm.

# 10 The Mumbai Hoagie

Just about every street corner in Mumbai houses vendors with makeshift stalls, set up and broken down at a moment's notice, serving these addictive, grab-and-go sandwiches that have a lot of attitude, much like the passersby who can't get enough. No whole grain breads or sourdough hoagies here, just soft white bread perked up with a spread of chiles and cilantro and crammed with slices of spicy boiled potatoes, crisp-pungent onion, succulent tomatoes, and creamy cheese. And no, you can't just have one.

LACTO-VEGETARIAN
(VEGAN IF YOU LEAVE
THE CHEESE OUT)

**Makes 6 sandwiches**

I medium-size to large russet or Yukon Gold
   potato

I teaspoon cumin seeds

I teaspoon coarse kosher or sea salt

½ teaspoon ground red pepper (cayenne)

½ cup firmly packed fresh cilantro leaves and
   tender stems

2 fresh green serrano chiles, stems discarded

12 slices any kind of sandwich bread

I small red onion, cut into ¼-inch-thick slices
   (like you would for hamburgers)

I medium-size tomato, cut into ¼-inch-thick
   slices

6 slices cheddar, muenster or Jack cheese
   (about ¼ inch thick)

1 Peel the potato and slice it lengthwise into ¼-inch-thick slices. Put the potato slices in a small saucepan and add enough water to cover them. Bring the water to a boil over medium-high heat, uncovered, stirring the potato slices a bit to make sure they don't stick to each other. Let the water boil briskly, uncovered, until the slices are fork-tender, 2 to 4 minutes. Drain them and run cold water over them to stop them from continuing to cook.

2 While the potato slices cook, heat a small skillet over medium-high heat. Once the skillet is hot (when you hold the palm of your hand close to the bottom of the skillet you will feel the heat), usually after 2 to 4 minutes, add the cumin seeds

## Extra Credit

- Any sandwich toppings are fair game here. I gave you the ones traditional to the streets of Mumbai. Slices of cool, crisp cucumber are also popular, as are daikon radish and red beets.

- Grilling the sandwiches is always an option (I do love those during the cooler months with a mug of Ginger-Cumin Tomato Soup, page 144). Brush the outside of the sandwiches with butter and cook them until golden brown and crisp on both sides (3 to 5 minutes per side) in a nonstick skillet or griddle

or even one of those fancy panini makers.

- I admit I love kitchen gadgets. I do have them all. My prized one happens to be a brand of mandoline that is considered the Cadillac among mandolines. Slick, sexy, and safe, I use it every opportunity I get to slice, shred, julienne, or mince. Even an inexpensive, but good mandoline will do the job for you. To get even slices for these sandwiches, use the slicer to make your task easy.

and toast them, shaking the skillet, until they turn reddish-brown and smell nutty, 15 to 30 seconds. Immediately transfer the seeds to a small heatproof bowl or plate to cool. Once cool, place the cumin seeds in a spice grinder (you can also use a coffee grinder) and grind them to the consistency of finely ground black pepper. Tap the ground cumin back into the same small bowl or plate and stir in ½ teaspoon of the salt and the cayenne.

3 Pour ¼ cup of water into a blender and sprinkle in the remaining ½ teaspoon of salt. Pile in the cilantro and the chiles and puree, scraping the inside as needed, to make a smooth, bright green, pungent, slightly thin but spreadable paste.

4 To assemble the sandwiches, take 2 slices of bread and spread a liberal amount of the cilantro paste on one side of each slice. Arrange 1 or 2 slices of potato, a few rings of onion, and a tomato slice or 2 over the cilantro paste on 1 slice of bread. Sprinkle a generous pinch of the cumin spice blend over the vegetables. Top them with a slice of cheese and place the other slice of bread, cilantro paste side down, on top of the cheese. Slice the sandwich in half diagonally and serve.

5 Repeat with the remaining slices of bread and fillings.

#  Naan Pizzas with Roasted Vegetables

LACTO-OVO VEGETARIAN

Naans are the perfect base for single serving pizzas. When grilled up with a green salad, they make for a great meal—cheap and easy never had it this good.

**Makes 4 pizzas (each about 8 inches in diameter)**

Naan (page 93), prepared through Step 5

2 tablespoons canola oil

I large russet or Yukon Gold potato, peeled, cut in half lengthwise, each half thinly sliced crosswise

I teaspoon coarse kosher or sea salt

8 ounces prewashed baby spinach leaves

2 fresh green serrano chiles, stems discarded, thinly sliced crosswise (do not remove the seeds)

All-purpose flour, for rolling out the dough

2 cups store-bought, tomato-based pizza sauce

4 cups assorted shredded cheeses, such as mozzarella, cheddar, fontina, and Romano

1 Once you've prepared the naan dough and set it aside to rest, get the toppings ready. Heat the oil in a large nonstick skillet over medium heat. Once the oil appears to shimmer, add the potato slices and the salt and fry them, uncovered, stirring occasionally, until they are sunny brown, slightly crisp on the outside, and just tender when cut with a fork, 12 to 15 minutes. Increase the heat to high and add the spinach, stirring briskly and constantly to wilt the leaves without allowing them to rest in one spot long enough to release any water, 1 to 2 minutes. Stir in the chiles and turn off the heat.

2 Place a pizza stone or unglazed pottery tiles on the grill rack. *If you are using a gas grill,* preheat it to the highest heat setting. *If you are using a charcoal grill,* build an intensely hot fire so the charcoal turns red-hot and ash-white. The temperature

## Extra Credit

- Any toppings you have a passion for can be for the taking. If you are using vegetables, I recommend roasting them, either on the stovetop or in the oven, for great flavor.

- It is hard to generate that same intense heat in a kitchen oven because they are not designed to generate more than 550°F, but you can bake the pizza in it if you don't have a grill (or if it's snowing outside). If yours is a conventional oven, place the pizza stone, unglazed pottery tiles, or a cookie sheet on the lowest rack and preheat it at the highest bake setting. Cook the pizza as described in Step 4, adding the sauce, vegetables, and cheese all at once, once the dough gets slightly browned.

- A convection oven generates the same heat but distributes it more evenly, and you can place the pizza stone on any of the racks. You will need to bake the crust a little longer (3 to 5 minutes) than you would on an outdoor grill.

- If you plan on a pizza party, make a batch or two of the dough beforehand. It will keep for up to 1 week wrapped in plastic wrap and refrigerated. Make it interactive and have all of your guests roll out their own crusts and adorn them their way. If you have refrigerated the dough, let it return to room temperature before rolling it out. It is much harder to roll chilled dough but at room temperature, it becomes effortless.

it. Press it down to form a patty. Roll the patty out to form a round roughly 8 to 9 inches in diameter, dusting it with flour as needed. Make sure the round is evenly thin, with no tears on the surface. Lift the round (here is where a wooden paddle that often comes with a pizza stone kit comes in handy) and slide it onto the hot pizza stone.

4 Within seconds, the dough will start to bubble in spots. Ladle ½ cup pizza sauce on the dough and spread it evenly to cover almost the entire surface, leaving about ½-inch dough bare around its periphery. Spread a quarter of the vegetable topping over the sauce. Cover the grill and cook until the dough turns crispy brown on the underside and the edge acquires light brown patches, 3 to 4 minutes. Lift the cover and spread 1 cup shredded cheese atop the vegetables. Place the cover back on the grill and let the cheese melt, about 1 minute. Lift the pizza from the stone onto a cutting board and slice it as desired.

5 Repeat with the remaining dough, pizza sauce, potato and spinach topping, and cheese. Serve each pizza as soon as it is ready.

should hover between 600° and 700°F (see Extra Credit).

3 Lightly flour a small work area near the grill, and place a dough round on

#  Mac and Cheese Outsourced

By now you must know we Indians don't like to leave anything alone. It started with telemarketing and then spread to handling all sorts of complaint calls for large companies, followed by manufacturing everything from action dolls to zippers at throwaway prices. So why would you think something as iconic in the American culture as mac and cheese is not fair game for that touch of masala? Just know that next time you talk about white and creamy mac and cheese and say "that's all my Timmy will eat for dinner" to the curious Indian on the other end of the phone who's in Bangalore but pretending to be in Kansas, he or she will of course want to take that pan of buttery smooth comfort and see what can be done to make it appealing since "my Rahul is very picky and wants only American pizza." Here is my version, with all of that cheesy, bubbly American panache fortified and reinforced with Indian gusto.

**LACTO-VEGETARIAN
GLUTEN FREE (IF YOU USE
GLUTEN-FREE MACARONI)**

**Serves 4**

Coarse kosher or sea salt

3 cups uncooked elbow macaroni

2 tablespoons ghee, homemade (page 31) or store-bought, or butter

1 cup finely chopped red onion

2 to 3 fresh green serrano chiles, stems discarded, finely chopped (do not remove the seeds)

2 tablespoons chickpea flour (see **Extra Credit**, page 91)

1 tablespoon Raghavan's Blend (page 39) or store-bought **Madras** curry powder

2 cups half-and-half

2 cups shredded cheese, such as a mix of cheddar, Jack, mozzarella, or **Colby**

¼ cup finely chopped fresh cilantro leaves and tender stems

Fill a large saucepan more than halfway with water and bring it to a rolling boil over medium-high heat. If you like to salt the water when boiling pasta, by all means use as much as you need at this juncture. Add the macaroni to the boiling

## Extra Credit

• You can easily turn this into more of a substantial pasta meal by folding in slightly steamed broccoli or asparagus, ribbons of fresh spinach or mustard greens, and yes, cooked meats too (like pieces of leftover remains of chicken, the turkey from the holiday gathering, maple-glazed ham, crispy bacon, or browned ground beef).

• There are many versions of mac and cheese that are baked with a bread crumb crust on top. I usually don't care for that since the starchy pasta has a tendency to suck up all the sauce and render the macaroni dry. You would almost have to double the quantity of sauce when baking the macaroni to leave behind some succulence that will make your mouth happy.

water and let it return to a boil, stirring once or twice. Vigorously boil the macaroni uncovered, stirring occasionally, until it is cooked just right, tender but not mushy, 8 to 10 minutes.

2 While the macaroni cooks make the cheese sauce. Heat the ghee in a small saucepan over medium-high heat. Once the ghee appears to shimmer, stir in the onion and chiles and stir-fry until the onion is light brown around the edges and the chiles smell pungent, 3 to 4 minutes.

3 Sprinkle the chickpea flour over the onion and chiles and stir to mix. Cook the flour, stirring constantly so it cooks evenly, until it is light brown and the aromas that waft from the pan smell nutty, about 1 minute. Stir in the spice blend; the heat in the pan will be just right to cook the spices without burning them, 5 to 10 seconds. Pour in the half-and-half, a little at a time, whisking it in quickly to make sure there are no lumps. Let the sauce come to a boil, still uncovered, stirring occasionally, until it thickens a bit, 3 to 5 minutes. Stir in 1 teaspoon of salt and the cheese and cilantro and turn off the heat. The hot sauce will melt the cheese.

4 By now the macaroni should be cooked just right. Drain the noodles, giving the colander a good shake. Transfer the macaroni back to the pan you cooked it in. Pour the lip-smacking cheese sauce over the noodles and stir the two together to coat the ho-hum pasta with the zesty blanket of cheese.

5 Spoon or scrape the mac and ooey-gooey cheese into a serving dish. Serve the mac and cheese warm and bubbly, oozing with chiles-heat; an addiction that brings out the sophisticated toddler in all of us.

# 13 Root Vegetable Pot Pie

Pot pies warm the cockles of everyone's heart with morsels of meat and vegetables bonded in a creamy béchamel sauce. My version delivers all of that, sans meat, and with coconut milk instead of cream. The nutritional value of the root vegetables makes it a bit less of a guilty pleasure. The buttery puff pastry top may tilt the scale toward the sinful side, but in my opinion it is always more fun to live life on the edge (okay, sometimes). The flavors in this curry (called *ishto*—an Indianized word perhaps for stews) are very much in keeping with southwestern India's coastal cooking in Kerala, where coconut milk flows in abundance, swathing the aromatic spices (cumin, peppercorns, and cloves, among others) in the masala. In Kerala they serve it with a lacy crepe called *appam* on the side, but my Western half turned this into a rendition with a convenient puff pastry on top.

**Serves 6**

3 tablespoons canola oil

3 medium-size russet or Yukon Gold potatoes, peeled and cut into ½-inch cubes

2 medium-size sweet potatoes, peeled and cut into ½-inch cubes

1 medium-size turnip, peeled and cut into ½-inch cubes

1 small onion, cut into ½-inch cubes

2 to 3 fresh green serrano chiles, stems discarded, finely chopped (do not remove the seeds)

1 tablespoon Raghavan's Blend (page 39) or store-bought Madras curry powder

1½ teaspoons coarse kosher or sea salt

1 can (13.5 ounces) unsweetened coconut milk (see Extra Credit, page 181)

Flour, for dusting the puff pastry

1 sheet frozen puff pastry, completely thawed

## Extra Credit

Even in the cold months I crave greens and since kale seems to be omnipresent, hearty, and as tough as the winters of my Midwestern home, I boil some a bit until tender (5 to 8 minutes), then drain and chop the kale to add to the vegetables as they cook.

1 Position a rack in the center of the oven and preheat the oven to 350°F. Evenly grease the inside of a large ovenproof casserole dish with 1 tablespoon of the oil (I use a 10-inch round dish that is 3 inches deep).

2 Heat the remaining 2 tablespoons of oil in a large skillet over medium-high heat. Once the oil appears to shimmer, add the potatoes, sweet potatoes, turnips, onion, and chiles and cook them, uncovered, stirring occasionally, until some of them brown and the chiles smell pungent, about 5 minutes.

3 Stir in the spice blend and salt and continue to cook the vegetables, uncovered, stirring occasionally, until the spices cook gently but do not burn, about 2 minutes.

4 Pour in the coconut milk, scraping the bottom of the skillet to incorporate the browned bits of vegetables and spices into the sauce. Reduce the heat to medium and let the vegetables simmer vigorously, uncovered, stirring occasionally, until the creamy sauce, mottled with the aromatic spice blend, starts to thicken and the vegetables barely give in and are still firm looking when pierced with a knife or fork, about 10 minutes. Turn off the heat.

5 Lightly flour a cutting board or countertop. Dust both sides of the puff pastry with flour. Roll out the puff pastry so that it is large enough to cover the top of the prepared casserole dish with an overhang of about ½ inch around the edge. Transfer the vegetables and sauce to the casserole dish and top it with the puff pastry. Press the overhang of the puff pastry against the outside of the dish on all sides, forming a secure seal.

6 Bake the pot pie until the pastry is a sunny brown, crisp, and, yes, puffy, 40 to 50 minutes.

7 Bring the pot pie to the table and slice through the pastry into serving portions. Spoon the pastry topping and the vegetable filling onto serving plates.

# Chapter 8

# Side Dishes Unfolded

**I CANNOT STRESS** enough the importance of vegetables, rice, and grains in India. They often take the lead role in the daily mealtime performance, pushing protein-rich fare to the sidelines. It is not uncommon to find two vegetables on the dinner plate in India along with rice—and other grains—next to a small helping of meat, fish, poultry, or legumes. For the vegetables, I did not take the traditional route of placing the recipes in alphabetical order. Instead, I focused on teaching you a range of spicing techniques starting with the use of a single spice and progressing to blends that create savory magic in vegetables that populate neighborhood grocery stores. Follow the spice trail in this chapter and you will expand your culinary prowess, Indian style.

## The Lesson Plan

**Lesson 1  Sweet-Scented Pilaf**
A rice pilaf with a sweet perfumed scent makes a perfect bed for the Ultimate Chicken Curry and the Smoky Yellow Split Peas that are the main dishes in our special foldout menu.  Learning how to cook a perfect pot of rice may be the most important lesson I teach when it comes to cooking Indian cuisine.

**Lesson 2  Turmeric Hash Browns**
Everyone's favorite tuber (mine for sure)—the potato—here shredded, tossed with hot chile, salt, and one spice, turmeric. Panfried, it's a crispy mound of heaven that breathes India.

**Lessons 3 and 4  Cayenne-Crusted Eggplant and Coconut Squash with Chiles**
Each of these two recipes also focuses on one spice: in one, thick slices of eggplant are coated in chickpea flour and cayenne and panfried, while in the other, yellow squash

is rounded out with a nutty finish of cumin seeds sizzled in ghee.

**Lessons 5 and 6  Tart Eggplant Pâté and Blistered Smoky Peppers**  The next two recipes build the momentum, each with two spices. An eggplant pâté with turmeric and sizzling cumin seeds delivers the smoky goods and that same smoky presence is felt with peppers using the same two spices and seared at a high temperature. Same spices, dissimilar techniques, spectacular results.

**Lessons 7 and 8  Not-So-Cool Cucumbers and Cumin Potatoes**  What makes Indians such experts in the world of spices? Spinning multiple flavors from one spice is the hallmark of layered cooking and the Not-So-Cool Cucumbers and Cumin Potatoes show you that magic with cumin used in two different ways within the same recipe.

226

**Lessons ⑨, ⑩, and ⑪ Green Bean Almondine with Nutmeg, Warm Citrus Cabbage, and Cauliflower and Peas** Enhance the vegetables in these three recipes with freshly ground spices. The classic green bean almondine gets a makeover in this Indianized version, while warm cabbage retains that al dente crunch but gets a surprising burst of citrus. The simple masala of cumin, coriander, cayenne, and turmeric turns cauliflower and peas sexy and intoxicating.

**Lessons ⑫ and ⑬ Curry House Cauliflower and Nutty Broccoli with Mustard** Popping mustard seeds in hot oil sets the nutty tone for a symphony of ground spices in these two recipes. This is a technique quite instrumental in learning to cook the southern Indian way. It's painlessly simple but it's important that you follow exactly the order in which you add the ingredients, including the spices, or the mustard seeds will turn on you, Mr. Hyde style, resulting in a pungent, bitter taste experience.

**Lessons ⑭, ⑮, ⑯, and ⑰ Ginger Raisin Bok Choy, Spinach with Cranberries, Sweet Corn with Toasted Coconut, and Saucy Green Beans** Finally you will be ready to create my signature spice blends to get you to a mastery level that may please your mother-in-law even if she's Indian—and believe me that's not an easy task! My simple Raghavan's Blend turns bok choy into a complex-tasting side dish that incorporates stir-frying and then stewing, two techniques that are essential to deliver outstanding sweet, pungent, and sour flavors.

If you keep a jar of homemade garam masala on hand, preparing Spinach with Cranberries is a cinch to make. The key to this recipe's success also lies in stir-frying at a relatively high temperature to deliver the smoky undertones.

The Sweet Corn with Toasted Coconut does not have either of my blends, but instead, walks you through the process of seasoning these sweet corn kernels with a simple mélange of ground, roasted coconut, coriander, and chiles (a classic combination in the Tamilian Brahmin kitchens of southeastern India).

The vibrant sauce that beds the green beans combines tomatoes, onions, and chiles and benefits from mustard seeds used in two ways—whole, popped in oil for a sweet, popcornlike nuttiness, and ground for a slightly bitter, pungent kick.

**Lesson ⑱ Mustard Rice with Peppers** There are no more starchy, gloppy results when rice is cooked properly and the way we flavor the water, broth style, with whole spices enhances India and Pakistan's prized basmati rice.

**Lesson ⑲ Savory Cream of Wheat** Cream of Wheat undergoes a chameleonlike transformation in a savory classic from southern India, proving that it can be more than boring breakfast fare.

**Lesson ⑳ Orzo with Chile-Spiked Eggplant** Now that you have learned what to do with so many spices, expand that knowledge into the way you really cook—marry Indian spices with a Western pasta that is elegant and easy.

227

tight-fitting lid and reduce the heat to the lowest possible setting. Let the rice steep for 8 to 10 minutes (8 if you are using an electric burner, 10 for a gas burner). Then turn off the heat and let the pan stand on that burner, undisturbed, for 5 minutes.

5 Uncover the pan, fluff the rice with a fork, and serve. You may choose to remove the cloves, bay leaves, cardamom pods, and cinnamon sticks before you serve the rice. I usually leave them in since they continue to perfume the rice and just instruct the

folks eating the rice to watch for those whole spices and eat around them.

**1** Place the rice in a bowl and have all your ingredients prepped.

**2** Fill the bowl with enough water to gently rinse the rice, separating the grains with your fingers.

**3** When the water gets cloudy, gently rinse the grains without breaking the slender grains.

**4** Once the rice is ready, sprinkle the whole spices into the hot ghee and allow them to sizzle.

# Sweet-Scented Pilaf

## Masala Pulao

1 cup Indian or Pakistani white basmati rice or long-grain white rice

2 tablespoons ghee, homemade (page 31) or store-bought, or canola oil

1 teaspoon cumin seeds

½ teaspoon whole cloves

6 green or white cardamom pods

2 fresh or dried bay leaves

2 cinnamon sticks (each about 3 inches long)

1 small red onion, cut in half lengthwise and thinly sliced

1 teaspoon coarse kosher or sea salt

P erfuming oils with whole spices has been classic to north Indian cuisine for thousands of years (no, I am not exaggerating). Western cultures call it blooming (or tempering) but we call it *tadka*. Whatever the nomenclature for this technique, the results play a pleasing game with your palate of how-much-can-you-eat-without-stopping. Give in and savor the pilaf as a side to any main dish, salad, soup, or even a starter. It makes an elegant bed for the Ultimate Chicken Curry and Smoky Yellow Split Peas in our foldout menu.

1 Place the rice in a medium-size bowl. Fill the bowl with enough water to cover the rice. Gently rub the slender grains between the fingers of one hand, without breaking them, to wash off any dust or light foreign objects (like loose husks), which will float to the surface. The water will become cloudy. Drain this water. You don't need a colander for this; I just tip the bowl over the sink to pour off the water, making sure the rice stays in the bowl. Repeat this 3 or 4 times until after you rinse the grains the water remains relatively clear. Now fill the bowl halfway with cold water and

let the rice sit at room temperature until the kernels soften, 10 to 15 minutes, then drain the rice.

2 Heat the ghee in a medium-size heavy pot or saucepan over medium-high heat. Once it appears to shimmer, sprinkle in the cumin, cloves, cardamom, bay leaves, and cinnamon sticks. The spices will sizzle, turn reddish brown, crackle, and scent the air with sweet aromas in 30 seconds to 1 minute. Add the onion and stir-fry the slices until lightly brown around the edges, 3 to 5 minutes.

3 Add the drained rice to the spiced onions, tossing them gently to coat the rice. Add 1½ cups of cold water and the salt. Stir the rice once or twice to incorporate the ingredients. Bring the water to a boil, uncovered, still over medium-high heat and let boil without stirring, until the water has evaporated from the surface and craters are starting to appear in the rice, 5 to 8 minutes.

4 Now (and not until now) stir once or twice to bring the partially cooked layer of rice from the bottom of the pan to the surface. Cover the pan with a

**5** Quickly add the sliced red onion to the sizzling spices to prevent them from burning.

**6** Stir-fry the medley to coat the onion with ghee.

**7** Allow the onion to brown around the edges.

**8** Add the rice and fresh water to the pot and cook until most of the liquid evaporates from its surface and craters start to appear.

**9** Once cooked, uncover the pan and fluff the rice to release any pent-up steam.

## Extra Credit

The whole spices used here are some of the spices most commonly used in versions of garam masala. Here they are left whole, gently infusing the nutty clarified butter with subtle aromas and tastes—great proof that in northern India not all garam masalas are ground.

# Turmeric Hash Browns

VEGAN
GLUTEN FREE

I am not lying when I say this is one recipe I succumb to every Saturday or Sunday for breakfast. Not having potatoes piled into the beautiful ceramic bowl given to me by my friend Richard Bresnahan, a potter of national and international renown, is cause for panic and a quick trip to the store. For you see, I am a self-confessed potato-holic. I need them, I want them, and I covet them with unabashed lust. In India we were not privy to this tuber prior to the sixteenth century and we thank the Spanish and the Portuguese settlers for that gift from the New World. Now, no meal in India is replete without the inclusion of potatoes in some shape, size, or form. These shredded wonders incorporate one spice (turmeric) and two flavorings (cilantro and chile) to yield a golden-colored, perfumed, and pleasingly hot cake that is crisp on the outside and moist inside.

**Serves 4 as a side or 2 as a breakfast**

**2 pounds russet or Yukon Gold potatoes (see Extra Credit)**

**½ cup finely chopped fresh cilantro leaves and tender stems**

**1½ teaspoons coarse kosher or sea salt**

**½ teaspoon ground turmeric**

**I habanero chile, stem discarded, and finely chopped (do not remove the seeds; see Extra Credit)**

**2 tablespoons canola oil**

1 Peel the potatoes. Shred them in a food processor using the shredding attachment or by scraping them against the large holes of a box grater. Pile the potato shreds into a medium-size bowl. Mix in the cilantro, salt, turmeric, and chile. Because you are dealing with the heat of a habanero, use a spoon to do the mixing.

2 Heat the oil in a large nonstick skillet or well-seasoned cast iron pan over medium-high heat. Once the oil appears to shimmer, spread the turmeric-colored potatoes in the skillet in an even layer that is about 2 inches deep. The sizzle as soon as the potatoes hit the skillet is a good sign that the skillet is the right temperature.

## Extra Credit

- A combination of turnips and rutabagas, instead of or in addition to the potatoes, adds a deeper dimension (keep in mind the total amount for the recipe is 2 pounds). Using sweet potatoes adds a sugariness that markedly offsets the habanero chile's capsaicin (the chemical that gives chiles their characteristic heat). If you really want to take the easy way out, buy pre-shredded potatoes from the refrigerated section of your supermarket. I won't judge, I promise.

- The Cubans may be known for their infamous cigars but let's not lose sight of their other gift to the world—that addictive member of the capsicum family called the habanero (which means "from Havana"). Potent, perfumed, pungent, the habanero may sometimes be labeled as a Scotch bonnet, even though the latter is a different variety of the same species. It is widely available among the chiles and the peppers in the vegetable bins of neighborhood grocery stores. It is the second hottest cultivated chile and with a reputation to hurt so good. Please be advised to use disposable gloves while chopping it. The habanero's fruity aromas are unmistakable as soon as you cut it open. Discard the veins and seeds if you wish a gentler heat. Serranos or jalapeños are okay alternatives but keep in mind they don't possess that fragrance I so adore.

Reduce the heat to medium and cook the potatoes covered, without stirring, until they are nice and crispy brown on the underside, 10 to 12 minutes. Turn the thick patty over using 2 spatulas and brown the second side the same way, 10 to 12 minutes.

3 Serve the potatoes immediately to experience the crispy exterior and the soft interior.

# Cayenne-Crusted Eggplant

## Baadaam Baingan

LACTO-VEGETARIAN
GLUTEN FREE

Not all Indian recipes have painstakingly layered and complex flavors. Often one spice can be the diva in the dish and refuse cluttered companionship. When freshly panfried, these finger-friendly, addictive, crispy, nutty, subtly hot, and tender morsels of eggplant will make you appreciate that divine presence. You just can't stop at one, much like the ubiquitous potato chip, and by comparison it fares a whole lot better in the nutrition department.

**Makes about a dozen slices (serves 4 as a side)**

1 cup buttermilk

1 cup chickpea flour (see Extra Credit, page 91)

½ cup almond slivers or slices, ground (see Extra Credit)

1 teaspoon ground red pepper (cayenne)

1 teaspoon coarse kosher or sea salt

Canola oil for panfrying

1 pound eggplant, stem discarded, cut crosswise into ¼-inch-thick slices (see Extra Credit)

1 Pour the buttermilk into a shallow bowl or pie plate. Thoroughly combine the chickpea flour, almonds, cayenne, and salt in another shallow bowl or pie plate.

2 Line a plate with paper towels to ready it for draining the crisped eggplant slices.

3 Pour oil to a depth of ⅛ inch in a large nonstick skillet or a well-seasoned cast-iron pan and heat over medium heat. Once the oil appears to shimmer, take 4 to 6 slices of the eggplant and dunk them in the buttermilk. Make sure they are well coated, and the buttermilk has formed a thick paintlike sheen. Dredge each slice on both sides in the spiced chickpea flour (make sure the coating adheres well to the eggplant's surface; I often shower the slices with the flour mixture and press

## Extra Credit

- To pulverize the almonds to a fine grind I use my spice grinder (like a coffee grinder). In this instance running the machine for too long is not necessarily better because the fat in the nuts will turn them to a pasty consistency, not unlike peanut butter. A blender will also work for grinding the almonds, but a food processor may make them much coarser in consistency.

- Eggplant, a member of the nightshade family (think potatoes, tomatoes, peppers, chiles, tomatillos, and tobacco) is a vegetable known to have existed in India (where it is called *brinjal*) and China around the birth of Christianity. It made its way to Europe and the rest of the world around the eighth century CE. The varieties of eggplant grown in the world are diverse, but the most common ones found in grocery stores are often mistakenly called Italian eggplants. Each is usually firm, a pound in weight or larger, and dark purple. These work great for this recipe. Avoid eggplants that have soft spots, which indicate a diminished shelf life due to being overripe.

- Make sure the eggplant slices are evenly thick. Slices of differing thicknesses or crooked ones will yield irregular results with respect to cooking times. Mandolines are great for perfectly even slices (if you have one in storage, now's the time to get it out).

- Turn your leftover cooked eggplant slices into an Italian favorite. Spoon some store-bought pasta sauce in the bottom of a greased casserole dish and layer some of the eggplant slices over it. Top with mozzarella or cheddar cheese and repeat the sauce, eggplant, and cheese layers once more. Bake, covered, in a 350°F oven until the sauce is bubbly and the cheese has melted, about 30 minutes.

it onto the vegetable's surface). Gently add the dredged eggplant to the oil. You want to hear the instant sear and sizzle of the coating, which is essential in making the bottom crisp. Cook the slices until reddish-brown and crisp, 3 to 4 minutes. Turn the eggplant slices over and repeat with the second side, 3 to 4 minutes. Transfer the slices to the paper towel–lined plate to drain. Wipe the skillet clean with paper towels. Add more oil to the skillet and heat it before repeating with the remaining eggplant slices.

4 Serve the eggplant slices immediately. They are optimum in texture when served right away but will keep if placed on a rack in an oven that has been preheated to 200°F. The goal is to make sure you don't let the eggplant get soggy (hence the rack to elevate it) and 15 to 20 minutes is about the limit for keeping them warm. Even though the eggplant slices are perfectly edible when cold and soggy, do enjoy them piping hot.

# Coconut Squash with Chiles

Shorakkai Aviyal

his simple curry (and no, this has neither curry powder nor turmeric in it) showcases two ingredients that are so common to some of the sauces in southeastern Indian kitchens: coconut and chiles. Ideally, freshly shredded coconut is the way to go, but if it is not available, the dried shreds are a good enough alternative. Even though this is a side dish, when I have leftovers for lunch, I often will serve myself a couple of warmed-up whole wheat tortillas with the squash and some yogurt with grapes (page 108) alongside. Since I have a tendency to skip breakfast during the week (I know, hold your lectures please), I resort to an early lunch, instead.

LACTO-VEGETARIAN
(VEGAN IF YOU USE OIL)
GLUTEN FREE

**Serves 4**

I pound yellow squash or zucchini

½ cup dried unsweetened coconut shreds
   (see **Extra Credit**, page 121)

I to 2 fresh green serrano chiles, stems
   discarded

2 tablespoons ghee, homemade (page 31) or
   store-bought, or canola oil

I teaspoon cumin seeds

I teaspoon coarse kosher or sea salt

2 tablespoons finely chopped fresh cilantro
   leaves and tender stems

1 Slice about ½ inch off both ends of each squash and discard. Cut the squash in 1-inch cubes and place them in a small saucepan. Pour 1 cup of water over the squash and bring it to a boil over medium-high heat. Reduce the heat to medium, cover the pan, and cook the squash, stirring occasionally, until it is fork-tender but still firm looking, 5 to 8 minutes.

2 Meanwhile, transfer about ½ cup of the simmering liquid from the pan with the squash to a blender. Add the coconut and chiles and puree them, scraping the inside

## Extra Credit

- Often labeled summer squash, the thin-skinned yellow variety, available year round, is a common sight next to zucchini in the produce department of supermarkets. Mild flavored, this is the perfect vegetable to soak in vibrant flavors.

- On a trip to Texas for a series of classes, I was pleasantly surprised to see freshly shredded coconut in the freezer section of mainstream grocery stores. It was sold under a well-known national brand that specializes in frozen vegetables. If you see it in your store use that in a heartbeat. A full cup of freshly shredded coconut will work well as an alternative to the ½ cup of dried coconut called for in this recipe.

of the blender as needed, to make a thick paste mottled with green flecks of hot chiles amid a sea of naturally sweet coconut. Add this to the pan of squash. At this point, I usually scoop some of the liquid from the pan, add it to the blender, swish it around to make sure I get every last bit of paste, and then pour it back into the pan.

3 Heat the ghee in a small skillet over medium-high heat. Once the ghee appears to shimmer, sprinkle in the cumin seeds; they will instantly sizzle and perfume the air with their nutty aroma, 5 to 10 seconds. Pour the cumin seed oil over the squash and stir it in along with the salt.

4 Serve the squash curry warm sprinkled with the cilantro.

# 5 Tart Eggplant Pâté

## Bharta

Called *bharta* in Hindi, meaning a mishmash of sorts, this eggplant pâté folds in ingredients typical among the peasant community in the northwest region of India. A whole eggplant (pierced to vent or it will burst) is often placed on an open flame and charred black to create a smokiness. Once peeled, as you would a roasted bell pepper, the pulp is sweet and bitter-free, offering a smooth, albeit slightly grainy, backdrop to pearl-like bits of red onion, earthy ginger, and sun-yellow turmeric. Great as a side dish for any of the mains in the book, I also serve the eggplant pâté slathered on pieces of toasted baguette slices for an appetizer for a froufrou cocktail party.

LACTO-VEGETARIAN
(VEGAN IF USING OIL)
GLUTEN FREE

**Makes 2 brimming cups**

2 to 2½ pounds eggplant (see **Extra Credit**, page 236)

½ cup finely chopped red onion

2 tablespoons finely chopped fresh ginger

2 fresh green serrano chiles, stems discarded, finely chopped (do not remove the seeds)

I teaspoon coarse kosher or sea salt

½ teaspoon ground turmeric

2 tablespoons ghee, homemade (page 31) or store-bought, or canola oil

I teaspoon cumin seeds

Juice from I medium-size lime

2 tablespoons finely chopped fresh cilantro leaves and tender stems

1 Preheat a gas (or charcoal) grill, or the broiler, to high.

2 Prick the eggplants in multiple spots with a fork or knife (this prevents them from bursting when you grill or broil them).

Don't bother to remove the stems, since they will be discarded once you skin the eggplants.

3 *If you are grilling the eggplants,* place them on the grill grate, cover the grill,

## Extra Credit

- If you would like a smoother texture, put the pâté in a food processor after it cooks and puree it until smooth. This works great for spreading on toast points.

- Any leftover eggplant pâté is great spread on top of smashed avocadoes. It makes an unusual guacamole that is sure to perk up your conversations at the dinner table.

them and discard the stems along with the skins. You will notice that there are eggplant juices pooled in the bowl; make sure you do not discard them. If a lonesome piece of charred skin still lingers on the eggplant, don't sweat the small stuff.

5 Return the eggplants to the bowl and mash them and their juices well with a potato masher (I often use a clean hand to do this if a masher is not handy). Add the onion, ginger, chiles, salt, and turmeric to the mashed eggplant and stir to mix.

6 Heat the ghee in a medium-size skillet over medium heat. Once the ghee appears to shimmer, sprinkle in the cumin seeds; they will instantly sizzle and perfume the air, 5 to 10 seconds. Add the eggplant pâté and cook it, stirring occasionally and scraping the bottom of the skillet to make sure it does not stick, until the flavors get a chance to mingle, emerge, and win you over, about 15 minutes.

7 Stir the lime juice into the eggplant pâté and serve it warm sprinkled with the cilantro.

and cook, turning them periodically to ensure even grilling, until the skins are evenly charred, about 25 minutes.

*If you are broiling the eggplants,* position the broiler rack so the eggplants will be about 6 inches from the heat. Place the eggplants on the rack and broil them, turning them periodically until the skins are evenly charred, 25 to 30 minutes.

4 Place the grilled eggplants in a medium-size or large bowl, cover it with plastic wrap, and sweat eggplants in their own heat until the skins appear shriveled, about 15 minutes. Once the eggplants are cool to the touch, working over the bowl, peel

# Blistered Smoky Peppers

Simla Mirch aur Suva

VEGAN
GLUTEN FREE

What I admire in this combination of ingredients is the inclusion of three members of the capsicum family—bell peppers, dried cayenne chiles, and fresh serrano chiles—to create a depth of flavor that ranges from hot to smoky to sweet. Fresh dill, often used like greens, is a typical herb in the Sindhi community of northwestern India near the Pakistan-India border. The dill lends not only color but a grassy, earthy texture to the mix of peppers. I recommend serving this as a side dish with the Buttermilk Fried Chicken (page 172) for a balance of color, nutrition, and taste.

**Makes 4 cups; serves 4**

I pound assorted bell peppers, green, red, orange, yellow, purple—your pick

2 fresh green serrano chiles, stems discarded

2 tablespoons canola oil

2 dried red cayenne chiles (like chile de árbol), stems discarded

2 dried or fresh bay leaves

¼ cup finely chopped fresh dill

I teaspoon coarse kosher or sea salt

I teaspoon ground cumin

¼ teaspoon ground turmeric

I Discard the stem from each bell pepper. Slice each pepper in half lengthwise and remove the seeds and ribs (those are the white, slightly spongy parts that look like flimsy half-opened partitions). Cut each pepper half into squares about 1 inch in size and place them in a medium-size bowl.

Thinly slice each of the serrano chiles crosswise and add them to the bell peppers. Do not remove the seeds from the chiles.

2 Heat the oil in a large skillet over medium-high heat. Once the oil appears to shimmer, add the dried red chiles and

## Extra Credit

- When slicing bell peppers (and eggplant too), it is easier to cut them from the inside (once they are halved) as the skin can be a bit resilient. The sharper the knife you use, the easier it is to glide the blade through the vegetable, lowering the chances of an accident.

- Just like eggplant (again), when seared and blistered, peppers deliver smoky-sweet results. It's similar to when you make roasted peppers—you completely blacken the skins and peel them to experience the juicy, honeyed flavors.

bay leaves. The chiles will blacken almost immediately as you stir them, 15 to 20 seconds. Add the bell peppers and serrano chiles to the skillet and continue to stir-fry. You want the peppers to sear (not stew)

and start blistering in spots; you may need to increase the heat to high. This normally takes about 5 minutes. Make sure you have adequate ventilation as you do this lung-cleaning step.

3 Turn off the heat and add the dill, salt, cumin, and turmeric, stirring once or twice. The heat from the skillet and its contents will be just enough to cook the ground spices without burning them while the dill will maintain its spritely green brightness.

4 Discard the bay leaves and serve the pepper medley warm. I leave the dried chiles in it for the person at the table who thumps his or her chest with machismo joy at the challenge of munching them.

# 7 Not-So-Cool Cucumbers

Zeera Kakadi

VEGAN
GLUTEN FREE

When you have a surplus of juicy cucumbers from your garden and get tired of canning, pickling, or slicing them atop salads, try turning them into the cooked vegetable du jour to accompany grilled meats or what-have-you. We Indians, especially from northwestern India, delicately spice cucumbers with cumin and turmeric, and cook them until just tender. This is one of those vegetables that when cooked exudes surprising succulence with each bite. The cucumber has an almost squashlike quality (no surprise since it is from that family) that seems to come through much more sharply when warmed.

**Serves 6**

4 medium-size to large cucumbers (about 3 pounds)

2 teaspoons cumin seeds

2 tablespoons canola oil

I large green or red bell pepper, stem, core, ribs, and seeds discarded, flesh cut into ¼-inch cubes

2 fresh green serrano chiles, stems discarded, finely chopped (do not remove the seeds)

I teaspoon coarse kosher or sea salt

¼ teaspoon ground turmeric

Juice from I medium-size lime

Peel the cucumbers with a potato peeler. Slice off and discard about ¼ inch from both ends of each cucumber. Cut each cucumber in half lengthwise. Using a spoon, scoop out and discard the slippery, watery seeds. Working with one cucumber half at a time, slice that again lengthwise into 2 halves. Each cucumber should yield 4 equal slender slices. Group 3 or 4 of these slices together with the long sides parallel to you. Using a sharp knife, cut the slices crosswise into ½-inch-wide slices to end up with ½-inch pieces. Repeat with the remaining slices.

You should have about 5 cups of cubed cucumbers.

2 Place 1 teaspoon of the cumin seeds in a spice grinder (you can also use a coffee grinder) and grind them to the consistency of finely ground black pepper. Set the ground cumin aside.

3 Heat the oil in a large skillet over medium-high heat. Once the oil appears to shimmer, sprinkle in the remaining teaspoon of cumin seeds, which will instantly sizzle and turn reddish brown and fragrant, 5 to 10 seconds. Add the bell pepper and the chiles and stir-fry until the bell pepper softens a bit and the chiles start to smell pungent, about 2 minutes.

4 Stir in the ground cumin, salt, and turmeric; the heat will be just right to cook the spices without burning them, 15 to 30 seconds. When the spices cook, their aromas change into a more sophisticated nuttiness. Add the cucumbers, stir well once or twice, and cook, uncovered, stirring occasionally, until the cucumbers are tender but still firm looking, 10 to 12 minutes.

5 Stir in the lime juice and serve the cucumbers warm.

## Extra Credit

- This recipe illustrates a technique very typical of Indian food: layering the flavors in a dish with one spice used in different forms. Cumin seeds, when sizzled in hot oil, perfume the cucumbers with nutty sweetness and an aroma that scents not only the air but provides essential aromatics that help you savor the vegetable. The same seeds, when ground, intensify the earthy component and balance the heat from the chiles.

- If you have preground cumin, use it in Step 4 instead of grinding a teaspoon of cumin seeds. Because preground cumin is less assertive than freshly ground, you will need to add 2 (not 1) teaspoons (so, 1 teaspoon cumin seeds and 2 teaspoons ground cumin).

- Should you wish not to use cucumbers, yellow summer squash makes a great backdrop to the flavors in this stir-fry. You can use any winter squash but keep in mind these require longer cooking times and you may need to add a little water to help them steam better. Also, the winter squashes are naturally sweeter and will mask the other flavors a bit more. Add an extra chile and a bit more salt to balance that added sweetness.

- Cold leftovers of this dish can be converted to a healthy snack. Toss the cucumbers with unsweetened puffed rice cereal and serve them sprinkled with some finely chopped red onion and finely chopped fresh cilantro leaves and tender stems. I usually recommend twice the amount of puffs as cucumbers. The textural difference is quite addictive and this snack idea is a version of a classic street food favorite in Mumbai called *bhel.*

# 8 Cumin Potatoes

## Zeera Aloo

VEGAN
GLUTEN FREE

This uncluttered potato side dish also features cumin used in two ways: whole seeds sizzle in oil to give it a nutty perfume; ground seeds pan roast with the potatoes for an intensely earthy flavor, transporting you to the *terroir* they originate from. Crisp on the outside (hence the importance of having a nonstick skillet), with slow-burning tender heat on the inside, these potatoes are just as good as a breakfast side as my Turmeric Hash Browns (page 232).

**Serves 4**

1½ pounds russet or Yukon Gold potatoes (see Extra Credit)

2 tablespoons canola oil

1 teaspoon cumin seeds

2 teaspoons ground cumin

1½ teaspoons coarse kosher or sea salt

½ teaspoon ground turmeric

½ teaspoon ground red pepper (cayenne)

2 fresh green serrano chiles, stems discarded, thinly sliced crosswise (do not remove the seeds)

2 tablespoons finely chopped fresh cilantro leaves and tender stems

1 Peel the potatoes. Slice them lengthwise into long planks, each roughly 1 inch thick. Stack a few of the planks and cut them into 1-inch-wide strips. Turn the strips 90 degrees and slice them into 1-inch-wide pieces; you will end up with 1-inch cubes of potatoes.

2 Heat the oil in a large nonstick skillet over medium-high heat. Once the oil appears to shimmer, sprinkle in the cumin seeds, which will almost instantly sizzle, turn reddish brown, and smell nutty, 10 to 15 seconds. Add the potato cubes, ground cumin, salt, turmeric, cayenne, chiles, and cilantro. Stir once or twice. Reduce the heat to medium. Cook the spiced potatoes,

covered, stirring occasionally, until they are golden yellow, crisp on the outside, with hues of brown, red, and green, and tender on the inside without being mushy, 18 to 20 minutes.

3 Serve the potatoes warm.

## Extra Credit

The variety of potato most common in India is similar to the russet, which is a good choice for this dish. I also recommend Yukon Gold potatoes as an option because of their golden yellow appearance and a perfect balance of starch and mouthfeel. They are a bit sweeter and their skins are much thinner, making it okay to use them without peeling.

The assortment of tubers available in supermarkets nowadays is phenomenal and I have yet to meet a potato I did not like. The tender baby ones, which at the peak of late spring are about the size of marbles, are my favorite. If you decide to use them in this recipe, rinse them well and use them whole. For a varied and colorful presentation, include purple, red, white, gold, and fingerlings when you make this recipe.

# Green Bean Almondine with Nutmeg

LACTO-VEGETARIAN
(VEGAN IF YOU USE OIL
INSTEAD OF GHEE)
GLUTEN FREE

Perky green beans are moistened with nutty-rich clarified butter and flavored with sweet nutmeg and aggressive mustard—quite typical of home kitchens in Calcutta in eastern India. On a night that I served these, I also made Tandoori Chicken (page 174) and a gargantuan mound of creamy garlic-mashed potatoes (just because). The filled dinner plates looked colorful and had great form; the aromas that wafted from them were highly intoxicating and, yes, made our taste buds dance with joy.

**Serves 4**

I pound fresh green beans

I medium-size lime

2 tablespoons ghee, homemade (page 3l) or store-bought, or canola oil

I small red onion, cut in half lengthwise and thinly sliced

¼ cup almond slivers or slices

½ teaspoon freshly grated nutmeg (see **Extra Credit**, page 283)

½ teaspoon ground mustard

½ teaspoon ground red pepper (cayenne)

I teaspoon coarse kosher or sea salt

1 Snap off and discard the stem end of each green bean. String the beans if necessary by removing the thin strand of thread-like filament that peels off the side of the beans when you snap the stem end. Keep the tail end intact (I think the beans look pretty with a curved tail to provide grace to an otherwise gangly vegetable). Rinse the green beans in a colander under cold running water and drain them. Pat the green beans dry with paper towels.

2 Using a Microplane or the smallest holes of a box grater, remove the zest from the lime in shreds. Set the shredded zest aside. Juice the lime and set the juice aside.

3 Heat the ghee in a large skillet over medium-high heat. Once the ghee appears to shimmer, add the onion and almonds and stir-fry until both are light brown around the edges, 2 to 3 minutes.

4 Sprinkle in the shredded lime zest, and the nutmeg, mustard, cayenne, and salt and stir once or twice. The heat in the skillet will be just right to cook the ground spices for 5 to 10 seconds without burning them.

5 Add the trimmed green beans, stirring to coat them with the spices. Pour in ½ cup of water and scrape the bottom of the skillet to loosen the browned bits of onion and spices. Reduce the heat to medium, cover the skillet, and let the beans simmer, stirring occasionally, until they are fork-tender but not mushy, 12 to 15 minutes.

6 Stir in the lime juice and serve warm.

## Extra Credit

- The common variety of fresh green beans is also known as string beans or snap beans (they should break easy with a snap between your fingertips) and belongs to the family of *Phaseolus vulgaris*. I find nothing uncouth about them when it comes to their availability, frugality, and taste.

  During the summer season, use the yellow wax beans (my favorite) or even the slinky French kind called haricots verts (these are particularly expedient for cooking because of their slender bodies).

- I am a huge fan of freshly ground spices. Even though I have recommended using ground nutmeg and mustard here, start with the whole spice if you can. Whole nutmeg, when freshly grated against a Microplane or box grater, imparts an essence rich with sweet oils. When pulverized in a spice grinder, which works like a coffee grinder, black or yellow mustard seeds yield a stronger pungency with that up-the-nose heat so typical of mustard.

# 10 Warm Citrus Cabbage

Nimboo Bund Gobhi Ki Subzi

VEGAN
GLUTEN FREE

I am a sucker for cooked cabbage (I may be in the minority here in the United States but, hey, I am used to it) and relish each opportunity I get to savor it. Its texture provides a noodlelike comfort, and I admit I can make a meal out of this side dish. Available at all times, here and in India, this inexpensive member of the Brassica family (think cauliflower, broccoli, mustard), is tight-headed and full of intoxicating aromas when cooked (revered by some and not by others), and is rich in vitamin C and other essential nutrients. My colleagues Harold McGee and Shirley Corriher (highly respected authorities on food science in the culinary world) agree that the longer cabbage is cooked, the sharper the unpleasant smells. Some of that is counterbalanced in this recipe by what Indians are masters at—using spices to manipulate tastes and aromas that leave behind a pleasingly lasting impression on the palate. Serve the cabbage as a side dish with any of the main courses in this book.

**Makes 6 cups; serves 6**

1 small head of cabbage (about 2 pounds) or 2 bags (14 ounces each) coleslaw mix

2 teaspoons coriander seeds, or 1 tablespoon ground coriander

1 teaspoon cumin seeds, or 2 teaspoons ground cumin

1 teaspoon coarse kosher or sea salt

¼ teaspoon ground turmeric

2 tablespoons canola oil

2 tablespoons finely chopped fresh ginger

2 fresh green serrano chiles, stems discarded, finely chopped (do not remove the seeds)

Juice from 1 medium-size lime

2 tablespoons finely chopped fresh cilantro leaves and tender stems

If you are using a head of cabbage, cut it in half from top to bottom (position it with the bulbous base resting on the cutting board). Remove the tough rib from

250

the bottom of each cabbage half by slicing through it on the diagonal; you will end up with a V-shaped opening at the base of each half. Cut each cabbage half in half from top to bottom again, then slice these into shreds, as thin as you can. Place the cabbage shreds in a large bowl (for photos illustrating these steps, see the foldout at the beginning of Chapter 5). If you are using a preshredded coleslaw mix (which usually has a few shreds of carrots and purple cabbage in it for color), empty the contents of the bags into a large bowl.

2 If you are using the coriander and cumin seeds, place them in a spice grinder (you can also use a coffee grinder) and grind them to the consistency of finely ground black pepper. The intensity of those two freshly ground spices will make you wonder why you never ground spices fresh before with more regularity. Sprinkle the ground coriander and cumin, salt, and turmeric over the cabbage. Stir to mix the spices thoroughly with the cabbage.

3 Heat the oil in a wok or large saucepan, over medium-high heat. Once the oil shimmers, add the ginger and chiles and stir-fry until the ginger browns and the chiles smell pungent, 1 to 2 minutes.

## Extra Credit

- I have spoken at length about the virtues of grinding your spices fresh but if you don't happen to have the seeds on hand and the preground variety is available, use it by all means. Weak spices are better than no spice at all. I hope the preground spices have not been sitting on your shelf for years (in which case no spice is a better option) as their essential oils will have completely dissipated by now and all the spices are doing is taking up shelf space—I call them shelf squatters.

- To get more juice out of a lime (or any citrus fruit for that matter), before you cut it rub it firmly with the palm of your hand against a countertop or cutting board. The warmth of your hand and the pressure you exert will soften the skin and loosen up the juices.

4 Take a couple of handfuls of the spiced cabbage, add it to the pan, and stir-fry until the cabbage wilts, 1 to 2 minutes. Repeat until all of the cabbage has wilted. Reduce the heat to medium and let the cabbage simmer, covered, stirring occasionally, until it is fork-tender and has the texture of cooked (al dente) noodles, 12 to 15 minutes. Cabbage contains enough water to provide the moisture to braise it gently.

5 Stir the lime juice and cilantro into the cabbage and serve it warm.

# Cauliflower and Peas

## Gobhi Mutter

I am going to teach you to use the entire cauliflower head and you will like it (you will also clean my house and do the windows—or is that asking too much?). Normally a humdrum mélange of vegetables, this combination of cauliflower and peas blossoms with the right touch of spices and cilantro, especially when some of the spices in the blend, freshly ground, release intoxicating and perfumed essential oils. The night I tested this recipe, I also served Cardamom Fennel Scallops (page 185) to my family. No leftovers made the evening fruitful.

**Serves 4**

| | |
|---|---|
| 1 medium-size (1½ pounds) cauliflower | ½ teaspoon ground red pepper (cayenne) |
| 2 tablespoons canola oil | ¼ teaspoon ground turmeric |
| 1 tablespoon coriander seeds | 1 cup frozen green peas (no need to thaw) |
| 2 teaspoons cumin seeds | ¼ cup finely chopped fresh cilantro leaves and tender stems |
| 1½ teaspoons coarse kosher or sea salt | |

Rinse the head of cauliflower under cold running water. Let it drip-dry a bit before you cut it. When ready, remove the leaves that cup the cauliflower. Slice them into thin strips and pile them on one side of a large plate. Cut the tougher, stalklike pieces—if any—into thin strips. Heap them on top of the leaves. Cut the cauliflower head in half and cut out the thick rib that runs through the base of each half by making a V-shape cut to dislodge the rib. Slice the rib into thin strips and add them to the pile of stalks and leaves. Cut the cauliflower head into 1-inch florets (if you wish to get technical, if you take a ruler or tape measure, when measured across the top, the florets should be 1 inch across). Group the florets separately from the stalks and leaves.

2 Heat the oil in a large skillet over medium-high heat. Once the oil appears to shimmer, add the pile of stalks and leaves and stir-fry them uncovered until slightly softened, 1 to 2 minutes (this gives them a head start since they take a bit longer to become tender than the florets). Cover the skillet and cook, stirring, occasionally, until the stalks and leaves are still very firm looking but give in slightly when cut with a fork, about 5 minutes more.

3 As the stalks steam, place the coriander and cumin seeds in a spice grinder (you can also use a coffee grinder) and grind the blend to the consistency of finely ground black pepper. Add the salt, cayenne, and turmeric to the ground coriander and cumin, giving you the joy of having just created your own spice blend.

4 Once the stalks are ready, add the florets and the spice blend to the skillet. Cook the medley, uncovered, stirring occasionally, to allow the ground spices to cook gently without burning, 1 to 2 minutes. Add ½ cup of warm water, scraping the bottom of the skillet to release any browned bits of cauliflower and spices, effectively deglazing the skillet to create a depth of flavor in the cauliflower. Reduce the heat to medium-low, cover the skillet to let the cauliflower steam, stirring occasionally, until it is all fork-tender, 12 to 15 minutes.

5 Stir in the peas and cilantro. Cover the skillet again and let the steam thaw and just cook the peas, about 2 minutes.

6 Serve the Cauliflower and Peas warm.

## Extra Credit

If you are out of the whole spices (coriander and cumin) and only have the ground version on hand, use 1½ tablespoons of ground coriander and 1 tablespoon of ground cumin when you make the spice blend for the recipe.

# 12 Curry House Cauliflower

## Aloo Gobhi

VEGAN
GLUTEN FREE

honestly think there is a gnome of Indian descent sitting under a tree stamping out menus that he disperses to anyone who is about to open a north Indian restaurant (a curry house, mate) in the Western Hemisphere. And the menu item that always makes the cut is *aloo gobhi,* florets of cauliflower and chunks of potatoes cloaked in a dark sauce of onion, ginger, garlic, and tomatoes stewed with a host of spices. This version of mine removes all that clutter and maintains the integrity of the flavors of the simple, cruciferous cauliflower and starchy potato with a few simple spices. It makes a great side to Mustard Cannellini Beans (page 209) and a stack of either homemade All-Wheat Griddle Breads (page 84) or store-bought whole-wheat tortillas.

**Serves 4**

I small head (about I pound) cauliflower

2 medium-size russet or Yukon Gold potatoes

2 tablespoons canola oil

I teaspoon black or yellow mustard seeds

2 slices fresh ginger (each about the size of a 25-cent coin; no need to peel the skin), cut into matchstick-thin strips

2 fresh green serrano chiles, stems discarded, cut lengthwise into thin strips (do not remove the seeds)

2 teaspoons ground cumin

I teaspoon coarse kosher or sea salt

½ teaspoon ground turmeric

2 tablespoons finely chopped fresh cilantro leaves and tender stems

Rinse the head of cauliflower under cold running water. Let it drip-dry a bit before you cut it. When ready, remove the leaves that cup the cauliflower. Slice them into thin strips and pile them on one side of a large plate. Cut the tougher, stalklike pieces— if any—into thin strips. Heap them on top of the leaves. Cut the cauliflower in half and cut out the thick rib that runs through the base of each half by making a V-shape cut to dislodge the rib. Slice the rib in thin strips and add them to the pile of stalks and leaves. Cut the cauliflower head into 1-inch florets (if you wish to get technical, if you take a ruler or tape measure, when measured across the top, florets should be 1 inch across). Group the florets separately from the stalks and leaves.

2 Peel the potatoes and cut them into 1-inch cubes. Transfer the cubed potatoes to a bowl large enough to hold them. Add enough cold water to cover the potatoes to prevent them from oxidizing and turning black.

## Extra Credit

The Curry House Cauliflower will keep in the refrigerator for up to 4 days. I don't recommend freezing any leftovers. Potatoes don't do too well when they freeze and thaw. The result is a mealy texture.

3 Heat the oil in a large skillet over medium-high heat. Once the oil appears to shimmer, add the mustard seeds, cover the skillet, and wait until the seeds have stopped popping (not unlike popcorn), about 30 seconds. Immediately add the pile of stalks and leaves along with the ginger and chiles and stir-fry to partially cook them, 3 to 4 minutes.

4 Meanwhile, drain the potatoes and pat them dry with paper towels. Add the potatoes, florets, cumin, salt, and turmeric to the skillet. Continue stir-frying the vegetables to cook the spices, 1 to 3 minutes. Pour in ½ cup of warm water and scrape the bottom of the skillet to release any browned bits of vegetables and spices. The water will start to boil almost instantly, thanks to the heat of the skillet. Reduce the heat to medium-low, cover the skillet and let the vegetables simmer, stirring occasionally, until they are tender when pierced with a fork, 10 to 12 minutes.

5 Serve the vegetable mix sprinkled with the cilantro.

#  Nutty Broccoli with Mustard

abbage and cauliflower, part of the *Brassica* family, are hugely popular all over India year round. But their close sibling, broccoli, was never part of my childhood years and I can't recall ever seeing it in my neighborhood's open-air markets either. In recent years, thanks to India's visibility in the global marketplace, broccoli appears in numerous vendors' gunnysacks. It cooks quickly and its strong flavors hold up well against the spice palate I've created here.

VEGAN
GLUTEN FREE

**Serves 4**

1½ pounds broccoli with stems

2 tablespoons canola oil

I teaspoon black or yellow mustard seeds

2 teaspoons ground coriander

1½ teaspoons coarse kosher or sea salt

I teaspoon ground cumin

½ teaspoon ground red pepper (cayenne)

¼ teaspoon ground turmeric

½ cup almond slivers or slices, ground (see **Extra Credit**)

1 Cut off the broccoli stems and, using a potato peeler, peel off the outer layer as it can be slightly fibrous. Cut the stems into thin slices or strips (the stems are usually tough so thinly slicing them lets them cook faster and more evenly). Cut the head of the broccoli into about 1-inch florets (if you were to measure the floret size, you would measure it across its crowned head). Keep the stems and the florets separate.

2 Heat the oil in a large skillet over medium-high heat. Once the oil appears to shimmer, add the mustard seeds, cover the skillet and cook until the seeds have stopped popping (not unlike popcorn), about 30 seconds. Immediately add the sliced stems to keep the mustard seeds from continuing to cook (and thus burn) at the high heat. Sprinkle in the coriander, salt, cumin, cayenne, and turmeric and stir-fry to toast the spices, about 30 seconds. The aromas emanating from the skillet

# Extra Credit

- Cauliflower and Broccoflower (a cauliflower-broccoli hybrid) are equally good as alternatives to the broccoli. They all cook similarly with respect to time, and the quantity of spices will produce the same balanced flavor. If acid is your thing, squeeze in the juice of a small to medium-size lime just before you serve.

- If the nuts I am grinding are whole, I use a food processor. I like the resulting coarse bread crumb consistency for a textural crunch. For a finer grind, use that spice grinder of yours. It's a great way to clean out your grinder and add more flavor to the recipe. Cashews, peanuts, Brazil nuts, pistachios, hazelnuts, and pecans are equally nutty if you wish

to use what you have on hand and don't want to make that extra trip to the grocery store. Keep whole nuts in the refrigerator (a good place to store them so you keep the rancidity at bay).

- You can turn any leftover nut-coated broccoli to a smooth puree by processing it in a food processor. Drizzle in a tablespoon or more of canola oil or ghee if you wish a richer finish as you process it. Serve the puree with toasted baguette slices or store-bought crostini for an appetizer.

   Another option is to turn the broccoli into patties. If you do, first process it to a chunky crab cake-like texture. Form the broccoli into patties and panfry them in a little oil. Serve the patties with any dipping sauce.

will be complex and layered. Add the florets, stir to coat them with the spices, and cook them for 1 to 2 minutes.

3 Pour in ½ cup of water, which will instantly bubble up. Scrape the bottom of the skillet to release the browned bits of broccoli and spices. Cover the skillet, reduce the heat to medium, and let the broccoli stems and florets simmer, stirring occasionally, until they are fork-tender, about 15 minutes.

4 Stir in the ground almonds, which will absorb any residual liquid, and serve the broccoli warm.

#  Ginger Raisin Bok Choy

Even though bok choy is not a vegetable that is eaten in India (in spite of being part of the popular *Brassica* family with such well-known siblings as cabbage, cauliflower, and broccoli), the spices and combinations here of sweet, tart, and hot ingredients are very reflective of the way northwestern Indians cook. The succulence of just-cooked bok choy appeals to my sensibilities and the day I made this, I served it alongside Creamy Wild Salmon with Kale (page 179) and Blistered Smoky Peppers (page 241). A glass of bubbly sparkling wine and scintillating conversation with my dear friend and colleague, the cookbook author Mary Ellen Evans, made it a sinful, alcohol-kissed lunch on a weekday. The joy of testing recipes!

VEGAN
GLUTEN FREE

**Serves 6**

1 large bunch bok choy (about 1½ pounds)

2 tablespoons canola oil

2 tablespoons finely chopped fresh ginger

¼ cup golden raisins

2 teaspoons Raghavan's Blend (page 39) or store-bought Madras curry powder

1 teaspoon coarse kosher or sea salt

1 can (14.5 ounces) diced tomatoes, drained (I usually save the drained juice and use it for something else)

1 Cut off the bottom bunched end of the bok choy to get rid of the tough base (about ½ inch cut from the bottom should do it). Slice the stalks crosswise into thin slices, making sure you include the bright green tops. Place the sliced bok choy in a colander and rinse it well under cold water. Let it drain as you continue the preparation.

2 Heat the oil in a large skillet over medium-high heat. Once the oil appears to shimmer, add the ginger and raisins. Stir-fry the medley until the ginger becomes fragrant and light brown and the raisins plump up, turning the base of the skillet sugary brown, about 2 minutes.

3 Add the bok choy (you may need to do this in handfuls, stirring a few times in between additions to make sure it wilts a bit and makes room for the remaining bok

choy) and stir-fry for 2 to 3 minutes. Stir in the spice blend and salt. The watery liquid that the bok choy releases will rinse out the skillet, effectively releasing the browned bits of ginger and sugary raisins from the bottom of the skillet.

4 Increase the heat to high and let the bok choy cook, uncovered, stirring occasionally, until the slices are still firm looking and maintain a juicy crisp tenderness, about 5 minutes.

5 Stir in the tomatoes and cook until warmed through, 1 to 2 minutes.

6 Serve the bok choy warm.

## Extra Credit

- Even though I used the variety of bok choy that looks more like a celery bunch, if you find the shorter, leafy bunches of bok choy called baby or Chinese bok choy in your supermarket use them. They may not be as juicy as the larger variety, but are just as flavorful. Spinach, mustard greens, the longer cooking kale, or even collard greens (or a combination of any or all of these) also yield addictive results.

- Because of its juicy personality, I have served this bok choy as an appetizer on garlic-rubbed slices of grilled focaccia and crusty baguette, making for an exciting alternative to the ho-hum tomato bruschetta.

# 15 Spinach with Cranberries

VEGAN
GLUTEN FREE

Perky red among a sea of greens, the cranberries in this dish offer hope and flavor, especially at the Thanksgiving table, when the view outside the window can be dismal, gloomy, and marred by piles of white snow (especially in the tundra of Midwest topography). Embarrassingly simple to make, the key in this recipe is to make sure you stir it constantly, sear and cook the spinach, sealing in that slightly smoky undertone that comes with this style of cooking. Serve it with the Mint-Massaged Leg of Lamb (page 165).

**Serves 4 as a small side**

I tablespoon canola oil

½ cup finely chopped red onion

½ cup dried cranberries

I pound prewashed baby spinach leaves

½ teaspoon garam masala, homemade (page 4I) or store-bought

½ teaspoon coarse kosher or sea salt

1 Heat the oil in a large skillet, sauté pan, or wok over medium-high heat. Once the oil appears to shimmer, add the onion and cranberries and stir-fry until the onion slices are light brown, about 2 minutes.

2 Increase the heat to high and add handfuls of the spinach leaves to the skillet, stirring constantly to make sure the spinach sears and then wilts (as opposed to releasing its internal water so that it wilts and stews). Adding spinach in batches will take 3 to 5 minutes of cooking time.

3 Turn off the heat and stir in the garam masala and salt.

4 Serve the spinach warm.

## Extra Credit

Dried cranberries are sweetened, very much raisin-like, and are common year-round at the grocery store. Raisins (the regular kind and also golden) are a great alternative to cranberries but don't look as pretty (sometimes it's okay to judge someone or something by looks).

# 16 Sweet Corn with Toasted Coconut

### Thénga Makkaí

VEGAN
GLUTEN FREE

Unfortunately the corn in India can be rather resilient in texture, not as sweet and juicy as the ears we find here, especially in my Midwestern backyard. The spices in the blend for this recipe make their presence felt, balancing the corn's sugariness with smoky heat from the dried red chiles and the citruslike fragrance of coriander seeds. This is a perfect consort to the Grilled Baby Back Ribs (page 167) and may very well be the showstopper for late summer grilling parties.

**Makes 4 cups; serves 4 to 6**

I tablespoon coriander seeds

2 to 3 dried red cayenne chiles
  (like chile de árbol), stems discarded

¼ cup dried unsweetened coconut shreds
  (see **Extra Credit**, page I2I)

2 tablespoons canola oil

I teaspoon black or yellow mustard seeds

I small onion, finely chopped

4 cups sweet corn kernels (fresh or frozen;
  see **Extra Credit**)

I medium-size tomato, cored and finely chopped
  (do not remove the seeds)

I teaspoon coarse kosher or sea salt

Heat a large skillet over medium-high heat. Once the skillet is hot (when you hold the palm of your hand close to the bottom of the skillet you will feel the heat), usually after 2 to 4 minutes, add the coriander seeds and chiles. The seeds will start to crackle a bit and turn reddish brown and the chiles will blacken slightly, after 1 to 2 minutes. Quickly add the coconut and keep stirring constantly as the coconut will start to brown and smell nutty almost instantly and impart a slight oily sheen. Transfer the spicy coconut to a small bowl or plate to cool. Keeping the coconut mixture in the skillet will burn the blend, making it unpalatable.

## Extra Credit

Sweet corn on the cob, enrobed in leathery husks with those tufts of corn silk, fills every grocery store bin, roadside farmer's stall, and neighborhood farmers' markets to the brim at the tail end of summer. Bursting with sugary succulence, each golden kernel is easy to separate from the cob.

Once you shuck the cob and get rid of the corn silk (a few golden threads running down the cob are okay) position the ear of corn so that it stands on its head. Hold the corn with one hand and with the other hand slice the kernels off the cob with a sharp knife. The milky liquid that exudes from the cob will add to the sweetness. Depending on the size of the ears of corn, you will need 4 or 5 large ears for this recipe. Frozen sweet corn kernels (no need to thaw) work fine but please refrain from using the canned variety.

2 Pour the oil in the hot skillet. It will instantly appear to shimmer. Add the mustard seeds, cover the skillet, and cook until the seeds have stopped popping (not unlike popcorn), about 30 seconds. Immediately add the onion and stir-fry until light brown, about 2 minutes.

3 Add the corn and ½ cup of water. Stir once or twice and cover the skillet. Reduce the heat to medium and let the corn cook gently, stirring occasionally, until it is still juicy sweet when tasted and not overly cooked, 5 to 7 minutes.

4 Meanwhile, transfer the cool, red, spiced coconut to a spice grinder (you can also use a coffee grinder) and grind it to the consistency of slightly coarse black pepper.

5 Add the ground coconut spice blend to the corn along with the tomato and salt. Let it all simmer, uncovered, stirring occasionally, until the tomato is warmed through, about 1 minute.

6 Serve the corn warm.

# 17 Saucy Green Beans

### Chaulee Ki Subzi

**VEGAN
GLUTEN FREE**

Savory Indian cuisine is all about balance, and these boisterous green beans do a good job of helping you understand what that means. I have you cut the beans and chiles in equal pieces because I want you to get a jolt of heat when you think all's well in mellowville. Mean? Well, before you make that judgment, the acidity of the tomatoes will come to your rescue along with the texture and juicy sweetness of green beans. These beans go really well with Buttermilk Fried Chicken (page 172).

**Serves 4**

I pound fresh green beans

2 tablespoons canola oil

I teaspoon black or yellow mustard seeds

I small red onion, cut in half lengthwise and thinly sliced

2 fresh green serrano chiles, stems discarded, cut lengthwise in half, each half sliced diagonally into ½-inch pieces (do not remove the seeds)

2 teaspoons ground cumin

I teaspoon ground mustard

¼ teaspoon ground turmeric

I cup canned diced tomatoes with their juices

1½ teaspoons coarse kosher or sea salt

1 Snap off and discard the stem end of each green bean, and string the beans if necessary by removing the thin strand of threadlike filament that peels off the side of the beans when you snap the stem end. Cut the beans diagonally into ½-inch pieces, place them in a colander, and rinse them well under cold running water.

2 Heat the oil in a large skillet over medium-high heat. Once the oil appears to shimmer, add the mustard seeds, cover the skillet, and cook until the seeds have

stopped popping (not unlike popcorn), about 30 seconds. Immediately add the onion, chiles, cumin, ground mustard, and turmeric. Stir-fry until the spices are fragrant, about 1 minute.

3 Add the green beans, tomatoes, salt and ½ cup water and scrape the bottom of the skillet to loosen the browned bits of spices and onion. Reduce the heat to medium-low, cover the skillet, and let the beans cook, stirring occasionally, until they are fork-tender, 10 to 12 minutes.

4 Serve the green beans warm.

## Extra Credit

During the warm summer months, when my otherwise frozen state of Minnesota defrosts, I throw together a combination of bright green and yellow wax beans that I've purchased at the farmers' market for a quick weekday side dish. Make sure the green beans you buy are of top-notch quality. When bent, they should snap with a slight crisp sound. If they are limp, don't waste your money on them—they may have a fibrous texture when cooked, which will make the experience unremarkable.

If you can't find really good fresh beans, you are better off using a bag of frozen green beans. And no to your unspoken question of "Can I use canned beans?"

# 18 Mustard Rice with Peppers

Rai Pulao

Seasoned rice dishes in India are called *pulaos* (pilafs here in the Western world) and to get that single-grain appearance, plump and inviting, we invoke the queen of the rice world—basmati (the perfumed one), grown in the foothills of the Himalayan mountains. Even though the obvious way to serve this is as a side to a main course (vegetarian or otherwise), have a bowlful or two for lunch with a side of salad.

LACTO-VEGETARIAN (VEGAN IF YOU USE OIL) GLUTEN FREE

**Makes 3 cups (serves 6 as a side)**

· · · · · · · · · · · · · · · · · · · · · · · · · · · · · · · · · · · ·

I cup white Indian or Pakistani basmati rice or
   long-grain white rice

2 tablespoons ghee, homemade (page 3I) or
   store-bought, or canola oil

I teaspoon black or yellow mustard seeds

2 to 3 dried red cayenne chiles
   (like chile de árbol), stems discarded

I small red onion, finely chopped

I medium-size green or red bell pepper, stem,
   core, ribs, and seeds discarded, flesh finely
   chopped

I teaspoon coarse kosher or sea salt

Place the rice in a medium-size bowl. Fill
the bowl with enough water to cover the
rice. Gently rub the slender grains between
the fingers of one hand, without breaking
them, to wash off any dust or light foreign objects (like loose husks), which will
float to the surface (see page 27 for a photo
illustrating this technique). The water will
become cloudy. Drain this water. You don't
need a colander for this; I just tip the bowl
over the sink to pour off the water, making sure the rice stays in the bowl. Repeat
this 3 or 4 times until after you rinse the
grains the water remains relatively clear.
Now fill the bowl halfway with cold water
and let the rice sit at room temperature
until the kernels soften, 20 to 30 minutes,
then drain the rice.

2 Heat the ghee in a medium-size saucepan over medium-high heat. Once the
ghee appears to shimmer, add the mustard seeds, cover the pan, and wait until
the seeds have stopped popping (not unlike
popcorn), about 30 seconds. Add the chiles,
stir them a few times, and watch them
blacken relatively quickly; they will smell
smoky and pungent, about 30 seconds. Add
the onion and bell pepper and stir-fry until
the onion is lightly brown around the edges

## Extra Credit

• Your healthy mind might coax you to make this pilaf with brown rice or another whole grain. Should you choose to, because they are quite textured in nature, you'll find that the more you chew, the more saliva you generate and that dilutes the flavor of the spices and other ingredients. Up the amounts of spice and salt by about 50 percent to compensate for that increase in texture.

• This rice reheats really well in the microwave. Just place it in a covered dish and reheat on high 2 to 3 minutes. You can freeze the rice for up to a month and frozen rice can also be resteamed in the microwave until warm.

and the pepper pieces appear limp, 5 to 7 minutes.

3 Add the drained rice to the mustard-speckled onion-pepper mélange, tossing them gently to coat the rice. Add 1½ cups of cold water and the salt. Stir the rice once or twice to incorporate the ingredients. Bring the water to a boil, uncovered, still over medium-high heat and let boil until the water has evaporated from the surface and craters are starting to appear in the rice, 5 to 8 minutes. Now (and not until now) stir once or twice to bring the partially cooked layer of rice from the bottom of the pan to the surface. Cover the pan with a tight-fitting lid and reduce the heat to the lowest possible setting. Let the rice steep for 8 to 10 minutes (8 if you are using an electric burner, 10 for a gas burner). Then turn off the heat and let the pan stand on that burner, undisturbed, for 10 minutes.

4 Uncover the pan, fluff the rice with a fork (don't remove the chiles), and serve. The chiles can be eaten or set aside, if you'd rather keep things on the milder side.

# 19 Savory Cream of Wheat

## Uppama

A breakfast food the world over, in North America, Cream of Wheat swirls in creamy mouthfuls with sugar and milk, nudging you with a comforting wake-up call. But in southern India it gently slaps you awake with chiles, onion, and vegetables. My childhood favorite, I still make it every few weeks on a Sunday morning, after downing three cups of coffee and *The New York Times*. I vary the vegetables according to what's on hand or what summer bounty sprouts from my backyard's raised vegetable bed. At dinnertime, it makes a great side to serve with a fish or chicken dish. The next time I will try it with a mimosa, all in the name of research.

**Serves 4**

. . . . . . . . . . . . . . . . . . . . . . . . . . . . . . . . . . . . . . . . . . . . . . .

2 tablespoons canola oil

1 teaspoon black or yellow mustard seeds

¼ cup unroasted and unsalted cashews

1 cup finely chopped red onion

2 medium-size carrots, peeled and finely chopped

2 fresh green serrano chiles, stems discarded, finely chopped (do not remove the seeds)

8 ounces prewashed baby spinach leaves

1 cup Cream of Wheat (not quick cooking)

1½ teaspoons coarse kosher or sea salt

1 Heat the oil in a Dutch oven or a medium-size saucepan over medium-high heat. Once the oil appears to shimmer, add the mustard seeds, cover the pan, and cook until the seeds have stopped popping (not unlike popcorn), about 30 seconds. Immediately add the cashews and pan roast, stirring very often, until they are light brown and smell nutty, 1 to 2 minutes.

2 Add the onion, carrots, and chiles and stir-fry until the carrots give in easily

when you bite into a piece, 3 to 5 minutes. Take handfuls of the spinach and add them to the pan one batch at a time, stirring each handful for a few seconds to wilt it before adding the next, 1 to 2 minutes total.

3 Sprinkle the Cream of Wheat over the spinach, spreading it evenly so as not to let it clump in mounds and stirring as you sprinkle to prevent lumps. Continue to cook the Cream of Wheat, stirring occasionally, until it smells fragrant, 1 to 2 minutes.

4 Pour in 4 cups of water and sprinkle in the salt. Stir well to make sure everything gets well combined. Let the liquid come to a rolling boil, then reduce the heat to medium-low and cover the pan. Let steep, without stirring, until the creamy wheat appears porridge-like and the vegetables are tender, about 20 minutes.

5 Stir the porridge once or twice to release the trapped steam and serve warm.

## Extra Credit

The resemblance here to the Italian polenta is uncanny and if you have any of this left over, press ¼ cup of the cold porridge into a mold (like a ramekin, perhaps) then turn it out onto a plate. Spray a nonstick skillet or a griddle with nonfat cooking spray and cook, turning once, until crisp on the outside and warm on the inside, 5 to 8 minutes. Serve it with your favorite tomato-based sauce or even as is with a dipping chutney for a great starter.

# Orzo with Chile-Spiked Eggplant

**20**

The texture and look of orzo, known as barley rice in Italy (because the pasta was made from barley), is a perfect foil, creamy and nutty, for this pleasantly hot eggplant curry. Curries in India are always ladled over rice and this combination works just as well. Some of the other pasta shapes may not work, and don't try whole grain pastas either. The texture of whole grain pasta creates a chewier experience, which dilutes the curry's spices.

**Serves 4**

2 pounds eggplant

I medium-size red onion, coarsely chopped

6 medium-size cloves garlic

4 pieces fresh ginger (each about the size and thickness of a 25-cent coin; no need to peel the skin)

3 fresh green serrano chiles, stems discarded

2 tablespoons canola oil

I tablespoon Raghavan's Blend (page 39) or store-bought Madras curry powder

I can (14.5 ounces) diced tomatoes with their juices

1½ teaspoons coarse kosher or sea salt plus extra for salting the orzo water (optional)

½ pound orzo pasta

1 Cut the stem ends off the eggplants, slicing about ¼ inch below the stem. Discard the stems. Stand the eggplants on their sliced end and cut them lengthwise into long planks about ¼ inch thick. Stack two or three planks and cut them into ¼-inch-wide strips. Holding the strips in place, turn them 90 degrees and cut them into ¼-inch-wide pieces to end up with cubes that are ¼ inch in size. Transfer the cubes to a bowl large enough to hold them.

2 Place the onion, garlic, ginger, and chiles in a food processor. Using the pulsing action, mince the pungent medley, making sure not to let the processor run constantly or you will end up with a watery mess.

3 Heat the oil in a Dutch oven or large saucepan (one that will accommodate all that eggplant) over medium-high heat. Once the oil appears to shimmer, add the spicy minced onion and stir-fry until the chiles smell pungent and some of the minced onion is light brown, 6 to 8 minutes.

4 Stir in Raghavan's Blend; the heat will be just right to cook the ground spices without burning them in 15 to 30 seconds.

## Extra Credit

- For a heartier curry in the peak of winter use a combination of root vegetables and kale (of the same poundage) instead of or in addition to the eggplant. If you are using root vegetables and kale instead of eggplant, sprinkle on another teaspoon of the spice blend in Step 4 to compensate for the assertive tubers and for the water (about I cup) you may need to add in Step 5 to provide more moisture to render them fork-tender.

- If you are adding 2 pounds of root vegetables and kale to the 2 pounds of eggplant, double all the other ingredients and be prepared to add some water to the pot in Step 5.

- Yes, you can obviously use steamed white rice instead of the pasta.

- For a burst of protein, serve the orzo with a liberal sprinkling of freshly shredded Parmigiano-Reggiano cheese.

5 Add the eggplant cubes and the tomatoes with their juices and the 1½ teaspoons salt, giving them a good stir. Cover the pan and stew, stirring occasionally. Once the eggplant releases some of its water and the juices from the tomato pool at the base, scrape the bottom of the pan to loosen the browned bits and cook, covered, stirring occasionally, until the eggplant is tender, 10 to 12 minutes.

6 As the eggplant simmers, fill a large saucepan three quarters full with water and bring it to a rolling boil over medium-high heat. Salt the water if you wish and scatter in the orzo, stirring it to make sure the pasta doesn't stick together. Let the orzo simmer briskly, uncovered, stirring occasionally, until it is tender but still firm (al dente), 8 to 10 minutes.

7 The eggplant should be ready by now. Drain the orzo in a colander and give it a good shake to get rid of some of the excess water. Spread the orzo out on a platter and spoon the eggplant curry over it.

8 Serve the eggplant orzo curry while still hot.

# Chapter 9

# Sweet Endings and Thirst Quenchers Unfolded

**I AM THE** first to admit I am not a very sweet person. What I meant to say was I am very nice but don't have a sweet tooth. If I have the choice between a third helping of something savory and a dessert, I'm likely to skip the sweets. Except when it comes to chocolate! Most of the desserts in India are milk-based, relying on a ton of sugar and often one or two spices, namely cardamom and saffron. They are perfectly delicious and do take care of the old Indian grandma's adage "Eat lots of sweets in the hope of saying sweet things." My desire in offering the recipes here is a reflection of my having lived in two countries for major portions of my life. The main criterion was that they needed to have classic Indian flavors with a more Western je ne sais quoi. My American half now understands that term to mean quick and easy. (That's not the literal translation, just so you know that I know!)

. . . . . . . . . . . . . . . . . . . . . . . . . . . . . . . . . .

# The Lesson Plan

**Lesson ① Funnel Cakes in Saffron Syrup**
Known as *jalebis* in India, these crispy coiled cakes may very well remind you of a summer outing to a local state or street fair. Most often they are coated in a honeyed syrup, but in northern India, it is a classic street food that is dipped in a sweet-tart syrup incorporating two of the world's most expensive spices: saffron and cardamom. Easy to master, once you get the hang of shaping the coils, funnel cakes are a perfect sweet finish to a classic Indian meal.

**Lesson ② Yogurt "Cheesecake" with Nutmeg** The fact that you can create a cheesecakelike consistency and mouthfeel with no eggs or cream cheese and only four ingredients (including nutmeg and cardamom) is reason enough for you to start your dessert class with the yogurt "cheesecake." Based on a classic baked yogurt dish from Calcutta, you will find

yourself making this for family and friends time and again.

**Lesson ③ Creamy Rice Pudding** The next in the lineup unravels a classic wedding dessert from southern India. This rice pudding has just three ingredients and the technique of condensing whole milk and then incorporating store-bought sweetened condensed milk to sugarcoat the rice is nothing short of brilliant.

**Lesson ④ Cranberry Mango Compote**
Spicing mango and cranberries with savory ingredients like mustard and red chiles is based on a pineapple condiment from the northeastern state of Assam, which is in close proximity to the Himalayan mountains. An unusual attention grabber, the compote is an addictive winner served warm over vanilla ice cream.

**Lesson ⑤ Cashew Pistachio Bars** These bars are a classic dessert, originating in the northeastern parts of India. The key flavoring in these bars relies on the queen of dessert spice—green cardamom—as well as the world's most expensive spice—saffron. If you're going all out, this is the dessert to make. Painlessly simple but addictive.

**Lessons ⑥ and ⑦ Mango Bread Pudding with Chai Spices and Crème Anglaise** This bread pudding combines mangoes with a medley of spices that are typical of *masala chai* in northwestern India: black peppercorns, cloves, cardamom, and cinnamon (what's not to love?). Freshly ground is the way to go and you will agree with me once you take your first spoonful. The bread pudding is a great dessert to prepare on a cold evening, and if you are entertaining, this can be baked ahead (even up to a day or two) and reheated (covered in a preheated 300°F oven for about 15 minutes).

**Lessons ⑧ and ⑨ Chocolate Chile Brownies and Bombay Biscotti** Chocolate creeps in to cloak brownies and biscotti with its deep darkness. When I was growing up in India, the chocolate of choice was always Cadbury's, and should you wish to pay homage, then look for these bars in your neighborhood stores. The decadent brownie swirls in pungent chiles for that distinctively Indian desire for heat, providing the right balance for these dense, rich bars. For Bombay Biscotti, I strongly recommend Cadbury's Fruit and Nut bars. The almond extract in the dough brings out the chocolaty goodness in each cookie, making it the ideal accompaniment to your afternoon chai.

**Lesson ⑩ Saffron-Pistachio Ice Cream Bars** Ice creams are huge in the Indian culture; families often walk after a heavy meal to the nearest ice cream parlor to imbibe cool comfort in the suffocating heat. Saffron-pistachio ice cream bars are a classic, based on India's well-known ice cream *kulfi*.

**Lessons ⑪ and ⑫ Mango Yogurt Shakes and Ginger Cardamom Tea** Beverages are a must as part of a meal. However, contrary to popular belief lassi—those frothy yogurt shakes with pureed ice and fruit—are never consumed with the meal, always after! Even though peasant lassis are always plain, and either sweet or salty, this mango version of mine is a favorite in restaurants all over the world. Chai, too, is never served with the meal. A spiced milky tea that has gained popularity in the U.S., in India no gathering—whether of two or two hundred people—goes without an offering of chai.

**Lesson ⑬ The Slumdog Martini** And the Bette Davis in all of us should scream elegance as we lift up our martini glasses, pinky finger pointing toward the sky, and sip mint-muddled martinis. How adult is that?

parchment paper. As the funnel cakes will sit on the rack and drip the excess syrup onto the sheet below, it makes for an easy cleanup.

4 To fry the funnel cakes, pour oil to a depth of about 2 inches into a medium-size sauté pan. Heat the oil over medium-high heat until a deep-fry thermometer inserted into the oil (without touching the bottom of the pan) registers close to 275°F.

5 When you are about to fry the cakes, turn the heat back on under the syrup to the lowest setting to keep the syrup warm. Pour the batter into a squirt bottle (like those diner ketchup bottles), and squeeze out the batter directly into the hot oil, making concentric circles until they are about 2 inches in diameter. Quickly squeeze out 3 more funnel cakes into the oil. Fry them, turning each occasionally, until they are golden brown and crisp,

5 to 7 minutes. Using a slotted spoon, transfer the cakes from the hot oil to the saffron syrup. Completely coat each cake with the syrup, then transfer it from the syrup to the rack. Repeat with the remaining batter.

6 I usually serve the funnel cakes warm alongside a bowl of cold ice cream to highlight a pleasing temperature difference.

I  Place the yeast in a bowl and add a tablespoon of warm water..

2  Whisk the yeast and water to combine, making sure the yeast is completely dissolved.

3  Add the all-purpose and chickpea flours to the dissolved yeast.

4  Pour in ½ cup water over the flours.

VEGAN

# Funnel Cakes in Saffron Syrup

### Jalebis

Vendors hunched over a gargantuan wok filled with hot oil are a common sight, especially on the streets in northern India. They pipe oodles of these funnel cakes, called *jalebis,* with impressive dexterity, flipping them in one melodious motion from the oil to the syrup and then stacking them on platters. Those juicy, crunchy cakes beckon passersby as they go about their business, and they are usually hard-pressed to resist that temptation. Sweet, crunchy, and aromatic funnel cakes are one of my favorite ways to end a meal, and they always leave me feeling guilty because I cannot stop at one. I think your guests will be very happy you served them—with coffee or tea, of course—as the ending to your gatefold meal.

**Makes 8 to 10 funnel cakes; serves 4**

FOR THE FUNNEL CAKES

½ teaspoon active dry yeast (from ¼-ounce package)

½ cup unbleached all-purpose flour

I teaspoon chickpea flour (see Extra Credit, page 91)

½ teaspoon unrefined sugar

½ teaspoon canola oil

FOR THE SAFFRON SYRUP

I cup unrefined sugar

I tablespoon freshly squeezed lime or lemon juice

4 to 6 green or white cardamom pods

½ teaspoon saffron threads (see page 18)

Canola oil for deep-frying

Ice cream (optional), for serving

YOU'LL ALSO NEED

Squirt bottle

1 Get the batter for the funnel cakes ready: Sprinkle the yeast into a medium-size bowl and pour in about 1 tablespoon warm tap water. Mix the two well (or as we Indians might say, do it "nicely yaar") to make sure the yeast dissolves. Stir in the all-purpose and chickpea flours, the ½ teaspoon of sugar and the ½ teaspoon oil. Whisk in ½ cup of water, beating it to create a smooth, lump-free batter. Let the batter sit for 1 to 2 hours in a warm spot.

It will bubble and get lighter in color. This will help make the funnel cake light and crispy.

2 While the batter rests, make the saffron syrup: Place the 1 cup of sugar and the lime or lemon juice, cardamom, saffron, and ½ cup of water in a small saucepan and stir to mix. Heat, uncovered, over medium heat. Once the mixture comes to a boil, let it boil, uncovered, until it reaches a

single-thread consistency (if you scoop a bit of the syrup into a spoon, dip your forefinger in it, and then touch your thumb and forefinger together and separate them. When ready, that drop of syrup should connect your thumb and finger very briefly by a sugary thread), about 5 minutes. Turn off the heat.

3 Place a cake rack on a baking sheet. I usually line the baking sheet with

5  Whisk the batter well to make sure you have no lumps. Set it aside to rest for an hour or two.

6  Bring the ingredients for the sugar syrup to a boil.

7  Continue to boil the syrup until it reaches a single-thread consistency. If you have a candy thermometer, use it to confirm the consistency.

8  Squeeze the batter directly into the hot oil to make 2-inch concentric circles.

9  Remove the fried funnel cakes from the oil and coat them in the sugar syrup. Allow them to rest on a rack set on a baking sheet.

## Extra Credit

These cakes are really simple to form once you get the hang of making those coil-like concentric circles. Don't be heartbroken if they are not perfect because they will still taste incredible. The beauty of these funnel cakes is their ability to last in the refrigerator, stored in an airtight container, for up to two weeks. Rewarm them in a microwave for barely a minute before you eat them. These do not freeze well at all.

# Yogurt "Cheesecake" with Nutmeg

## Bhapa Doi

LACTO-VEGETARIAN
GLUTEN FREE

**M**any moons ago when I was visiting Calcutta in eastern India, home to India's confections, at a well-known sweetshop, I happened to stick a spoon in a small clay pot filled with something creamy. Called *bhapa doi,* it was love at first bite. Decadent, velvet smooth, devoid of any spice, it appeased my cheesecake urges instantly. Imagine my surprise when I found out there was neither eggs nor cream cheese in it, just sweetened house-made condensed milk and plain yogurt baked until set. So here's my rendition, equally simple, made with store-bought condensed milk and two over-the-counter (no prescription needed) spices—cardamom and nutmeg.

**Makes 6 individual "cheesecakes"**

2 cups Greek-style plain yogurt

I cup sweetened condensed milk

½ teaspoon ground cardamom (see Extra Credit, page 43)

Freshly grated nutmeg (see Extra Credit), for sprinkling

Seasonal fresh fruit (cut up into bite-size pieces) for topping the "cheesecakes"

YOU'LL ALSO NEED

6 small ramekins or heatproof bowls, each about 3½ inches in diameter and 2 inches deep

1 Position an oven rack in the middle of the oven and preheat it to 350°F.

2 Place the yogurt, condensed milk, and cardamom in a medium-size bowl and whisk to mix. Spoon the yogurt mixture into the ramekins, dividing it evenly among them and making sure you fill them at least halfway. You will probably have enough to fill the ramekins three quarters full. Sprinkle a light dusting of nutmeg over each serving.

3 Place the ramekins in a rectangular baking dish (like a cake pan) large enough to contain them without overcrowding. Pour enough hot water into the baking dish to come about halfway up the sides of the ramekins, creating a water bath to keep the yogurt moist while baking.

4 Place the baking dish with the ramekins in the oven and bake the "cheesecakes" in the water bath, uncovered, until a knife inserted in the center comes out clean, about 25 minutes.

5 Remove the baking dish from the oven, then remove the ramekins from the baking dish. Let the "cheesecakes" cool at room temperature, then refrigerate them for at least 2 hours or even overnight.

6 Serve the "cheesecakes" topped with the cut-up fresh fruit.

## Extra Credit

Nutmeg graters are available in any kitchenware store. You can also use a box grater or a Microplane that has really small holes to grate the whole nutmeg.

# 3 Creamy Rice Pudding

### Pal Paysam

You may glance at the ingredient list and question the choice of flavors in this obviously nothing-to-it dessert. Haven't you heard it's not the quantity that matters but the quality? Here, it's also the technique that delivers a Brazilian *dulce-de-leche* complexity by creating homemade condensed milk from whole milk. Simple as that may be, the result is nothing short of spectacular. No wonder this version is the main attraction at south Indian weddings, family gatherings, and any special occasion.

LACTO-VEGETARIAN
GLUTEN FREE

**Serves 6**

½ gallon whole milk

½ cup uncooked Indian or Pakistani white basmati rice or long-grain rice

I can (14 ounces) sweetened condensed milk

1 Place the whole milk and rice in a Dutch oven or large saucepan and bring it to a boil, uncovered, over medium-high heat, stirring very frequently. Once the milk starts to boil you may need to reduce the heat a bit but make sure to keep the milk at a vigorous boil (no need to stir so frequently now since the chances of scorching are much lower). Occasionally scrape the side of the pan to release any bits of cream and milk solids that have collected there; when they fall back into the milk they will provide texture and color.

2 Continue to cook the milk and rice, uncovered, stirring occasionally, until the combination reduces to about 5 cups and the rice thickens the pudding slightly with its starchy presence, 30 to 35 minutes.

3 Pour in the condensed milk and let the mixture continue to simmer, uncovered, stirring occasionally, until the pudding is the consistency of watered-down porridge, light brown in color, and swollen with cooked rice, about 15 minutes.

4 Ladle the pudding into bowls or mugs and serve warm (during winter) or chilled (during the dog days).

## Extra Credit

- You may wish to serve the rice pudding alongside a bowl of fresh seasonal fruit.

- Some versions of the pudding (especially in the north of India) include ½ cup more rice, thickening the milk substantially.

- If you wish, flavor the pudding with ½ teaspoon fresh ground cardamom, ½ cup ghee-sautéed golden raisins, ½ cup cashews, and ½ cup pistachios.

- You may think of using low-fat milk in the pudding, but I don't think the flavors are as good. I find those versions not as succulent, and when I did test the pudding with low-fat milk, I found myself serving it with a scoop of premium vanilla ice cream. So much for good intentions!

#  Cranberry Mango Compote

T his simple fruit stew packs an unexpected punch thanks to the blackened red chiles. Often served with fish in the northeastern communities in India, I serve the compote warm over a bowl of premium vanilla ice cream for a conversation-stopping experience. It is surprising—even to me—how much heat the chiles provide, so the chilling comfort of ice cream is welcoming.

VEGAN
GLUTEN FREE

**Makes 2 cups (serves 4 over ice cream)**

I tablespoon canola oil

I teaspoon black or yellow mustard seeds

2 to 3 dried red cayenne chiles
   (like chile de árbol), stems discarded

I cup fresh or frozen cranberries
   (no need to thaw)

I cup fresh mango cubes (about ¼-inch cubes;
   see Extra Credit, page 299)

½ cup golden raisins

¼ cup firmly packed dark brown sugar

½ teaspoon freshly grated nutmeg
   (see Extra Credit, page 249)

8 scoops (¼ cup each) premium vanilla
   ice cream

1 Heat the oil in a small saucepan over medium-high heat. Once the oil appears to shimmer, add the mustard seeds, cover the pan, and wait until the seeds have stopped popping (not unlike popcorn), about 30 seconds. Stir in the chiles and let them blacken and smell smoky, about 30 seconds. Make sure you have adequate ventilation as the fumes from the capsaicin within the chiles will send you into a coughing fit. It's good for your lungs!

2 Add the cranberries, mango, and raisins. Reduce the heat to medium and cook, uncovered, stirring occasionally, until the raisins are plump, 3 to 5 minutes.

3 Sprinkle in the brown sugar and nutmeg and cook, uncovered, stirring occasionally, until the sugar melts, 2 to 4 minutes. Stir in ½ cup water and let simmer, uncovered, stirring occasionally, until the sauce turns syrupy thick, 15 to 20 minutes. Serve

the compote warm over scoops of ice cream. The compote can be kept in the refrigerator, covered, for 2 to 3 weeks. I don't recommend freezing it as the texture of the fruits becomes mealy and unpleasant.

# 5 Cashew Pistachio Bars

## Kaaju Pista Burfi

LACTO-VEGETARIAN
(VEGAN IF YOU USE
VEGAN BUTTER)
GLUTEN FREE

Diamond-shaped bars of off-white, ground cashew nuts, speckled with cardamon and veiled with a wisp-thin veneer of beaten silver, are a common sight in confectioners' display windows all across India. My childhood favorite, these bars are something I still bring back with me on frequent visits to my birth land. My version is an adaptation of a recipe from my friends Jai and Bee, who blog (extremely well, I might add) at jugalbandi.info. It combines two prized nuts—cashews and pistachios—and flavors them with menthol-like cardamom and the diva among spices, saffron. It's great having these bars around, especially with a cup of afternoon chai on a cold winter's afternoon.

**Makes 20 bars (each about 1½ inches square)**

Ghee, homemade (page 31) or store-bought or unsalted butter, for greasing the pan

I cup raw (unroasted) unsalted cashew nuts

I cup raw (unroasted) unsalted shelled pistachio nuts

¼ teaspoon cardamom seeds (removed from the green or white cardamom pods)

½ cup unrefined sugar

¼ teaspoon saffron threads (see page 18)

1 Prepare an 8- or 9-inch square pan by greasing the bottom with ghee or butter. Set the pan aside.

2 Place ½ cup each of the cashew and pistachio nuts in a blender. Using the pulsing action, grind the nuts to the consistency of fine bread crumbs. Letting the blender run consistently instead of using quick pulses will create a wet mass, akin to nut butter (think peanut butter). I often have to scrape down the inside of the blender to make sure everything gets evenly ground. Tap the ground nuts out into a medium-size bowl. Repeat with the remaining ½ cup each of cashew and pistachio nuts, but this time add the cardamom seeds. Add the second batch of ground nuts to the first, making sure you give it all a good mix.

3 Place the sugar, saffron, and ¼ cup of water in a small saucepan and heat, uncovered, over medium heat. Once the mixture comes to a boil, let it boil, uncovered, until it reaches a single-thread consistency (if you scoop a bit of the syrup into a spoon, dip your forefinger in it, and then touch your thumb and forefinger together and separate them, when ready that drop of syrup should connect your thumb and finger very briefly by a sugary thread), about 5 minutes. Turn off the heat.

4 Take a handful of the cardamom-scented nuts and sprinkle it into the sugar syrup, quickly stirring it in to make sure there are no lumps. Vigorously stir in the remaining nuts (you will notice it getting harder to do this as the mixture starts to cool a bit).

5 Quickly scrape the fudgelike batter into the prepared pan, spreading it out to the edges (it will be about ½ inch thick). Let the nut batter cool for about 15 minutes.

6 Cut it into 1½-inch squares. The bars can be stored in a container with a tight-fitting lid in the refrigerator for up to 2 weeks.

## Extra Credit

- I personally prefer if these bars aren't overly sweet. Some of them tend to be on the sweeter side in India; if you wish, double the amount of sugar and water in the recipe while everything else remains the same.

- These bars are incredibly rich tasting, even if they are not swimming in clarified butter. I usually can nibble on one piece and that's plenty for my not-so-sweet tooth.

# Mango Bread Pudding with Chai Spices and Crème Anglaise

LACTO-OVO VEGETARIAN

There is nothing as comforting as a bowl brimming with warm bread pudding. Add mangoes and spices inspired by the world's love affair with Indian chai (tea), and you will make every excuse in the book to indulge in this soothing treat. Even though it makes a stunning meal-ender, I didn't say you couldn't eat it for breakfast too.

**Serves 8**

Nonfat cooking spray

4 cups stale (but not dry) ½-inch cubes white bread (preferably a day-old crusty French baguette)

2 large ripe mangoes, peeled, and cut into ½-inch cubes (about 4 cups; see Extra Credit, page 299)

½ teaspoon black peppercorns

½ teaspoon whole cloves

½ teaspoon cardamom seeds (removed from the green or white cardamom pods)

I piece (½ inch) cinnamon stick, broken into smaller pieces (see Extra Credit, page 125)

2 cups whole milk

2 large egg whites, slightly beaten, or ½ cup egg substitute (like Egg Beaters)

½ cup tightly packed dark brown sugar

I teaspoon pure vanilla extract

Crème Anglaise, for serving (optional; recipe follows)

1 Position a rack in the center of the oven and preheat the oven to 350°F. Lightly spray a 9-inch-square baking dish with cooking spray.

2 Pile the bread cubes and mango cubes into the prepared baking dish, distributing them evenly.

## Extra Credit

I am a sucker for sousing puddings with alcoholic sauces. Your local liquor store will carry mango-flavored rums. Whip up a crème anglaise and fortify it with I tablespoon mango rum instead of the vanilla.

Pour a liberal amount of the sauce over each serving of the pudding and sprinkle a bit of coarsely ground black peppercorns on top. Trust me, you will have a second helping.

4 Place the milk, egg whites, brown sugar, vanilla, and the freshly ground spices in a medium-size bowl and whisk to mix. Pour the spiced milk over the bread and mangoes, making sure they get completely drenched. Allow the bread cubes to rest as they soak up the liquid, about 5 minutes.

5 Bake the bread pudding, uncovered, until the pudding appears to have set and a knife inserted in its center comes out clean, about 1 hour and 15 minutes.

6 Slice the pudding into serving pieces and serve it warm topped with spoonfuls of crème anglaise, if using, for optimum flavors.

3 Place the peppercorns, cloves, cardamom seeds, and cinnamon stick in a spice grinder (you can also use a coffee grinder) and grind them to the consistency of finely ground black pepper.

## Crème Anglaise

An elegantly rich sauce, crème anglaise makes a standout topping for puddings and fruit desserts. Clearly it is a non-Indian, spice-free concoction, but don't let that stop you from adding it to your dessert repertoire. Or see Extra Credit for how to spice it up.

**Makes about 3 cups**

I cup whole milk

I cup heavy (whipping) cream

½ teaspoon pure vanilla extract

6 large egg yolks

6 tablespoons sugar

1 Pour the milk and cream into a medium-size saucepan and bring them to a boil over medium heat. Once boiling, reduce the heat to low and stir in the vanilla.

2 Whisk the egg yolks and sugar together in a large bowl until light yellowy in color and well blended, about 2 minutes.

3 Slowly pour the hot milk and cream mélange into the sugared yolks, whisking vigorously as you pour. Once all is well blended, transfer the custard mixture to the saucepan and cook, stirring it occasionally with a wooden spoon until the custard nicely coats that spoon, about 5 minutes. For a smooth custard, strain it before putting it in the refrigerator. It is best served chilled.

# 8 Chocolate Chile Brownies

My dear friend and colleague Mary Ellen Evans is an amazing teacher, cookbook author, and above all a sweet soul. She was the first one who gave me a break in my teaching career, inviting me to teach at a well-known cooking school she ran for ten years. Her well-rounded career has spanned all courses; her desserts are exceptional. I particularly have a soft spot for her chocolate creations. If you think chocolate is not Indian, you may wish to spend a little time in India and see the influence of Cadbury all across the subcontinent. Mary's killer brownies pack an extra punch with my chiles, and feel free to serve them with a dollop of premium vanilla ice cream.

LACTO-OVO VEGETARIAN

**Makes a 13- by 9-inch pan of brownies**

8 ounces bittersweet chocolate

4 ounces unsweetened chocolate

I cup (2 sticks) unsalted butter, at room temperature, plus butter for greasing the baking pan

3 to 4 fresh green serrano chiles, stems discarded, finely chopped (do not remove the seeds)

4 large eggs, at room temperature

I cup firmly packed dark brown sugar

I cup granulated sugar

1½ teaspoons pure vanilla extract

1⅓ cups unbleached all-purpose flour

½ teaspoon coarse kosher or sea salt

## Extra Credit

If you wish a more distinct Indian flair, stir ½ teaspoon of ground cardamom into the batter before you bake it.

1 Place a rack in the center of the oven and preheat it to 350°F. Lightly grease the bottom of a 13- by 9-inch baking dish. Set the baking dish aside.

2 Divide the bittersweet chocolate into two piles; one pile should weigh 6 ounces, the second pile 2 ounces. Chop the 6 ounces of bittersweet chocolate into coarse chunks; set them aside in a small bowl. Coarsely chop the 2-ounce pile of bittersweet chocolate and the unsweetened chocolate into smaller pieces and transfer them to a microwave-safe bowl.

3 Cut the butter into slices (these do not have to be perfect since the butter is soft and not easy to handle) and add it to the bowl with the mixed chocolates along with the chiles. Microwave the chocolate and chile mixture at 50 percent power until it is fully melted and smooth when stirred, 2 minutes. If necessary, continue to microwave the chocolate mixture at 50 percent power in 15-second increments.

Let the chocolate mixture cool to room temperature.

4 Crack the eggs into a medium-size bowl. Using a hand or stand mixer set on low speed, beat the eggs until the yolks and the whites combine. Sprinkle in the brown sugar and continue to beat on low until the sugar blends with the eggs. Add the granulated sugar and beat, scraping down the side of the bowl as needed to ensure an even mix. Using a spatula or wooden spoon, stir in the chile-spiked melted chocolate and the vanilla until just combined.

5 Now sprinkle in the flour and salt and stir it into the chocolate batter with that same spatula or wooden spoon until no white streaks remain. Stir in the reserved bittersweet chocolate chunks until just combined. Pour and scrape the batter into the prepared baking dish and bake, uncovered, until a toothpick inserted in the center comes out looking slightly oily, 20 to 25 minutes.

6 Remove the baking dish from the oven and let the brownies cool until the chocolate chunks are firm, several hours. Slice the brownies into 1-inch pieces. The brownies will keep in an airtight container at room temperature for up to 4 days.

# Bombay Biscotti

rowing up in Mumbai (Bombay) during the sixties and seventies was not boring. You could stay put on the balcony of your apartment and watch the world go by. All your shopping needs were easily met without leaving that vantage point, since every hawker would pass by, either pushing or pulling their wares of fruits, vegetables, legumes, rice, milk, clothing, recycling, and my favorite, cookies. The seller had not just one kind of cookie, but at least ten varieties neatly packed in a large rectangular aluminum chest that rested on his head. No words were ever spoken from the street level since it would be fruitless against the backdrop of horns, whistles, barks, and hawkers. Eye contact was all that was needed and he would make his way up the chipped stairs and wait at the doorstep. Once he unlocked his treasure chest of baked temptations, we saw all our favorites—the layered flaky, puffy rectangles of buttery, melt-in-your-mouth biscuits; shortbread-type round cookies; and bent, wand-shaped, slightly sweet crisps that we all knew simply as toasts.

Flash forward to the United States where I became reacquainted with those "toasts"—same shape, different name—as Italian biscotti (meaning "twice baked"). Here's my version that punctuates the biscotti with decadent chocolate and chunks of my favorite childhood sin—Cadbury fruit and nut bars.

LACTO-OVO VEGETARIAN

**Makes about 3 dozen biscotti**

½ cup whole almonds

2 cups unbleached all-purpose flour, plus flour for dusting

1 cup granulated sugar

½ cup unsweetened cocoa powder

2 teaspoons baking powder

½ teaspoon coarse kosher or sea salt

6 tablespoons (¾ stick) unsalted butter, chilled and cut into thin slices

1 bar (3.5 ounces) Cadbury Dairy Milk Fruit and Nut chocolate bars, coarsely chopped

3 large eggs

¼ teaspoon pure almond extract

1 Position a rack in the center of the oven and preheat it to 325°F. Line a baking sheet with parchment and set aside.

2 Heat a small skillet over medium-high heat. Once the skillet is hot (when you hold the palm of your hand close to the bottom of the skillet you will feel the heat), 2 to 4 minutes, add the almonds. Toast the almonds, shaking the skillet every few seconds, until they smell aromatic and some of the nuts have acquired patchy blisterlike spots, 2 to 4 minutes. Transfer the almonds to a food processor to cool. Once the almonds are cool, pulse them two or three times until they break up into slightly smaller pieces (you don't want them to be ground any more than that). Tap the almonds out onto a plate.

3 Place the flour, sugar, cocoa powder, baking powder, and salt in the food processor and pulse it a few times to mix well. Add the butter slices and pulse again a few times to create a coarse meal-like texture. Return the almonds to the food processor along with the chopped chocolate.

4 Crack the eggs into a small bowl, add the almond extract, and whisk until the eggs are uniformly light yellow and slightly frothy.

5 Pour the egg mixture through the feeder chute of the food processor and pulse the machine a few times to form a wet dough. Empty the dough out onto a work surface. Knead the chocolate brown dough until it comes together into a neat ball studded with almonds, chocolate chunks, and raisins (from the chocolate bar).

6 Divide the dough in half by slicing it lengthwise down the middle. Lightly dust the work surface with flour. Working with one half, roll the dough out into a log about 14 inches in length and 2 inches wide. Repeat with the other half. Transfer the logs to the prepared baking sheet, placing them about 3 inches apart to make sure they don't stick together.

## Extra Credit

- I love serving these with my Yogurt "Cheesecake" with Nutmeg (page 282) since I feel no meal is complete without a little chocolate.

- For a midnight snack, melt some premium vanilla ice cream and swirl in some crushed cardamom seeds.

Dunk these biscotti into the ice cream and don't worry about the calories you are adding at night— you can pretend you were sleepwalking and everyone knows that anything you eat while sleepwalking doesn't count.

7 Bake the logs until they appear dry and opaque on the surface—almost like a parched landscape—20 to 25 minutes. Remove the baking sheet from the oven and let it rest on a rack until the logs feel cool to the touch, about 15 minutes. Reduce the oven temperature to 275°F.

8 Carefully transfer each log to a cutting board and cut it at an angle, making diagonal slices about ¾ inch apart. Transfer the slices back to the baking sheet, making sure you lay them down on a cut side. Bake the slices for 10 minutes. Turn the slices over and bake them until they look dry and crisp, 10 minutes longer. Transfer the biscotti to a wire rack to cool.

9 Store the biscotti in a plastic zip-top bag or a jar at room temperature for up to 2 weeks.

## 10 Saffron-Pistachio Ice Cream Bars

### Kulfi

LACTO-OVO
VEGETARIAN
GLUTEN FREE

This is my rendition of the classic Indian ice cream called *kulfi*. Scented with alluring saffron and speckled with decadent pistachios, this is what ice cream should be all about. Smooth, opulent, sinful, but not as fat-laden as one might think, the ice cream draws its intense flavors from a simple technique of condensing the milk. This enriches the milk solids, and the film of cream that comes from boiling whole milk provides texture, an integral mouthfeel, to the succulence of *kulfi*. Stick a wooden stirrer into the ice cream as it freezes and you have what every child and childlike adult cannot resist—an ice cream bar to lick until the cows come home (or until you come home to the cows).

**Makes 6 ice cream bars**

4 cups (I quart) whole milk

¼ teaspoon saffron threads (see page 18)

½ cup egg substitute (like Egg Beaters; see Extra Credit)

½ cup granulated sugar

I cup heavy (whipping) cream

I teaspoon pure vanilla extract

¼ cup raw (not roasted) unsalted pistachio nuts

YOU'LL ALSO NEED

6 narrow freezerproof containers (see Extra Credit)

6 flat wooden stirrers (like the ones in coffee shops)

1 Make sure the inside container of your ice cream maker is frozen and ready for the ice cream mixture. Keep it in the freezer until you add the ice cream mixture in Step 6.

2 Place the milk in a Dutch oven or large saucepan and bring it to a boil, uncovered, over medium-high heat, stirring very frequently. Once the milk starts to boil you may need to reduce the heat a bit but make sure to keep the milk at a vigorous boil (no need to stir so frequently now since the chances of scorching are much lower). Keep scraping the side of the pan to release any collected bits of cream and milk solids that have collected there; when they fall back into the milk, they will provide texture and color.

3 Once the milk has reduced to about 1½ cups, about 20 minutes, stir in the saffron threads. The heat from the milk will extract what saffron is so revered for: flavor, aroma, and color—deep yellow with an orange hue, the color of the setting sun, especially around the threads when you see them suspended in the milk. Let the condensed milk cool, then transfer it to a bowl and place it in the refrigerator until cold, 2 to 3 hours. If you wish to rush it, stick it in the freezer for 30 minutes.

4 *If you are using a stand mixer,* once the saffron milk is chilled, pour the egg substitute into the mixer bowl. Beat it on medium speed while gradually sprinkling in the sugar. Once all the sugar is used up, let the mixer run for an additional 1 to 2 minutes.

*If you are using a hand-held mixer,* beat the egg substitute and sugar together on medium speed until the mixture is light yellow in color, 2 to 3 minutes.

5 Pour in the saffron milk, cream, and vanilla. Continue to beat the mixture on medium speed until it looks frothy, 2 to 3 minutes.

6 Pour the ice cream mixture into the frozen container of the ice cream maker and turn on the machine. While the batter churns, place the pistachio nuts in a spice grinder (you can also use a coffee grinder) and grind them to the consistency of coarsely ground black pepper. Once the batter is slightly frozen, (a gelato-like soft freeze), sprinkle in the ground pistachios and continue to run the machine to make sure the nuts get evenly dispersed.

7 Divide the soft freeze equally among the 6 narrow freezerproof containers and stick a wooden stirrer in the center of each of them. Freeze overnight and get ready to devour.

## Extra Credit

- Freezerproof ice cream bar molds are not hard to find in kitchenware stores, department stores, and even dollar stores.

- The basis for this egg batter is an adaptation of everyone's favorite Ben & Jerry's ice cream recipe. I wish I could call them my pals but the only things we have in common are the same publisher and editor who published their iconic ice cream cookbook *Ben & Jerry's Homemade Ice Cream & Dessert Book.* They use raw eggs as the starter to their mixtures, but I have used egg substitute instead with equally succulent results. That's where the adaptation ends. Everything else is purely vintage Indian.

- I will admit I walked into my neighborhood's coffee shop and, without even purchasing coffee, walked away with 6 of those wooden coffee stirrer sticks. I half expected to hear the police siren but thankfully that did not happen. I had full intentions of buying them at this grocery store but they ran out and I so desperately needed to test the recipe. So my apologies; the next time I stop by to buy coffee, I will give them an extra tip. Hindu guilt is alive and well!

# Mango Yogurt Shakes

## Aam Lassi

LACTO-VEGETARIAN
GLUTEN FREE

A staple at every Indian restaurant in the Western world, this yogurt shake, blended with mango puree, is a great end to a heavy meal. If done right, it should be light, refreshing, fruity, and satiating. Restaurants often use canned mango pulp and if you have access to the one imported from India called Alphonso mango pulp (see Extra Credit), use it in a heartbeat (a half cup of pulp for this recipe). Depending on how sour your yogurt is, you may need to up the ante on the sugar. The effervescent water is a nice touch as it levitates the shake, making it not so heavy. You may very well savor the company of this lassi, and may also be willing to forget about that cute namesake who happens to be a Scottish rough-coated collie. He may never come home again!

**Makes 4 cups; serves 4**

1½ cups plain yogurt

½ cup sparkling water

½ cup ice cubes

1½ cups fresh or frozen ripe mango cubes
(see Extra Credit)

¼ cup granulated sugar

1 Place the yogurt, sparkling water, ice cubes, mango, and sugar ingredients in a blender and puree to create a frothy shake.

2 Pour the lassi into 4 glasses and serve chilled (the ice in the shake will ensure that).

# Extra Credit

- More mangoes are consumed worldwide than any other fruit, a fact that's not surprising when you consider that there are more than one thousand varieties.

  I was fortunate to have been born in India, home to more than 125 varieties of mangoes (so, yes, that makes me a mango snob), cultivated there for more than 4,000 years. Dusseri, Payaree, Totapuri, and Langada are some varieties that elicit passionate debates as to which one is the best. Of course no one will be the loser with any of them. The one that stands out in my memory is the Alphonso from western India, salmon orange and musky smelling. When perfectly ripe, the flesh melts in your mouth, its sweetness overpowers your palate, and no fibers get in the way of nirvana.

  In my suburban supermarket in these United States, I see a mere handful of common mango varieties like the Haden, Tommy Atkins, Kent, Champagne (also called Ataulfo), and Keitt, grown and shipped from Florida, California, Mexico, or Hawaii. This tropical king of fruits is seasonal in India but available almost year round here at local supermarkets, wholesale outlets, natural food stores, and Asian and Latino groceries.

  Mangoes are usually picked green off the tree because if they are allowed to tree-ripen, chances are the insects (or monkeys) will get to them before we can. Ripen them on the kitchen counter, or enclose them in a brown paper bag to create the gases essential for speedier maturation. Or do as my mother used to do: Completely submerge the fruit in uncooked rice kernels until ripe.

- To peel a ripe mango, use a swivel vegetable peeler or a paring knife to remove the skin. Now you need to separate the ripe flesh from the large flat seed. Holding the peeled fruit firmly with one hand, set it down so its tip is resting on a cutting board. Slice down the length of the broad side of the mango, running the knife as close as possible to the seed, to yield an oval, concave slice. Swivel the mango on its tip and repeat on the other side. Now slice off the narrower sides. Frugal *moi* then continues to shave off as many slices as I possibly can, to leave behind a bald seed (okay, I have heard all the bald jokes, so nothing will surprise me!).

# 12 Ginger Cardamom Tea

## Adrak Elaichi Chai

**LACTO-VEGETARIAN
GLUTEN FREE**

Chai, that milky, sweet, and spicy brew, is the lifeblood of India's social, political, and business gatherings. In a store selling silk saris, faced with a choice of the flame red silk laced with gold or the midnight purple with a sea green border and green leaves, the owner will offer you a cup of hot chai in a stainless steel tumbler to enlighten your decision. Visit your best friend or close a hostile business deal, but first sip chai. Stroll down the dry streets of summer Mumbai or wade through a foot of standing water in the harsh monsoons, but do take a moment to sip chai. Available on every street corner, hawked by vendors everywhere, is chai: Darjeeling black tea steeped with milk, ginger, cloves, cinnamon, cardamom, and a kick of black pepper. This variation is more quintessentially Mumbai, very much like the metropolis—bold, spicy, sensuous, and habit forming. Please indulge my two-second soapbox moment: Chai means tea and so when you say chai tea, if I were Microsoft Word, I would ask you if I could delete the redundant word. It's chai, pure and simple!

**Makes 4 cups**

2 tablespoons coarsely chopped fresh ginger

10 to 12 green or white cardamom pods

2 cups whole milk

¼ cup Darjeeling or Assamese loose black tea leaves, or 8 black tea bags, tea leaves removed

¼ cup sweetened condensed milk, or 4 teaspoons granulated sugar

If you have a mortar, place the ginger and cardamom in it and, using the pestle, pound them a few times to release some of the juices and oils within. Alternately, put the ginger and cardamom in a mini chopper or food processor and pulse it a few times to break them down a bit to release those incredible aromas.

**2** Place 2 cups of water and the milk in a small saucepan over medium-high heat and bring to a rapid boil, uncovered, stirring regularly to prevent scorching. As soon as the liquid comes to a boil, stir in the tea leaves and the ginger-cardamom blend. Let the mixture return to a boil, uncovered, and boil, stirring occasionally, until the milk's color changes into a light brown tint scented with the strong, heady aromas of ginger and cardamom, 1 to 2 minutes.

**3** Stir in the sweetened condensed milk or sugar and turn off the heat. Strain the chai into serving cups and serve piping hot.

## Extra Credit

Even though I have recommended ginger and cardamom here, spices like ground cloves (¼ teaspoon), ground cinnamon (⅛ teaspoon), and even black pepper (¼ teaspoon) are great sprinkled in chai. Add any of these at the same juncture you would the ginger and cardamom.

## 13 The Slumdog Martini

Much like the popular movie *Slumdog Millionaire* that walked away with many an award, this adult beverage will charm your pants off. A muddled concoction, it combines north India's favorite herb, mint, with chiles and lime, and delivers a sophisticated drink, much like a sassy mojito that will make the Mumbaiite in you break into a Bollywood jig. And, yes, it should be shaken (the drink, that is) and not stirred.

VEGAN
GLUTEN FREE

**Makes 4 martinis (6 ounces each)**

¼ cup unrefined sugar

2 tablespoons finely chopped fresh ginger

1 teaspoon cumin seeds

½ cup firmly packed fresh mint leaves

2 fresh green serrano chiles, stems discarded, coarsely chopped (do not remove the seeds)

½ teaspoon coarse kosher or sea salt

2 cups crushed ice cubes (see **Extra Credit**)

¼ cup freshly squeezed lime juice

1 cup premium vodka or gin

1 Chill 4 martini glasses in the freezer.

2 Measure the sugar into a small saucepan and pour in ¼ cup water. Stir in the ginger. Bring it to a boil over medium heat, uncovered, stirring occasionally, until the sugar dissolves, about 2 minutes. Remove the pan from the burner, strain the syrup through a fine-mesh strainer into a small bowl or measuring cup, and chill in the refrigerator as you get the remaining ingredients ready.

3 Heat a small skillet over medium-high heat. Once the skillet is hot (when you hold the palm of your hand close to the bottom of the skillet you will feel the heat), usually after 2 to 4 minutes, add the cumin seeds and toast them, shaking the skillet every few seconds, until they turn an even reddish brown and smell incredibly nutty, 30 seconds to 1 minute. Immediately transfer the seeds to a small heatproof bowl to cool.

4 To make a single martini, place ⅛ cup of the mint leaves, a quarter of the chiles, ¼ teaspoon of the toasted cumin seeds, and ⅛ teaspoon of the salt in a cocktail shaker. Using a pestle or something you can use to pound, pummel the mélange to release the essential oils until the mint and chile breaks down a bit (not necessarily until it becomes pulpy), 1 to 2 minutes. Scoop in ½ cup ice cubes and pour in 1 tablespoon of the ginger syrup, 1 tablespoon of the lime juice, and ¼ cup vodka or gin. Screw the cocktail shaker's lid in place and shake to thoroughly mix the martini. Pour it into a chilled martini glass.

5 Repeat with the remaining ingredients and enjoy! If you drink all four, I will see you under the table.

## Extra Credit

There are some freezers that give you the option of choosing which form of ice you need. If you are one of us who does not have that fancy feature, put as much ice as you need into a blender and pulse it until it's crushed. Or, better yet, place a few cubes in a sealed plastic zip-top bag and beat them down to smaller pieces—a good way to release your anger and stress (yes, then there's that martini waiting for you, if that doesn't help).

# The Easy, Breezy Menus

# Menus for Great Indian Meals

Throughout my years as a cooking teacher, I've fielded many questions when it comes to learning how to cook the Indian way, but the question I hear the most is "How do I plan an Indian meal?" I always tell my students not to veer from the way they normally eat at home. If it's a protein that takes center stage (do you feel like eating chicken or fish or beans, and so on), then start with one of the choices I offer. Add a vegetable and/or starch and call it a day. It's that simple. But if you're planning on serving an Indian meal to company and need some more ideas, here are a few menus to titillate those taste buds starting with the one assembled from the step-by-step foldouts. I suggest prepping as much in advance of the dinner as possible. Certain dishes have no problem sitting in the fridge for a day or two!

## The Step-by-Step Foldout Menu

**Poppadums with Chile-Spiked Onion or Avocado Pomegranate Dip** (page 48)

**All-Wheat Griddle Breads** (page 84)

**Indian Slaw** (page 118)

**Ultimate Chicken Curry** (page 152)

**Smoky Yellow Split Peas** (page 194)

**Sweet-Scented Pilaf** (page 228)

**Funnel Cakes in Saffron Syrup** (page 278)

### TWO DAYS IN ADVANCE

- Flame-toast the poppadums—just remember to store them in a zip-top bag once they cool. If they do get exposed to a humid environment, they will lose their crispness—reheating in a microwave for 5 seconds will make them crispy again.

### ONE DAY IN ADVANCE

- Make the Chile-Spiked Onion and store it in a covered bowl in the refrigerator.

- Make the Avocado Pomegranate Dip and store it in an airtight jar in the refrigerator.

- Make the Indian Slaw and store it in a covered bowl in the refrigerator.

- Make the split peas and refrigerate them, covered.

- Make the curry and refrigerate it, covered.

### DAY OF

- Make the griddle breads, stack them in aluminum foil, and keep them warm in a preheated 200°F oven.

- Make the pilaf and keep it warm on the stove.

- Make the funnel cakes and let them drain on a rack till you serve dessert.

- Reheat the poppadums right before serving, if necessary.

• Reheat the curry and the split peas in the microwave or on low burners. If the peas are too thick, stir in water, a little at a time, until they are a nice saucy consistency.

**TO SERVE**

Place the poppadums in a cloth-lined basket and serve them with bowls of the onion topping and avocado dip, accompanied by iced tea or beer. Line a basket with parchment paper and arrange the griddle breads in it. Place it on the table alongside pretty bowls of the curry, pilaf, and split peas, and have guests serve themselves. The funnel cakes are crispy-sweet and sticky. Serve them on doily-lined plates with steaming cups of freshly brewed coffee. If this is your first home-cooked Indian meal, sit back and relish your accomplishment!

## The Indian Virgin

**Poppadums with Chile-Spiked Onion** (page 48)
**Tandoori Chicken** (page 174)
**Green Bean Almondine with Nutmeg** (page 248)
**Yogurt "Cheesecake" with Nutmeg** (page 282)

**TWO DAYS IN ADVANCE**

• Make the cheesecakes and keep them covered in the refrigerator.

• Flame-toast the poppadums—just remember to store them at room temperature in a zip-top bag once they cool. If they do get exposed to a humid environment, they will lose their crispiness—reheating in a microwave for 5 seconds will make them crispy again.

**ONE DAY IN ADVANCE**

• Marinate the chicken and keep covered in the refrigerator.

• Make the Chile-Spiked Onion and store it in a covered bowl in the refrigerator.

• Prepare and cook the beans but don't add the lime juice. Store them covered in the refrigerator.

• Peel and cut up or stem the fruit of choice (peaches, apples, melon, berries) that accompanies the cheesecakes and store it, covered, in the fridge.

**DAY OF**

• Reheat the poppadums right before serving, if necessary.

• Reheat the beans in a skillet and add the lime juice right before serving.

• Grill the chicken right before you plan to eat.

**TO SERVE**

Place the poppadums in a cloth-lined basket and serve them with the onion spread and icy cold beer. Follow with the chicken and green beans. End the meal with the individual cheesecakes topped with fresh fruit chunks.

# Breakfast at Tiffany's (the Indian version)

**Favorite juices**
**Spicy Indian Omelets** (page 198)
**Turmeric Hash Browns** (page 232)
**Mango Marmalade** (page 105)
  **and a store-purchased baguette**
**Bombay Biscotti** (page 293)
**Ginger Cardamom Tea** (page 300)

### ONE WEEK IN ADVANCE

- The biscotti are best prepared and baked a week ahead and stored in an airtight jar at room temperature.
- Make the marmalade and store it in an airtight jar in the refrigerator.

### DAY OF

- Let the marmalade come to room temperature before serving.

- Prepare and cook the hash browns. Keep warm.
- As your hash browns cook, prepare the eggs and toppings for the omelets.
- Toast the baguette slices, if you wish.

### TO SERVE

Place the toasts in a cloth-lined basket and cover with the cloth to keep warm. Spoon the marmalade into a pretty little bowl. Pour the juices into pitchers, if you have them. Make the omelets to order. Serve them with the hash browns on the side. Brew the chai toward the end of the meal. Sip the chai, being sure to dip your biscotti between sips.

# A Spring Menu

**Potato Leek Soup** (page 146)
**Braised Beet Salad** (page 127)
**Panfried Fennel Tilapia** (page 177)
**Mango slices and ice cream**

### ONE DAY IN ADVANCE

- Make the soup and refrigerate it in an airtight container. You can serve it warm or chilled (vichyssoise style).
- Prepare and cook the beets and the greens. Place the beets and greens in an airtight container, and refrigerate.
- Make the dressing and refrigerate it in an airtight container.
- If not prewashed, wash the salad greens, spin dry, lay in paper towels, and refrigerate.

### DAY OF

- Slice the mangoes and refrigerate the slices in an airtight container.
- If serving the soup warm, reheat it over very low heat.
- Panfry the tilapia while a friend helps you dress and assemble the beet salad.

### TO SERVE

Ladle the soup into pretty cups for guests to enjoy before dinner. It's easy to sip, spoon-free, while standing or sitting around. Lay platters of fish and beet salad on the table and ask guests to serve themselves. End the meal with scoops of ice cream accompanied by the mango slices.

# A Summer Menu

**Chilled Watermelon Soup** (page 136)
**Minty Cardamom Shrimp Salad** (page 133)
**Cayenne-Crusted Eggplant** (page 234)
**Potato Chile Bread** (page 97)
**Cashew Pistachio Bars** (page 286)

### ONE DAY IN ADVANCE

- Make the soup and keep it chilled in the refrigerator.
- Marinate the shrimp in a refrigerated airtight container.
- Make the salad dressing and refrigerate it in an airtight container.
- Slice the eggplant and keep the slices wrapped in plastic wrap in the refrigerator.
- Prepare the dough for the bread and shape it into a log. Wrap it in plastic wrap and refrigerate.
- Make the ice cream bars.

### DAY OF

- Remove the bread dough from the refrigerator and bring it to room temperature.

Cut off only enough to make the number of breads you'll need. Rewrap the remaining dough and return it to the refrigerator to cook at another time.

- Prepare and panfry the eggplant slices. Keep them on a rack in a preheated 200°F oven.
- Preheat the grill for the shrimp.
- Cook the breads in a skillet and keep them warm between pieces of aluminum foil in the preheated oven.
- Grill the shrimp.
- Once everything's ready, assemble the salad.

### TO SERVE

This is a great meal to enjoy outside, so if you have the space and the weather's good, be sure to take advantage. Serve the soup while the shrimp is being grilled or once the salad is assembled. Serve the shrimp salad, eggplant, and breads. Keep a pile of napkins at the ready when it's time to eat the ice cream bars.

# A Fall Menu

**Poppadums with Avocado Pomegranate Dip**
   (page 48)
**Pork Loin with Apples and Eggplant** (page 169)
**Mustard Rice with Peppers** (page 267)
**Mango Bread Pudding with Chai Spices** (page 289)

### TWO DAYS IN ADVANCE

- Flame-toast the poppadums—just remember to store them at room temperature in a zip-top bag once they cool. If they do get exposed to a humid environment, they will lose their crispiness—reheating in a microwave for 5 seconds will make them crispy again.

**DAY OF**

- Make the dip and transfer it to a serving bowl. Press a piece of plastic wrap directly onto its surface to make sure there is no air in between to initiate discoloration due to oxidation.
- Make the rice and either keep it covered in the cooking pot or transfer it to a microwave-safe bowl and reheat it before serving.

- Prepare and roast the pork.
- Prepare the ingredients for the bread pudding.

**TO SERVE**

Set out the dip and a basket or two of poppadums to enjoy before the main course. Just before serving the pork and rice, slip the bread pudding into the oven to bake. Nothing like warm pudding on a crisp night.

## A Winter Menu

**Minty Potato Cakes** (page 53)
  with **Tamarind Date Chutney** (page 103)
**Mint-Massaged Leg of Lamb** (page 165)
**Spinach with Cranberries** (page 262)
**Creamy Rice Pudding** (page 283)

**ONE DAY IN ADVANCE**

- Marinate the leg of lamb in the refrigerator covered with plastic wrap.
- Boil the potatoes and prepare and shape the cakes. Lay them on a flat plate or baking sheet, cover with aluminum foil, and refrigerate.
- Make the Tamarind Date Chutney and store in a serving bowl covered in the refrigerator.
- Make the rice pudding. Store it in its cooking pot in the refrigerator.

**DAY OF**

- Roast the lamb.
- Get all the ingredients prepped for the spinach.

- When the lamb has roasted for 1 hour, griddle-cook the potato cakes.
- When the lamb is cooked and finished resting, slice it and place the slices on a platter. Cover with foil to keep warm while you stir-fry the spinach.

**TO SERVE**

You might as well eat the potato cakes when they're fresh off the griddle, so have the chutney out and at the ready. That way you're not waiting for the main course to finish cooking before enjoying a little something. Once the spinach is ready, place it in a serving bowl and bring it to the table along with the platter of lamb. Warm the rice pudding over low heat as you eat your main course. Stir in a little extra milk and place the pot on a flame tamer, if possible, to prevent the pudding from sticking.

# ♪ Going on a Picnic, Leaving Right Away ♪

**Avocado Pomegranate Dip** (page 48)
  **with Plantain Chips** (page 58)

**Grilled Baby Back Ribs** (page 167)

**Indian Slaw** (page 118)

**Chocolate Chile Brownies** (page 291)

**Lemonade, iced tea, or other favorite beverages**

### ONE WEEK IN ADVANCE

- Most important: Make sure your picnic spot has a grill.

### ONE DAY IN ADVANCE

- Make the dip and store it in an airtight jar in the refrigerator.

- Marinate the ribs and store them covered in the refrigerator.

- Prepare the rib glaze and store it in a covered bowl in the refrigerator.

- Prepare the slaw and store it in a covered bowl in the refrigerator.

- Prepare and bake the brownies. When cooled, cover the pan with aluminum foil and store at room temperature.

### DAY OF

- Fry the plantain chips and when they're cooked, transfer them to a zip-top bag for easy transportation.

- Pack a cooler with plenty of your beverages of choice.

- Once at your picnic spot, glaze and grill the ribs.

### TO SERVE

Enjoy an iced tea, lemonade, or other favorite drink while you nibble on chips and dip as the ribs grill. Set out the slaw to eat with the ribs. Leave room for a big piece of chocolate brownie.

# Malt Shop Menu

**Raisin-Stuffed Lamb Burgers** (page 163)

**Hamburger buns or crusty rolls**

**Burger toppings such as sliced tomatoes, onions, and pickles**

**Crispy Okra Fries** (page 61)

**Tamarind Date Chutney** (page 103)

**Mango Yogurt Shakes** (page 298)

### TWO DAYS IN ADVANCE

- Make the Tamarind Date Chutney and store in an airtight container in the refrigerator. (This chutney keeps well for several weeks so you can really make it quite a bit in advance.)

### DAY OF

- Whip up a batch of the shakes and keep them chilled in the refrigerator.

- Prepare and shape the burgers. Don't cook them yet.

- Prepare all the toppings for your burgers.

- Prepare then fry the okra slices. Keep them warm on a rack in a 200°F preheated oven.

- Grill or fry the lamb burgers.

- Toast the buns or rolls if desired.

TO SERVE
Set out a platter with the burgers, a basket with the buns or rolls, and plates with a selection of your favorite toppings. Place the okra fries in a lined basket and serve the chutney on the side for dipping the fries. Have a pitcher of well-chilled shakes ready to pour.

## Indian Soul Food

**Collard Greens Roulade** (page 72)
**Buttermilk Fried Chicken** (page 172)
**Mac and Cheese Outsourced** (page 219)
**Sweet Corn with Toasted Coconut** (page 263)
**Corn Bread with Mustard Greens** (page 100)

ONE DAY IN ADVANCE
- Make the spice blend that you'll need for the mac and cheese.
- Marinate the chicken in the buttermilk mixture. Cover the pan with aluminum foil and refrigerate overnight.
- Prepare and bake the corn bread. Cover the pan with foil and keep at room temperature.

DAY OF
- Prepare the roulades, but don't fry them yet. Keep them covered and refrigerated.

- Make the corn and keep it covered in a microwaveable bowl for reheating.
- Prepare and fry the chicken pieces. Keep them on a rack to drain.
- Prepare and cook the macaroni and cheese.
- Panfry the roulade slices (I use the same oil that I fried the chicken in).

TO SERVE
Serve all the dishes in this meal at the same time. Set the table with a platter of roulade, a bowl of corn, and another of the mac and cheese. Pile the chicken pieces on another platter and place a basket with corn bread wedges by its side. Dig in to some great Indian soul food.

## The Vegan Table

**Poppadums with Avocado Pomegranate Dip** (page 48)
**Bean Sprouts Salad with Potato Croutons** (page 124)
**Truck Stop Beans** (page 213)
**Savory Cream of Wheat** (page 269)
**Funnel Cakes in Saffron Syrup** (page 278)

TWO DAYS IN ADVANCE
- Flame-toast the poppadums—just remember to store them at room temperature in a zip-top bag once they cool. If they do get exposed to a humid environment, they will lose their crispiness—reheating in a microwave for 5 seconds will make them crispy again.

- Make the dip and refrigerate it in an airtight jar.
- Make the funnel cakes. Keep them covered in the refrigerator.

**DAY OF**

- Make the bean sprout salad and keep it covered (I like serving this at room temperature).
- Get the Truck Stop Beans cooking and when they are almost finished simmering, make the Savory Cream of Wheat.

**TO SERVE**

Set out the poppadums and dip to tweak your friends' appetites while you finish up the Cream of Wheat. Place the salad, beans, and Cream of Wheat on the table and have friends serve themselves. Right before you're ready for dessert, reheat the funnel cakes slightly in a microwave (barely 30 seconds to take the chill off).

# Gluten-Free Gala

**Popeye's Dream Soup** (page 141)
**Creamy Chicken Kebabs** (page 75)
  **with Tangy Mint Chutney** (page 102)
**Cumin Potatoes** (page 246)
**Mustard Rice with Peppers** (page 267)
**Cashew Pistachio Bars** (page 286)

**ONE DAY IN ADVANCE**

- Prepare and cook the soup. Refrigerate the soup covered in the pot.
- Make the cashew bars (no need to keep them refrigerated if you plan on scarfing them down the next day). An airtight container should keep them fresh for one day.
- Skewer the chicken strips, then place them in the marinade. Keep covered in the refrigerator.
- Make the chutney and keep it covered and refrigerated.

**DAY OF**

- Make the potatoes and keep them covered in a microwaveable bowl for reheating a bit later.
- Prepare and cook the rice. Keep warm.
- Reheat the soup slowly on the stovetop or transfer to a microwaveable bowl and reheat in the microwave.
- Grill the chicken skewers.

**TO SERVE**

Pour the soup into teacups for guests to sip as the chicken grills. Bring the chicken to the table on a platter and place small bowls of chutney alongside. Transfer the potatoes and rice to pretty bowls. Finish up with a plateful of Cashew Pistachio Bars.

# Conversion Tables

Please note that all conversions are approximate but close enough to be useful when converting from one system to another.

## Oven Temperatures

| FAHRENHEIT | GAS MARK | CELSIUS |
|---|---|---|
| 250 | 1/2 | 120 |
| 275 | 1 | 140 |
| 300 | 2 | 150 |
| 325 | 3 | 160 |
| 350 | 4 | 180 |
| 375 | 5 | 190 |
| 400 | 6 | 200 |
| 425 | 7 | 220 |
| 450 | 8 | 230 |
| 475 | 9 | 240 |
| 500 | 10 | 260 |

Note: Reduce the temperature by 20°C (68°F) for fan-assisted ovens.

## Approximate Equivalents

1 stick butter = 8 tbs = 4 oz = 1/2 cup = 115 g

1 cup all-purpose presifted flour = 4.7 oz

1 cup granulated sugar = 8 oz = 220 g

1 cup (firmly packed) brown sugar = 6 oz = 220 g to 230 g

1 cup confectioners' sugar = 4 1/2 oz = 115 g

1 cup honey or syrup = 12 oz

1 cup grated cheese = 4 oz

1 cup dried beans = 6 oz

1 large egg = about 2 oz or about 3 tbs

1 egg yolk = about 1 tbs

1 egg white = about 2 tbs

## Liquid Conversions

| U.S. | IMPERIAL | METRIC |
|---|---|---|
| 2 tbs | 1 fl oz | 30 ml |
| 3 tbs | 1 1/2 fl oz | 45 ml |
| 1/4 cup | 2 fl oz | 60 ml |
| 1/3 cup | 2 1/2 fl oz | 75 ml |
| 1/3 cup + 1 tbs | 3 fl oz | 90 ml |
| 1/3 cup + 2 tbs | 3 1/2 fl oz | 100 ml |
| 1/2 cup | 4 fl oz | 125 ml |
| 2/3 cup | 5 fl oz | 150 ml |
| 3/4 cup | 6 fl oz | 175 ml |
| 3/4 cup + 2 tbs | 7 fl oz | 200 ml |
| 1 cup | 8 fl oz | 250 ml |
| 1 cup + 2 tbs | 9 fl oz | 275 ml |
| 1 1/4 cups | 10 fl oz | 300 ml |
| 1 1/3 cups | 11 fl oz | 325 ml |
| 1 1/2 cups | 12 fl oz | 350 ml |
| 1 2/3 cups | 13 fl oz | 375 ml |
| 1 3/4 cups | 14 fl oz | 400 ml |
| 1 3/4 cups + 2 tbs | 15 fl oz | 450 ml |
| 2 cups (1 pint) | 16 fl oz | 500 ml |
| 2 1/2 cups | 20 fl oz (1 pint) | 600 ml |
| 3 3/4 cups | 1 1/2 pints | 900 ml |
| 4 cups | 1 3/4 pints | 1 liter |

## Weight Conversions

| US/UK | METRIC | US/UK | METRIC |
|---|---|---|---|
| 1/2 oz | 15 g | 7 oz | 200 g |
| 1 oz | 30 g | 8 oz | 250 g |
| 1 1/2 oz | 45 g | 9 oz | 275 g |
| 2 oz | 60 g | 10 oz | 300 g |
| 2 1/2 oz | 75 g | 11 oz | 325 g |
| 3 oz | 90 g | 12 oz | 350 g |
| 3 1/2 oz | 100 g | 13 oz | 375 g |
| 4 oz | 125 g | 14 oz | 400 g |
| 5 oz | 150 g | 15 oz | 450 g |
| 6 oz | 175 g | 1 lb | 500 g |

# Bibliography

Achaya, K. T. *Indian Food: A Historical Companion*. Delhi: Oxford University Press, 1994.

Corriher, S. *CookWise*. New York: William Morrow, 1997.

Dalby, A. *Dangerous Tastes: The Story of Spices.* Berkeley: University of California Press, 2002.

Davidson, A. *The Oxford Companion to Food.* New York: Oxford University Press, 1999.

Iyer, R. *Betty Crocker's Indian Home Cooking*. New York: John Wiley & Sons, 2001.

—— *The Turmeric Trail: Recipes and Memories from an Indian Childhood*. New York: St. Martin's Press, 2002.

—— *660 Curries: The Gateway to Indian Cooking*. New York: Workman Publishing, 2008.

Joachim, D. *The Food Substitutions Bible*. Toronto: Robert Rose, 2005.

Katzer, G. *Gernot Katzer's Spice Pages*. Website gernot-katzers-spice-pages.com/engl/.

Montagné, P. *Larousse Gastronomique*. New York: Clarkson Potter, 2001. (American edition of a French book published by Auguste Escoffier and Philéas Gilbert in 1938)

Schneider, E. *Vegetables from Amaranth to Zucchini*. New York: William Morrow, 2001.

"The Spice Trade: A Taste of Adventure." Originally published in *The Economist* (n.d.). In "Encyclopedia of Spices" on theepicentre.com.

Tannahill, R. *Food in History*. New York: Stein and Day, 1973.

Trager, J. *The Enriched, Fortified, Concentrated, Country-Fresh, Lip-Smacking, Finger-Licking, International, Unexpurgated Foodbook*. New York: Grossman, 1970.

# Index

Page references in *italic* refer to photographs of prepared dishes.

# Photo Credits

Photography by Lucy Schaeffer

Food stylist: Simon Andrews

Prop stylist: Sara Abalan

Additional photography:
**fotolia:** p. 5 Uros Petrovic, p. 8 Whitebox Media, p. 10 (right and top) Kasia Bialasiewicz, p. 10 (bottom left) Stanley Marquardt, p. 12 (bottom) nito, p. 12 (top) volff, p. 13 (bottom) Yasonya, p. 13 (top) myfotolia88, p. 14 (bottom left) uckyo, p. 14 (bottom right) Schlierner, p. 14 (top) and p. 15 (bottom right) Elena Schweitzer, p. 15 (top) Songshu, p. 16 (bottom right) leeavison, p. 16 (left) preto_perola, p. 16 (right) Haris Rauf, p. 17 (left) Barbro Bergfeldt, p. 17 (right) Buriy, p. 18 (bottom) Nika Novak, p. 18 (top left) radarreklama, p. 18 (top right) Marco Speranza, p. 19 picsfive, p. 20 Ionescu Bogdan, p. 21 allison14, p. 21 (right) Orlando Bellini, p. 22 Edoma, p. 23 Roman Ivaschenko; **Getty Images:** p. 11 rubberball.